Justice and Security Reform

Justice and Security Reform: Development Agencies and Informal Institutions in Sierra Leone undertakes a deep contextual analysis of the reform of the country's security and justice sectors since the end of the civil war in 2002. Arguing that the political and bureaucratic nature of development agencies leads to a lack of engagement with informal institutions, this book examines the challenges of sustainably transforming security and justice in fragile states. Through the analysis of a post-conflict context often held up as an example of successful peacebuilding, Lisa Denney reveals how the politics of development agencies is an often forgotten constraint in security and justice reform and development efforts more broadly.

Particularly suited to upper-level undergraduates and postgraduate students, as well as practitioners, this book is relevant to those interested in security and justice reform and statebuilding, as well as Sierra Leone's post-conflict recovery.

Lisa Denney is a researcher at the Overseas Development Institute working on issues of security, justice, development and fragile states. She completed her doctorate in International Politics at Aberystwyth University on security and justice reforms in Sierra Leone.

Law, development and globalization

Edited by Julio Faundez

University of Warwick

During the past decades, a substantial transformation of law and legal institutions in developing countries has taken place. Whether prompted by market-based policies or the international human rights movement, by the relentless advance of the process of globalization or the successive waves of democratization, no area of law has been left untouched. The aim of this series is to promote cross-disciplinary dialogue and cooperation among scholars and development practitioners interested in understanding the theoretical and practical implications of the momentous legal changes taking place in developing countries.

Titles in the series:

State Violence and Human Rights: State Officials in the South
Andrew M. Jefferson and Steffen Jensen (eds)

The Political Economy of Government Auditing: Financial Governance and the Rule of Law in Latin America and Beyond
Carlos Santiso

Global Perspectives on the Rule of Law
James J. Heckman, Robert L. Nelson and Lee Cabatingan (eds)

Marginalized Communities and Access to Justice
Yash Ghai and Jill Cottrell (eds)

Law in the Pursuit of Development: Principles into Practice?
Amanda Perry-Kessaris (ed.)

Governance Through Development: Poverty Reduction Strategies and the Disciplining of Third World States
Celine Tan

Lawyers and the Rule of Law in an Era of Globalization
Yves Dezalay and Bryant Garth (eds)

Policing and Human Rights: The Meaning of Violence and Justice in the Everyday Policing of Johannesburg
Julia Hornberger

Lawyers and the Construction of Transnational Justice
Yves Dezalay and Bryant Garth (eds)

Gender, Justice and Legal Pluralities: Latin American and African Perspectives
Rachel Sieder and John McNeish

Social Movements, Law and the Politics of Land Reform
George Meszaros

Justice and Security Reform: Development Agencies and Informal Institutions in Sierra Leone
Lisa Denney

From the Global to the Local, How International Rights Reach Bangladesh's Children
Andrea Schapper

Land Law Reform in Eastern Africa: Traditional or Transformative?
Patrick McAuslan

Forthcoming titles in the series:

Multinational Integration, Cultural Identity and Regional Self-Government, Comparative Experiences for Tibet
Roberto Toniatti and Jens Woelk

Governing Refugees: Justice, Order and Legal Pluralism
Kirsten McConnachie

Law and Society in Latin America
Cesar Rodriguez Garavito

Policing and the Politics of Order-Making
Peter Albrecht and Helene Maria Kyed

Justice Reform and Development: Rethinking Donor Assistance to Developing and Transitional Countries
Linn Hammergren

Justice and Security Reform

Development agencies and informal institutions in Sierra Leone

Lisa Denney

Routledge
Taylor & Francis Group
a GlassHouse Book

First published 2014
by Routledge
2 Park Square, Milton Park, Abingdon, Oxon, OX14 4RN

and by Routledge
711 Third Avenue, New York, NY 10017

A GlassHouse Book

Routledge is an imprint of the Taylor & Francis Group, an informa business

British Library Cataloguing in Publication Data
A catalogue record for this book is available from the British Library

Library of Congress Cataloging-in-Publication Data
Denney, Lisa.
Justice and security reform : development agencies and informal institutions in Sierra Leone / Lisa Denney.
pages cm. – (Law, development and globalization)
ISBN 978-0-415-64250-7 (hardback) – ISBN 978-0-203-79727-3 (ebk)
1. Justice, Administration of–Sierra Leone. 2. Internal security–Sierra Leone. 3. Law reform–Sierra Leone. 4. Law and economic development. I. Title.
KTJ329.D46 2014
347.664–dc23
2013029444

ISBN: 978-0-415-64250-7 (hbk)
ISBN: 978-0-203-79727-3 (ebk)

Typeset in Garamond
by Cenveo Publisher Services

MIX
Paper from responsible sources
FSC® C013056
FSC www.fsc.org

Printed and bound in Great Britain by
TJ International Ltd, Padstow, Cornwall

Contents

Acknowledgements

I am indebted to many people who have helped me in writing this book. Beginning as my PhD thesis, Michael C. Williams, Hidemi Suganami, Alastair Finlan and Richard Rathbone provided me with rigorous supervisions that helped to forge the shape of the book. As examiners, Stephen Ellis and Jenny Mathers also helped to refine its scope and argument. The research would not have been possible without generous funding from the EH Carr Award, the Aberystwyth University Overseas Research Scholarship and the Gareth Jones Memorial Travelling Scholarship. In addition, I am grateful to my current employer, the Overseas Development Institute, for carving out some research time for me to complete this book – and to my colleagues there for creating an inspiring research environment.

I'd like to thank all those in Sierra Leone and the UK who generously gave me their time and shared with me their knowledge and personal experiences. I was honoured to meet such extraordinary people and to have the opportunity to tell some of their stories. The arguments and omissions in the book, however, are of course my own.

A number of experts kindly read parts of this book along the way and provided me with invaluable feedback that has strengthened the final product. To Peter Albrecht, Karen Barnes Robinson, Keith Biddle, Pilar Domingo, Paul Jackson, Clare Paine, Richard Rathbone and Mark White, your time and advice were very much appreciated. I would also like to thank the editorial team at Routledge for answering my many questions along the way and the anonymous reviewers for their helpful suggestions.

Some parts of this book have previously been published in other forms and I am grateful to the copyright holders for allowing their use here. An extract in Chapter 3 appeared in DAI's *Developing Alternatives* journal in Summer 2011; and parts of Chapter 5 have appeared as a journal article in *Development Policy Review* in January 2013 and as an Overseas Development Institute Briefing Paper in April 2012.

Thanks are also owed to Aubrey Wade, for providing the beautiful photo for the front cover, and to Professor John Innes Clarke, who kindly allowed use of his impressive maps of Sierra Leone originally printed in 1966 (and for which no publisher could be found to claim copyright).

To my friends who have sustained me through both the PhD and book process – I am immeasurably thankful for your humour, patience and wonderful company! To my parents and brothers back in Aus – thank you for your constant love, belief and support, even in the face of some not-so-popular trips to Sierra Leone.

Finally, to my husband Daniel – who not only knows more than he could ever have wanted to about Sierra Leone having read every word of this book, but also cooked almost every dinner of the first year of married life – thank you. The book, and I, would be sorely lacking without you.

Abbreviations

ACPP	Africa Conflict Prevention Pool
AFRC	Armed Forces Revolutionary Council
APC	All People's Congress
ASJP	Access to Security and Justice Programme
CCSSP	Commonwealth Community Safety and Security Project
CDF	Civil Defence Forces
CDIID	Complaints, Discipline and Internal Investigations Department
CDU	Civil Defence Unit
CGRP	Chiefdom Governance Reform Programme
CHAD	Conflict and Humanitarian Affairs Department
CISU	Central Intelligence and Security Unit
CPP	Conflict Prevention Pool
DDR	Disarmament Demobilization and Reintegration
DFID	Department for International Development
ECOMOG	Economic Community of West African States Monitoring Group
ECOWAS	Economic Community of West African States
FCO	Foreign and Commonwealth Office
FSU	Family Support Unit
GCPP	Global Conflict Prevention Pool
GoSL	Government of Sierra Leone
IGP	Inspector General of Police
ISU	Internal Security Unit
JSCO	Justice Sector Coordination Office
JSDP	Justice Sector Development Programme
LDP	Law Development Programme
LNP	Local Needs Policing
MLGRD	Ministry of Local Government and Rural Development
MoDUK	Ministry of Defence
MSWGCA	Ministry of Social Welfare, Gender and Children's Affairs
NPFL	National Patriotic Front of Liberia
NPRC	National Provisional Ruling Council
ODA	Overseas Development Agency

OECD	Organization for Economic Cooperation and Development
ONS	Office of National Security
OSG	Operational Support Group
PCRP	Paramount Chiefs Restoration Programme
PPJ	Promoters of Peace and Justice
PRSP	Poverty Reduction Strategy Paper
RSLAF	Republic of Sierra Leone Armed Forces
RUF	Revolutionary United Front
SILSEP	Sierra Leone Security Sector Reform Programme
SJSR	Security and Justice Sector Reform
SLA	Sierra Leone Army
SLP	Sierra Leone Police
SLPP	Sierra Leone People's Party
SSD	Special Security Division
SSR	Security Sector Reform
UNAMSIL	United Nations Assistance Mission in Sierra Leone
UNOMSIL	United Nations Observer Mission in Sierra Leone

Maps

Sierra Leone provincial and district boundaries

(Clarke 1969: 29)

Sierra Leone chiefdom boundaries

(Clarke 1969: 33)

Introduction

While interviewing a tribal headman[1] in Freetown in 2012, our discussions were interrupted by a man and woman who had come to see the chief to resolve a dispute. The man was standing for Parliament in the 2012 elections and one of the campaign posters he had paid for had been torn down. When the woman reproached the man allegedly responsible for tearing down the poster, he abused her. The couple had come to the chief to complain about the man's behavior and request that the chief punish him. After putting on his slippers and hat to listen to the couple, the chief reasoned there were two matters at hand. The first, involving interference with campaign posters, was a matter of electoral law under the formal legal system of Sierra Leone and was thus outside of the chief's jurisdiction. He encouraged the man to take this matter to the police – despite the man's plea that the chief could act much faster than the police, who he felt would probably do nothing. The second matter, that of abuse of the woman, the chief deemed within his jurisdiction under customary law. After establishing the name and address of the man accused, the chief wrote out a summons requesting that he attend a hearing at the chief's house that weekend. The woman paid the chief 25,000 Leones (the equivalent of about USD 5.80) for one of the chief's staff to 'get transport' to deliver the summons (transport would in fact cost substantially less than this – it is likely part of this amount was the chief's fee for service). The chief cautioned the woman to 'dress properly' for the hearing (she had come to see him in a *lapa*[2] and singlet), the couple departed and – hat and slippers off – our interview continued.

After 15 years of reform of the security and justice sectors in Sierra Leone, the UK continues to focus overwhelmingly on state systems, despite the fact that the majority of Sierra Leoneans access security and justice through informal means. It is not hard to see why they choose do so when, as in the case above, conflict resolution can be achieved within a week at relatively low cost, when compared with the alternatives. While experiences of informal dispute resolution in Sierra Leone are not always as benign as the above depiction, as this book will demonstrate, it does make clear the disconnection between donor-sponsored reforms and the reality of how security and justice are sought at the local level. This book addresses the question of why donors – in this case, the UK's Department for International Development (DFID) – seem unable to engage with such informal actors, in spite of their centrality to security and justice provision in Sierra Leone.

SJSR and informal actors

In contrast to conventional development initiatives, from 1997 to 2009, DFID's projects in Sierra Leone focused substantially on the police, military, intelligence service and judicial system. Its funding supported the provision of uniforms, training in teargas and baton use, supply of vehicles to members of the judiciary and building living quarters for the armed forces. Such work is indicative of the changing nature of development assistance, from being concerned primarily with education, healthcare and human rights throughout most of the 1990s, to focusing more heavily on security since the end of the 1990s (Duffield 2001). Security and, increasingly, justice are now seen as prerequisites for development (DFID 1998; DFID 2000b; World Bank 2011). As a result of this purported security-development nexus, 'programming in what traditionally were two discrete sectors is increasingly meshing' (Hurwitz and Peake 2004: 1).

This more proximate relationship between the concepts of security and development has combined with a renewed zeal for social-engineering, resulted in a proliferation of more expansive peacebuilding interventions since the 1990s that aim to recreate societies and supposedly ensure more peaceful and prosperous states (Paris and Sisk 2009: 6–7; Fukuyama 2004). In an effort to ensure that the peace being built is grounded in solid and sustainable foundations, rather than the 'quick wins' that earlier, and more limited, peacebuilding interventions focused on, an increased emphasis has been placed on building or strengthening the institutions of the state (Paris and Sisk 2009: 2–3). This has led to a conflation of peacebuilding and statebuilding agendas. The institutions of the state are now routinely seen as the vehicle through which security and development can be achieved (Paris 2004: 1–8). This focus on the state derives from the diagnosis that many of the challenges that post-conflict or fragile states encounter are the result of poor governance (Call and Wyeth 2008; Berdal 2009). As Francis Fukuyama notes, 'the ability to shore up or create from whole cloth missing state capabilities and institutions has risen to the top of the global agenda and seems likely to be a major condition for security in important parts of the world' (2004: xi–xii). Security and justice sector reform (SJSR) is one of the prime development strategies that the statebuilding agenda has spawned.

SJSR involves the restructuring of the security and justice apparatus to ensure democratic security governance and the rule of law, most commonly in post-conflict and fragile states (Donais 2009: 118). The rationale underpinning

SJSR is that well-functioning, disciplined and democratically controlled security and justice sectors will provide a secure, stable and predictable environment in which investment and development can occur, thus laying the foundations for economic growth (Bryden *et al.* 2008: 4). Given the presumed dependence of other developmental outcomes on security and stability, SJSR is often prioritized in statebuilding interventions, with a 'security first' approach adopted by the UK Government in Sierra Leone. SJSR programmes have since been implemented in diverse contexts – including Kosovo, Timor-Leste, Sierra Leone, Afghanistan, the Democratic Republic of the Congo (DRC), Haiti, Iraq, Liberia and South Sudan.

Despite this quickly growing catalogue of cases, SJSR is a relatively new concept that has, to some extent, emerged from what were the previously quite separate fields of security sector reform (SSR) and rule of law reform. Early SSR literature focused primarily on the technical capacities of the military and police and wider issues of security sector governance, drawing on civil-military relations theory (Chanaa 2002). Rule of Law reform underwent its own resurgence in the 1990s, after a hiatus since the perceived failure of the Law and Development Movement in the 1960s and 1970s (Trubek 2003). Both components of SJSR thus have their own distinct histories. Increasingly, however, as both fields were drawn into (and in some cases, co-opted by) the statebuilding agenda, they were brought into closer proximity. Separating out the two fields has become increasingly difficult given their interdependence, where gains in one sector can be set back without concomitant gains in the other. As a result, the two fields have become increasingly merged, though not without a good deal of tension and continuing 'siloed' approaches by programme staff who frequently have backgrounds in either police services or the judiciary (Stone *et al.* 2005: 24–26). Despite some quite justified concerns about this merger, it has also served to highlight the cross-cutting challenges that both fields confront. One of the most important of these challenges that has emerged over the last ten years, given that it speaks to how the power to discipline, punish and resolve disputes is divided within a society, is the role of informal actors and the challenge that they pose for SJSR efforts, which have been overwhelmingly state-centric in approach.

Throughout the 1990s, approaches to security and justice reforms, as with development programming more broadly, were largely based on the assumptions of the good governance agenda, suggesting that the promotion of 'a suite of essentially Western institutions: a separation of powers, free press, independent judiciary, pluralistic civil society, and respect for the rule of law', would lift the quality of governance in developing countries and promote economic growth (Kelsall 2008: 1). On this basis, donors frequently focused on transferring models perceived to be successful from Western political systems to those of developing countries, where corrupt and weak political structures were considered to be holding back development (Abrahamsen 2000). This was apparent in the security and justice sectors, where military personnel, police officers, lawyers and judges from Western countries were sent to post-conflict countries to help establish military, policing and justice structures that the reformers seemed to assume would evolve to look like their institutions back home. Yet, as it became apparent that the imposition of externally-derived models onto developing country realities was not producing the expected dividends, scholars and development practitioners turned towards embracing, rather than rejecting, the very stubborn local realities the good governance agenda had hoped to transform.

Merilee Grindle's (2004) concept of 'good enough governance', which came to influence DFID thinking (for instance, DFID 2005a), argued that the development community's focus on ideal governance standards was not appropriate for contexts with very different political configurations, often involving entrenched patrimonial behaviour. Rather, she advocated, the focus should be on making realistic improvements on the basis of what currently works within particular contexts. Increasing attention has since been paid to the limited role of the state in many developing (and especially fragile and post-conflict) countries and, as a result, the relative importance of informal actors in the governance of everyday life (see for instance Blundo and Le Meur 2009). Research looking specifically at the role of informal actors (the debate over the appropriate terminology is discussed below) has since mushroomed, with notable contributions from Kyed and Buur (2007), Anderson, Møller and Stepputat (2007), Baker (2005), Lund (2006; 2007), Isser (2011), Boege *et al.* (2009) and Scheye (2008). These authors have attempted to 'look beyond the normative Weberian model of what a state is supposed to look like ... [and rather] start with ... actual institutions and practices ... and explore the way in which they have evolved in the specific historical settings' (Anderson 2007: 23). Increasingly, it is actors beyond the state that are seen as the fulcrum of local authority, with broad agreement (despite no exact figures) that approximately 80–90 per cent of disputes in the Global South are resolved through informal means (Albrecht and Kyed 2011: 3; Lund 2006).

Alongside these shifts in thinking, donors have also been searching for new development approaches that take greater account of the social, political, economic and cultural contexts in which they operate. Indeed, the mantra of the development industry in recent times has been the worryingly obvious statement that 'context matters'. To operationalize this insight, donors have attempted to refine their analytical tools to understand context better – and have found that informal actors play important, and largely overlooked, roles. In 2003, for instance, DFID launched its 'Drivers of Change' analysis, in which over 20 country offices commissioned research to examine the 'formal and informal rules, power structures, vested interests and incentives' that drive local politics (DFID 2004c). The studies concluded that 'the realities of power and culture in Africa posed formidable obstacles to the implementation of Good Governance' (Kelsall 2008: 2). Other political and development initiatives have come to similar conclusions. The UK's Commission for Africa findings emphasized local realities, with a chapter entitled 'Through African Eyes' concluding that 'outside prescriptions only succeed where they work with the grain of African ways of doing things' (Commission for Africa 2005: 33). This resulted in the New Partnership for African Development (NEPAD) with an emphasis on 'African solutions to African problems' (Economic Commission for Africa 2007: 2). From 2007–12 DFID funded the African Power and Politics Programme, a research programme to investigate the role of informal and neo-patrimonial influences in African politics. The programme developed the argument that development practice should 'go with the grain' of African development (Kelsall 2008). Numerous donors are now utilizing 'political economy analysis' approaches that seek to reveal the formal and informal 'rules of the game'. The shift towards understanding and embracing local realities has led to an increased interest in the role of informal actors, like chiefs, trade associations, community dispute resolution mechanisms, and so forth. Not only are these actors recognized as often being the dominant providers of services, including security and justice, within their communities, they are also often seen to attract strong community loyalty (Fanthorpe 2005: 44). In Sierra Leone, chiefs are recognized as playing important roles in an array of governance, security and justice functions (Sawyer 2008: 388–389). It would seem that shifts in both academia and the development industry towards taking more realistic and pragmatic approaches to reform that begin with a better understanding of local realities would make engagement with informal actors attractive to those seeking to transform security and justice provision in post-conflict countries.

Yet despite the recognition in policy documents that local context is paramount, and that informal actors often play important roles in the constellations of power in fragile and post-conflict counties, the development community still struggles to operationalize these insights. Programming frequently remains based on blueprint approaches of transferring models of what works in one context to another (Sedra 2006; Krause and Jütersonke 2005). Engagements are overwhelmingly with state security and justice actors and not the informal actors that context analysis often reveals are integral (Albrecht and Kyed 2011). Indeed, as this book reveals, there has been minimal engagement with informal actors in Sierra Leone, despite their centrality as security and justice providers. This raises the question of why, despite clear recognition of the importance of informal security and justice actors in policy and academic literatures, does this largely fail to manifest on the ground? The answer, at least in part, has to do as much with the politics of the donors implementing SJSR programmes as it does with the contexts in which programming takes place.

The politics of development agencies

While this book argues for the need to work with informal actors in SJSR, it also recognizes how the politics of development agencies may limit their ability to do so. Despite the efforts made (however incomplete) to understand the politics and informal 'rules of the game' of the countries in which development programming is carried out, much less time has been devoted to understanding the politics of development agencies themselves, who are responsible for carrying out programming. This has contributed to an understanding of the problems of underdevelopment and insecurity as largely internal to developing countries, rather than also due to the process of development, determined to a large extent by donors and their own incentives and constraints, shaped by their own political environments in the West (Ayittey 1999). More to the point, when development programmes succeed, it is the programme staff, the theory of change underpinning the programme, or the quality of the projects implemented that are recognized as having succeeded. However, when development programmes fail to deliver, this is frequently blamed on a difficult operating environment, weak or corrupt local partners, lack of government commitment, and so on. To put it bluntly – success is due to donors whereas failure is due to aid recipients, recognizing the agency of aid recipients to a much greater degree in failure than in success. This does not occur because development agency staff are self-aggrandizing neo-colonialists, but rather due to a myriad of incentives and disincentives within development agencies that prioritize results rather than learning (Eyben 2005). Understanding these dynamics is critical, particularly given that development agencies work in multiple environments at any given time, and thus the impact of their internal workings is felt much further afield than in just one country. Therefore, while this book deals specifically with how DFID's political and bureaucratic characteristics play out in SJSR programming in Sierra Leone, these characteristics are also relevant for other contexts in which DFID works, as well as for places where other donors with similar operating procedures work.

Over the past few years, more attention has begun to be paid to the impact that development agencies – their political commitments, their multiple objectives, their procurement and staffing procedures, and their reporting requirements – have on how programming unfolds in developing countries. Building on perhaps the first major work in this regard, James Ferguson's *The Anti-Politics Machine*, a number of former-development professionals have attempted to pull back the curtain on the internal workings of donor organizations. Andrew Natsios, writing about the US Agency for International Development (USAID) (2010) and Sue Unsworth (2009), writing about DFID, as well as a number of other academics writing more broadly about development agencies, including Adrian Leftwich (2006), David Mosse (2004) and Will Hout (2012), have revealed some of the bureaucratic and political limits that development agencies work within and how they curtail programming in important ways. To understand why development happens in the ways that it does, these works shift the emphasis from focusing solely on the countries in which it happens, to focusing also on those who attempt to implement it. This book contributes to this burgeoning field, illuminating the ways in which the bureaucratic culture and political characteristics of, in this case DFID,[3] have shaped SJSR programming in important ways, to the detriment of engagement with informal actors.

DFID's SJSR in Sierra Leone

DFID is a leading innovator in SJSR, at the cutting edge (in donor terms) of research and programming on the issue (Wulf 2004). It has now been involved in SJSR for over 15 years, partnering with the Ministry of Defence (MoD) and the Foreign and Commonwealth Office (FCO) to provide 'joined-up' and sector-wide security and justice reforms in post-conflict and fragile states (Stone *et al.* 2005). Of particular note has been DFID's SJSR programme in Sierra Leone, often perceived as the most comprehensive and successful SJSR project to date and thus occupying something of an archetypal status in the international community (Olonisakin 2008: 1–3; UN Security Council 2008; Horn *et al.* 2008). Indeed, Sierra Leone is often talked about as having shaped the concept of SJSR as much as the country was itself shaped by the reforms it underwent (Albrecht and Jackson 2009: 17). Projects have been adapted from the Sierra Leone SJSR experience to other countries, with the Family Support Unit model (discussed in Chapter 3), for instance, being replicated in Liberia and the Democratic Republic of the Congo. This formative role played by Sierra Leone makes the analysis here relevant for contexts well beyond the small West African state.

DFID's SJSR in Sierra Leone has been one of the most comprehensive reform programmes undertaken by a bilateral donor, incorporating the restructuring, recruitment and retraining of the Republic of Sierra Leone Armed Forces and Sierra Leone Police, the revitalization of the Central Intelligence and Security Unit, reform of the judiciary and penal system, training of Parliamentary oversight committees and the Anti-Corruption Commission and the establishment of the Office for National Security and Justice Sector Coordination Office, to provide sector-wide coordination of the security and justice apparatuses. These reforms have been ongoing for over 15 years, with police reform commencing in 1997, and the Access to Security and Justice Programme commencing implementation in 2013, with a mandate until 2016. It is widely accepted that DFID's efforts in Sierra Leone have contributed to a more stable and secure post-conflict environment (Albrecht and Jackson 2009: 147–8; Olonisakin 2008). In fact, it is precisely because DFID's SJSR efforts in Sierra Leone have been – relatively speaking – so successful that it is an instructive case to examine. By explaining the organizational limitations of a leading SJSR donor in a sustained reform environment, this book contributes to an improved understanding of the roles that development agencies can play in transforming security and justice provision in fragile and post-conflict states.

What is the informal?

'Informal actors' is the rather imperfect term, used throughout the book, to refer to the diverse terrain of security and justice providers that exist in Sierra Leone – beyond the state and the related providers the state takes accountability for. The terminology used to capture this group of actors remains contested with multiple labels in use, none of which are entirely unproblematic and all of which seem to be based on caricatures of the state, rather than an accurate depiction of how it actually exists. While the general environment of diverse providers can perhaps best be described as one constituted by legal pluralism, institutional multiplicity, or multi-layered or hybrid governance, the designations given to those actors that render the environment plural, multi-layered or hybrid are unfortunately less nuanced (Scheye 2009a; 2009b; Bagayoko 2012). Nonetheless, there is a general understanding that despite the shortcomings of many of the terms frequently used, they all speak to the multiple systems and providers of security and justice in many societies that can be competitive, contested, or complementary and are almost always overlapping (Isser 2011).

The overlapping nature of security and justice providers is important. All of the available terminology – discussed briefly below – suggests a far greater distinction between the formal and informal, the state and the non-state, or the customary and the modern than exists in reality. In practice, these systems are interrelated and people move between them in often very fluid ways. As a result, there is an increasing focus in the literature on 'end-user' perspectives; that is, understanding security and justice from the perspectives of those who access the services (Luckham and Kirk 2012). From this standpoint, the classification of available services into formal versus informal, state versus non-state – and so on – has little meaning. Yet in order to highlight the neglect of those security and justice actors who are not a part of the immediate state apparatus, it remains useful to have a shorthand to capture the long list of actors that this can include (from chiefs, to secret societies, to trade associations, to alternative dispute resolution mechanisms, to gangs and militias). The conceptual baggage of the three most commonly used terms that were considered for use here – 'non-state', 'customary' and 'informal' – is set out below.

'Non-state' is popularly used to refer to those actors providing security and justice beyond the state (see for instance, Baker 2007; Albrecht and Kyed 2011). Yet chiefs in Sierra Leone, the primary focus of this book, do not fit neatly into this category because of their proximity to the state (Reno 1998; Fanthorpe 2005). As Albrecht notes:

> [Chiefs] belong neither to a pure non-state nor to a pure state category. This condition has made it difficult for international actors to engage robustly with chiefs, who have essentially refrained from clearly defining

> their functions and role as in-between state and non-state. In short, there does not seem to be a space for the type of actor that falls between categories.
>
> (Albrecht 2010: 7)

Chiefs are 'guaranteed and preserved' by The Constitution of Sierra Leone (1991) and have responsibilities set out in the Chieftaincy Act (2009). Chiefs are represented in Parliament by Paramount Chiefs, who have 12 reserved seats (one for each district). Indeed, chiefs at times refer to themselves as 'civil servants' and see their job as supporting the political party of the day (Tshombe Kargoi 2009). They are thus, at least in some ways, part of the state machinery, albeit in often poorly defined ways and, at times, sitting in tension with the state (for instance, in the competing jurisdictions of the state police and the chiefdom police). Indeed, terms such as 'twilight institutions' (Lund 2006) are used to highlight this inbetween nature of actors such as chiefs who play partly state and partly non-state roles. In the case of Sierra Leone, given the important connections with the state, 'non-state' does not accurately describe the kinds of actors that this book deals with.

Customary actors or traditional authorities are also popular terms in the literature (see for instance, Isser 2011; Ubink 2008; Kyed and Burr 2007). Given that chiefs perform customary functions and are often perceived as the 'custodians of tradition', these might seem more appropriate terms. Yet this terminology also suggests a strong link to tradition, in a way that can underplay the important modern governance functions that chiefs also carry out (for instance, collecting taxes on behalf of government). Ryann Manning notes this overlap of 'modern' and 'traditional' within the chieftaincy system:

> Local governance and justice in Sierra Leone involve a complex array of institutions and individuals, who draw their structure and legitimacy from a range of systems and heritages – customary, colonial, and modern – and interact with one another in a rich and sometimes unpredictable manner ... This process of mutual accommodation results in a hybrid system different from what was intended by either in isolation.
>
> (Manning 2009: 111)

Moreover, 'custom' and 'tradition' are far from fixed categories but rather highly political and contested. Using terminology, such as 'traditional' or 'customary' authority to refer to chiefs, suggests that they are the legitimate interpreters of what constitutes tradition or custom, and thus obscures their political and contested nature. Given the commitment of this research to presenting chiefs and secret societies in Sierra Leone not as ancient tribal traditions but rather as adaptive, modern institutions; and revealing 'custom' and 'tradition' to be highly political productions of power, terms that focus on custom or tradition, are also not appropriate here.[4]

While 'informal actors' suggests a stronger distinction between the 'formal' and 'informal' than in fact exists (Stephen Ellis suggests that the formal and informal realms are substantially more fluid than the terms themselves indicate (1996: 278)), it does not blur the relationship with the state in quite the same way as the 'non-state' label. It also draws on distinctions made in Sierra Leone, where state law is known as 'formal English law'. 'Informal' was also the term preferred by DFID, at least in the early 2000s when its policies began to address issues of the plurality of security and justice providers (DFID 2002b). Thus, while recognizing the exaggerated separation from the 'formal' that 'informal' implies, this term is used here, drawing attention to overlaps with the formal wherever possible.

A 'thick' method

Taking seriously the need to not just pay attention to, but also to actually start from, the context in which SJSR was happening, this book draws on the idea of 'thick understandings', developed by anthropologist Clifford Geertz. This means first understanding the historical, social and political situation in Sierra Leone, the causes of war, and how security and justice are accessed, before thinking about how to reform security and justice. 'Understanding' is also used here in a particular way. Geertz (1975) maintained that understandings could be 'thick' or 'thin'. Thin understandings merely describe what is apparent; thick understandings seek to look beneath the surface of what is apparent to get to culturally-specific but not immediately observable meanings (Geertz 1975). One can only achieve thick understandings by beginning with the culturally-specific context which gives behaviours, practices and ideas meaning. Employing the example of a wink, Geertz demonstrates that understood 'thinly', the action is described as a contraction of the eyelid; whereas a thick description probes beneath the action to examine its cultural significance, understanding it as a wink and thus a meaningful communicative gesture (Geertz 1975: 7). It is thus to understand practices as inextricably within their cultural context, involving an ethnography of practice which denies the possibility of separating practices from the cultures which constitute them (Geertz 1975: 27; Giddens 1979). Here, thick understandings are developed of the causes of war and the provision of security and justice in Sierra Leone, but also of DFID. It is not just complex post-conflict environments which require probing beneath the surface, but also the cultures of development agencies, especially because they are often perceived to be technical and value-neutral.

A thick method is also particularly pertinent in the case of Sierra Leone, where events and behaviours are often understood as having ulterior meanings to the obvious, apparent or observable one. As Marianne Ferme highlights:

> [V]isible and more easily accessible practices in Sierra Leone are presumed to be activated by forces and meanings 'underneath' them. These forces

> shape the perception of the visible world – the meaning of language and names, the history of places – and social relations ranging from the domestic to interactions with strangers. They infuse appearances with suspicion, and evoke instead a deeper understanding of what lies beneath the surface. The Mende word for meaning, *yembu*, 'that which is underneath' things, points explicitly to the primacy of the concealed in understanding the visible.
>
> (Ferme 2001: 3–4)

Thick description is thus all the more important in such a context, where events and actions are not taken at face value, but rather believed to mean something deeper. The differences in understanding are apparent in the common greeting in Sierra Leonean *Krio* '*Ow di bodi?*'. While at a thin level, this can be understood as the Sierra Leonean version of 'how are you?', the greeting takes on a more nuanced meaning when understood thickly as embedded within Sierra Leone experience and culture. Illness is an unfortunately common reality in Sierra Leone, making enquiries about the state of the body much more pertinent than in the West, where our greetings are more often about the state of someone's life and activities, than about their health. Moreover, Sierra Leonean culture has a particular interest in the corporeal, given the connection between the body and the spirit. The body is often seen as a vehicle for spirits and witchcraft, with spirits or witches gaining control by entering the body (for instance, while it is 'open' during childbirth) (Ferme 2001: 166–77). The corporeal is thus seen as intimately connected to deeper spiritual concerns. '*Ow di bodi?*' is therefore both a straightforward everyday greeting (at a thin level), as well as a description of what constitutes wellbeing within a particular culture and set of experiences (at a thick level). Similarly, a common response to '*Ow di bodi?*' is '*ah tel God tenki*' – literally, 'I tell God thank you'. At a thin level these may be understood to underscore the predominantly Christian religious beliefs of those who originally spoke *Krio* (primarily those from Freetown). Yet the response also reveals the sense in which the health of many Sierra Leoneans is perceived to be 'in God's hands', with healthcare only rarely accessible or affordable. It is these thicker understandings that are most revealing in *interpreting* local idiom, beyond straightforward externally-imposed translations.

Understandings of the causes of war in Sierra Leone, therefore, must go beyond simply an external description of what appeared to have happened and why, to interpret the causes in a manner that those involved would recognize. In attempting to develop a thick understanding of the causes of war and why people fought, fieldwork was conducted in Freetown, Bo and Kenema (covering three of the four provinces in Sierra Leone) involving interviews with ex-combatants, accessed through organizations set up by former-Revolutionary United Front (RUF) and Civil Defence Force (CDF) fighters to pursue more peaceful post-conflict lives. These organizations included Promoters of Peace and Justice and Bike Riders Associations in Freetown, Bo and Kenema. Interviews with former-combatants, combined with recent anthropological literature, aimed to understand the causes of war from the perspectives of those who fought. Extensive interviews were also undertaken with DFID and SJSR programme staff, representatives from the Sierra Leone Police, Office for National Security and High Court, as well as civil society (primarily NGOs and trade associations), academics and chiefs.

Plan of the book

The book is divided into five chapters that tell a story about how DFID's understanding of the causes of war led to SJSR programmes that focused primarily on state actors; how this focus has limited the effectiveness of SJSR; and why DFID finds engagement with informal actors so problematic. To be effective and sustainable, SJSR must go beyond technical improvements to the capacity of the police and judiciary to address the underlying causes of conflict that have undermined security and justice in the past. As Herbert Wulf explains, 'Ambitions to reform the security sector have to consider the underlying causes of violence for such programmes to succeed' (2004: 12–13). And indeed, the UK Government recognized this, with a ten-year Memoranda of Understanding (MoU) signed by the UK and Sierra Leone Governments setting out a broad development programme that 'was aimed at addressing both the symptoms and the root causes of the conflict' (White 2008b: 3). As Chapter 1 demonstrates, however, the UK Government appeared to largely conceptualize the war in Sierra Leone through a state failure lens – thus justifying a SJSR programme that has focused overwhelmingly on reform of state security and justice providers. Chapter 2 contrasts with the first, providing a thick account of the civil war in Sierra Leone that reveals how it was triggered as much by failures of informal systems of governance, such as chieftaincy and patrimonialism, as by failures of state government. A more detailed examination of informal governance, security and justice practices, with a particular focus on the chieftaincy system, and the secret societies that support or are closely related to chieftaincy, reveals the centrality of these informal actors to security and justice, as well as their role in causing the grievances that prompted many to fight (Richards 1996; Peters 2006). Any attempts to comprehensively address the causes of conflict and to transform the nature of security provision in Sierra Leone would therefore have to engage with these informal actors, as well as the state.

Yet this engagement is not apparent in programming, as the case studies in Chapters 3 and 4 demonstrate. A lack of engagement with informal actors is seen to limit the overall effectiveness of security and justice reforms. Chapter 3 provides a case study of the Family Support Units within the Sierra Leone Police. Laudable efforts to provide improved policing to women are demonstrated as limited to urban areas due to a focus on solely the formal police, overlooking the informal policing mechanisms that women are most likely to report to, especially in rural areas. Chapter 4 examines the limited engagements with informal actors through primary justice programmes[5] of the Justice Sector Development Programme (JSDP). These include efforts to codify customary law and to reform the Local Courts that are responsible for adjudicating customary law. While the JSDP engaged more extensively with informal actors than any other SJSR in Sierra Leone to date, its projects also displayed a lack of awareness of the nature and extent of informal justice in Sierra Leone. Taken together, these programmes can be seen to have engaged with overwhelmingly state security providers, leaving untouched and unreformed the informal security and justice actors that constitute the predominant providers in Sierra Leone. This means that DFID's SJSR efforts are having only a limited impact on the quality of security and justice provided in post-conflict Sierra Leone. A lack of engagement with informal security and justice actors also leaves the contributing causes of the war unaddressed. The key question thus becomes why, despite the fact that informal security and justice actors are often the dominant providers of security and justice in Sierra Leone, have DFID's SJSR programmes demonstrated such limited engagement with them?

Chapter 5 argues that DFID's lack of engagement with informal actors is due to the organization's bureaucratic and political nature. This nature makes it difficult to develop and act on a worldview that does not locate the state as the prime security and justice provider. Its bureaucratic and political nature biases DFID towards a particular vision of the state and security and justice that leads to an understanding of the causes of war as rooted in state failure. As a result DFID's post-conflict SJSR response focuses on reforming formal state institutions. Thus, ultimately, it is DFID's bureaucratic culture and political character that prevent it from engaging with informal security and justice actors and, by extension, from more successfully reaching its goals of sustainably transforming security and justice provision. Chapter 5 also sets out some of the uncomfortable implications of these political and bureaucratic constraints. Finally, the Conclusion posits some initial recommendations for how development agencies might deal with the difficult position that they find themselves in: environments in which security and justice are frequently provided by informal actors that donors struggle to engage with due to their own political and bureaucratic commitments.

Given the role that abuses of power played in triggering the civil war in Sierra Leone, supporting reforms to improve the quality of security and justice services in the country is clearly important. So too is ensuring that such support engages with the actual locus of power and does not leave informal actors, as the dominant providers of security and justice to the majority of the population, untouched. Only by engaging with the security and justice sectors *as a whole* – and not just with their state components – can real transformations be achieved. Whether development agencies are able to offer such comprehensive support remains an open question.

Notes

1 Tribal headmen are Freetown's equivalent of provincial 'chiefs'. Each tribal head is the customary authority for each of the ethnic groups in Sierra Leone. In theory, individuals would see the tribal head for their own ethnic group, however the Council of Tribal Heads decided that, due to the infeasibility of travelling across the city to meet the tribal head for a particular ethnic group, each head would provide services to any ethnic group who lived in their locale.

2 A piece of cloth worn by women tied around the waist.

3 It is important to note that, throughout the book, when referring to DFID and its world-view, this is not to suggest that individual DFID staff necessarily share the views of the organization. Rather, I am referring to DFID *as an organization* – its rules, policies, culture and bureaucratic processes and how these constituent parts coalesce to form something distinct from any of the single components.

4 Nor are they, in fact, in most developed country contexts, where the Catholic Church and Italian mafias are modern and adaptive institutions with long histories, often erroneously described as 'traditional' (Hobsbawm and Ranger 1983).

5 The Justice Sector Development Programme referred to justice outside of the formal English laws of Sierra Leone as 'primary justice'.

Chapter 1

The UK's 'African albatross'[1]

DFID policy on Sierra Leone

Walking along River Number Two, Sierra Leone's most popular beach, depicted in the 1970s as the 'taste of paradise' in a Bounty chocolate bar commercial, it is hard to image that this country once represented the archetypal 'new war' of the 1990s and would contribute to the precipitation of not only new understandings of security, but also new approaches to development and peacebuilding. The impact of Sierra Leone's post-conflict recovery upon security and development discourse has in no small way been facilitated by the UK's extensive engagement with its former colony and protectorate. In conducting the first comprehensive security and justice sector reform (SJSR) programme in Sierra Leone, Britain (and in particular the Department for International Development (DFID), as the lead agency) altered the mandate of the development industry and opened up the field of security to development specialists.

While SJSR has now been 'normalized', to some extent, as a development strategy, it should not be forgotten precisely how innovative (and controversial) it was when it was first developed in Sierra Leone. It is therefore important to trace how it emerged and understand the environment that enabled it. Furthermore, understanding the evolution of SJSR in the case of Sierra Leone is instructive for security and justice reforms more broadly. SJSR is often thought of as a top-down process 'applied' to countries. However, SJSR was as much shaped by the Sierra Leone encounter as post-conflict Sierra Leone has been shaped by it (Albrecht and Jackson 2009: 17). This formative influence of the Sierra Leone experience on security and justice reform therefore makes this story relevant to such reforms further afield.

This chapter seeks to examine how this sleepy country on the Atlantic coast, established as a colony for freed slaves and once regarded as 'the Athens of West Africa', became the test site for some of the latest thinking in liberal statebuilding. In order to do so, the wider political environment that enabled an innovative security-development strategy to emerge in Sierra Leone and the DFID policies underpinning that strategy need to be understood. This examination highlights the state-centric nature of the UK's DFID-led

SJSR programme. A narrative of the broader political trends underway internationally and in Britain helps to explain DFID's mandate within the civil service and how such an unconventional development programme was possible in a geopolitically insignificant country like Sierra Leone. This is followed by an analysis of DFID policy regarding the conflict in Sierra Leone, drawn together from document analysis and interviews, revealing how a particular understanding of the causes of war led to a rationalization of state-focused SJSR. This rationalization was not official policy, nor was the stated aim of SJSR to address the causes of war in Sierra Leone. However, the peacebuilding and statebuilding framework that SJSR emerges from is predicated on alleviating the underlying conflict causes. As Roland Paris notes:

> Creating the conditions for stable and lasting peace in the immediate aftermath of a civil war would not be an easy task ... As both [Kofi] Annan and [Boutros] Boutros-Ghali pointed out, peacebuilding involved identifying and alleviating the underlying sources of conflict within a war-shattered state, which required a thorough understanding of local conditions.
>
> (Paris 2004: 3)

However implicit, therefore, understandings of what caused a conflict get internalized within post-conflict peacebuilding responses such as SJSR and in this case focused on the failure of the state. DFID policies related specifically to informal security and justice are examined at the end of the chapter, but are shown to be dwarfed by state-centric approaches and uneven in their development within DFID.

This chapter sets out the international and domestic environments that shaped DFID and how these led the Department to understand the war in Sierra Leone in a particular manner, justifying SJSR as we now know it. It presents DFID's policy on Sierra Leone as neat and logical, not yet complicated by the messier interpretation of events set out in Chapter 2. The chapter therefore analyses the evolution of DFID and its policy that enabled the state-centric SJSR framework that the remainder of this book will critique. It demonstrates that the manner in which a conflict is understood, even if only implicitly, has important implications for how responses are formulated.

'A dirty war in West Africa'[2]

In March 1991, a group of predominantly Sierra Leonean (but also Liberian, Guinean and Burkinabe) irregulars calling themselves the Revolutionary United Front (RUF) launched a cross-border assault from Liberia into Kailahun and Pujehun Districts in eastern and southern Sierra Leone (Alie 2005: 51). They were assisted by special forces from the National Patriotic Front of Liberia (NPFL), led by Charles Taylor (the warlord, Liberian president and international war criminal).[3] Key members of the RUF had connections to former-Libyan leader Muammar al-Qaddafi, having been involved in Green Book[4] reading groups at Sierra Leonean university campuses and receiving guerrilla training in Benghazi, Libya in the 1980s (Kargbo 2006: 22; Richards 2005: 119–46; Members A, Promoters of Peace and Justice, Freetown 2009). The stated aim of the RUF was to overthrow the corrupt government of President Joseph Momoh who, along with his cronies, was manipulating patrimonial networks to extract a personal profit from the country, crippling the economic prospects for the majority of Sierra Leoneans.[5] Such a movement should have attracted the support of the general population, as the corruption and poor governance that the RUF claimed to be fighting against robbed the majority of citizens of opportunities and wellbeing (Dorman 2009: 37). However, the RUF miscalculated the people's willingness to accept gross violence against government officials, chiefs and, particularly in later stages of the civil war, the general population, and the rebels thus quickly lost the backing of their would-be support base (Peters and Richards 1998: 200).[6] As a result, the RUF lacked the legitimacy that could have transformed them into a broader-based popular movement. While the RUF did grow rapidly in size from a small base throughout the war, and have transformed themselves into a not-so-popular political party since the end of the conflict, they have not achieved widespread popular support outside their ranks at any stage.

The state responded to the threat posed by the RUF by deploying the poorly-paid and -trained Sierra Leone Army (SLA) to counter the rebels' increasingly violent onslaught. However, the SLA proved susceptible to the lure of loot and diamond access that the RUF boasted, particularly after a hasty SLA enlargement from approximately 2,500 to 15,000 troops between 1992 and 1995 (Peters and Richards 1998: 184). The soldier/rebel or 'sobel' phenomenon came to signify the overlap between the ostensibly opposed soldier and rebel forces (Williams 2001: 144). As a result of the weakness of Sierra Leone's state structure, manifested clearly in the inability and/or unwillingness of the SLA to protect the civilian population, communities formed their own civil defence forces (CDFs), which drew, to some extent, on the practices of secret societies, traditionally the forums for male and female initiation in Sierra Leone and West Africa more broadly (Fithen and Richards 2005: 128). All groups were involved in the recruitment of child soldiers and the use of drugs including marijuana, crack cocaine and amphetamines (often mixed with gunpowder to create *brown brown*) to prepare troops for battle (Peters and Richards 1998: 186; 188). Children were particularly favoured as recruits by the RUF because of their literacy skills, which allowed the RUF to convey orders and leave messages in towns they attacked promoting their message (Peters and Richards 1998: 188; 195).

Throughout the conflict, Sierra Leonean politics also underwent a proliferation of contesting factions. In 1992, a disgruntled SLA soldier, Captain Valentine Strasser, who had been fighting in Kailahun district, arrived in

Freetown with a small group of comrades to demand that President Momoh ensure better conditions for the fighting forces (Keen 2005: 93–4). The President, on hearing of the soldiers' arrival, fled Sierra Leone for Guinea, leaving Strasser to assume the presidency, with his band of soldiers forming the National Provisional Ruling Council (NPRC). Unable to repel the RUF and recognizing the weakness of the state, Strasser increased the size of the army and hired the South African private security company, Executive Outcomes (paid in mining concessions) to push the rebels back from mining areas (Dorman 2009: 28–9; Peters and Richards 1998: 184). The newly enlarged army of untrained recruits became increasingly difficult to control, committing abuses and making little headway in repelling the RUF. By the mid-1990s, Strasser and the NPRC came under strong pressure from the international community to hold the country's first elections since 1967. The atmosphere in the lead up to elections was threatened by an internal coup, in which Strasser was ousted by his NPRC colleague, Julius Maada Bio (who, more recently, contested the 2012 elections as the SLPP Presidential candidate) (Keen 2005: 154–5). Elections, however, went ahead as planned and saw Ahmad Tejan Kabbah, a former UN bureaucrat, assume the presidency in 1996 and enter into a peace accord with the RUF later that year (Peters and Richards 1998: 185). Democratic legitimacy did not ensure stability in the country. By 1997, the peace accord was in tatters, with continued RUF fighting. Kabbah was also suspicious of the SLA, given their support for the former NPRC government, and sidelined them in negotiations (Peters and Richards 1998: 185). Support was given instead to building up the CDFs, numbering between 15,000 and 25,000. Inevitably, this favouritism created resentment within the army and another coup was carried out in May 1997 by Major Johnny Paul Koroma and the Armed Forces Revolutionary Council (AFRC), forcing Kabbah into exile in neighbouring Guinea (Peters and Richards 1998: 185–6). The AFRC invited the RUF to join the new government, surprising many and resulting in Sierra Leone being suspended from the Commonwealth and the United Nations imposing arms and petroleum embargoes (Keen 2005: 212).

By 1998, rebel fighting had reached the capital of Freetown, which had hitherto been largely removed from the violence underway in the provinces. The fragility of the state was blatantly exposed. Nigerian peacekeepers under the auspices of the Economic Community of West African States Monitoring Group (ECOMOG) were deployed to push the rebels back with the help of the *Kamajor* CDF. A British private security company, Sandline International, was also engaged to support pro-Kabbah forces and was involved in the defence of the capital.[7] With the rebels forced out, Kabbah returned to Sierra Leone in 1998 and the United Nations Observer Mission in Sierra Leone (UNOMSIL) was established to monitor disarmament (Schümer 2008: 59). These victories, however, were short-lived, with the RUF again invading Freetown in January 1999 under 'Operation No Living Thing', in which approximately 6,000 people were killed.[8] As a result, the unarmed UN Observer staff were withdrawn (Schümer 2008: 59). RUF fighters were forced into retreat by ECOMOG, who in the process gained a reputation in Freetown for brutalities of their own (Schümer 2008: 71–2). Kabbah was forced by the international community to renew the peace process with RUF leader Foday Sankoh and both parties signed the Lomé Agreement in July 1999.[9] Despite 11,000 United Nations Assistance Mission to Sierra Leone (UNAMSIL) peacekeepers being deployed to enforce the Agreement,[10] it failed when the RUF captured UN peacekeepers and continued attacks and moves towards Freetown in early 2000 (Dorman 2009: 26). On 7 May 2000, approximately 700 British paratroopers, supported by 800 Royal Marine commandoes, were deployed to Sierra Leone, ostensibly to evacuate British nationals, but ultimately also to support UN and ECOMOG peacekeeping forces (Dorman 2009: 27; Kargbo 2006: 302; Kampfner 2003: 70; Olonisakin 2008: 63). A combination of Nigerian, UN and British forces eventually succeeded in driving the rebels from the capital, capturing Sankoh and having a stabilizing effect on the country (Olonisakin 2008: 63). UNAMSIL forces were later increased to a strength of 17,500 – the largest United Nations peacekeeping deployment in the world at the time (Schümer 2008: 59). Fighting across the rest of the country continued until March 2001. The war was officially declared over in January 2002. Elections were held in May 2002, with Kabbah re-elected as President and his SLPP party attaining a resounding majority of 83 of 112 parliamentary seats (Dorman 2009: 123). The RUF political party won no seats and received just 1.7 per cent of the national vote (Schümer 2008: 60).

The costs of Sierra Leone's 11-year civil war were substantial, resulting in between 75,000–200,000 deaths (Schümer 2008: 55), 12,000 amputee survivors,[11] 2 million displaced people (DFID, MoD and FCO 2003: 15; BBC 1999), 72,500 demobilized combatants (including 7,000 children), 42,300 weapons and 1.2 million pieces of ammunition collected, and 17,500 UN peacekeepers deployed (UN Disarmament Demobilization and Reintegration Resource Centre (undated)). This devastation prompted, and the massive international response reflected, innovations in development and security discourse, most noticeably in British development, foreign and defence policy. This is apparent in the status that post-conflict peacebuilding efforts in Sierra Leone have attained as an archetypal case of new ways of operating in complex emergencies (Olonisakin 2008: 1–3). Such innovations did not, however, occur in a vacuum and a sea-change in international thinking on how best to approach development, as well as shifting ideational sands within UK government structures and commitments from key stakeholders, provided fertile soil for the transformations to come. These international and domestic factors provided the context in which change was possible, and are examined in more detail below to explain the manner in which DFID came to engage with Sierra Leone.

Changing international times: Aid, development and security

Aid policy throughout the 1980s and early 1990s focused to a large degree on reforming fiscal policies within developing countries through structural adjustment programmes that de-emphasized the role of the state. These programmes promoted austerity measures and a liberal, free market economic agenda that would supposedly lure foreign investment and thus promote development. Yet by the end of the decade, little (if any) progress had been made. As James Ferguson notes:

> The idea that deregulation and privatization would prove a panacea for African economic stagnation was a dangerous and destructive illusion. Instead of economic recovery, the structural-adjustment era has seen the lowest rates of economic growth ever recorded in Africa (actually negative, in many cases), along with increasing inequality and marginalization.
>
> (Ferguson 2006: 11)

New thinking was needed to turn this deepening poverty around (Porteous 2005: 282). Opportunities were to be found in the space that opened up for non-traditional security thinking at the close of the Cold War (Waddell 2006: 535). As conflicts increasingly occurred within countries, rather than between them, civilian casualties increased, thus prompting humanitarian concerns and putting security issues firmly on the agenda of development practitioners.[12] Conflict was also seen to eat into the potential development dividend of aid. It has been calculated that armed conflict cost Africa approximately USD 284 billion between 1990 and 2005 – which is almost the total amount of aid the continent received in that time (IANSA, Oxfam and Saferworld 2007: 3). Improving the prospects for development thus depended on addressing the challenge of conflict.

With a nuclear stand-off between the United States and the Soviet Union no longer dominating security agendas, defence establishments (still wielding their Cold War-inflated budgets) also began to look elsewhere for the threats of the 1990s. These were to be found in the symptoms of the conflicts that were beginning to emerge in the developing world – such as civil wars in Somalia, Mozambique, Angola, Liberia and Sierra Leone; and genocide in Rwanda and Bosnia. Poverty, disease, inequality and resource scarcity came to be seen as the agitating factors that fractured countries, often along supposedly ethnic lines (Willett 2005: 576). Media coverage of these conflicts brought 'barbaric' (in fact just low-tech) fighting with machetes and hand-to-hand combat into the living rooms of an international community no longer hamstrung by superpower rivalries. The imperative to 'do something' was, at times, strong and international peacekeeping missions were deployed in the name of human suffering (albeit only where this was politically convenient).

The non-traditional instigating factors of these conflicts thus ascended the international security agenda as new major threats (Dalby 1997: 3–5).

Correlated to this change in threat perception, the very understanding of security also began to shift towards an increased focus on development. The human security agenda, which arose throughout the 1990s (its most emphatic enunciation in the United Nations Development Programme's 1994 Human Development Report), considered a variety of non-military variables as intrinsic to the security of the individual (in place of, or alongside, the state) (UNDP 1994). Rather than merely being concerned with state security from external military threats, human security propounded the idea that an individual's security was also influenced by their freedom from fear of hunger, disease and oppression and rights to education, healthcare and opportunity (Sen 2000). This expansion of the security agenda 'heralded certain versions of security that were much more conducive to integration with development concerns' (Waddell 2006: 525).

Thus, security policy was broadening its scope to prioritize traditional development concerns, such as poverty and inequality, on the threat agenda, while at the same time development policy was recognizing security concerns as major obstacles to progress, and therefore as legitimate areas for aid engagement (Williams 2002: 145; Duffield 2007). This more proximate relationship between security and development would later prove crucial for DFID's engagement with Sierra Leone. International events continued to justify the newfound complementarity between security and development. For instance, population flows from conflict zones created a fear in the West of being overwhelmed by the threats of crime and disease that supposedly attended such populations (Huysmans 2006). Borders were rendered increasingly permeable by the new threats, simultaneously creating security and development concerns. Importantly, UK Prime Minister Tony Blair was convinced of this transnational nature of threats, justifying humanitarian intervention in Kosovo by claiming in 1999: 'We are all internationalists now' (quoted in Penketh 2008). He went on to argue, 'We cannot turn our backs on conflicts and the violation of human rights within other countries if we want still to be secure' (quoted in Penketh 2008).

These trends were cemented by the 11 September 2001 terrorist attacks on the US, which profoundly influenced security and development policy making. The attacks brought home that not only were the new threats of underdevelopment and its associated symptoms of state failure threatening to those who experienced them in far off, developing countries – they were also threatening to the security of the West (Porteous 2008: 128–9; Waddell 2006: 546). As stated in the G8's Africa Action Plan, 'Poverty, underdevelopment and fragile states create fertile conditions for violent conflict and the emergence of new security threats, including international crime and terrorism. There will be no lasting security without development and no effective development without security and stability' (quoted in Willet

2005: 569). The UN High Level Panel on Threats, Challenges and Change also makes the point in its report entitled, 'A More Secure World: Our Shared Responsibility':

> Development is the first line of defence for a collective security system that takes prevention seriously. Combating poverty will not only save millions of lives, but will also strengthen states' capacities to combat terrorism, organised crime and proliferation. Development makes everyone more secure.
>
> (Quoted in Willet 2005: 569)

The UK endorsed this perspective with Foreign Secretary Jack Straw stating in a 2002 speech that 'as well as bringing mass murder to the heart of Manhattan, state failure has brought terror and misery to large swathes of the African continent, as it did in the Balkans in the early 1990s. And at home it has brought drugs, violence and crime to Britain's streets' (quoted in Abrahamsen 2004: 679). With the realization that underdevelopment posed a threat not just to those who live with it in their everyday lives but also to those abstracted from it in the West, efforts to address this threat have been afforded greater urgency. The recognition that, 'the security of the poor ... [is linked] to the security of the entire world' (Waddell 2006: 546) transforms the manner in which the developing world is engaged.

This political landscape meant that development and security were increasingly bundled together as mutually dependent concepts that policy could not neatly separate out, posing challenges for governments, in which independent departments have traditionally been responsible for relatively discrete fields of expertise. It is in this context that the New Labour government in the UK undertook transformational structural and policy changes in regard to security and development that set the stage for how they would respond to the situation in Sierra Leone.

The domestic context in the UK

Establishment of DFID

Development policy had been a central component of Blair's 1997 campaign, proposing the establishment of an independent department to oversee British aid. Aid had previously been dealt with by the Overseas Development Agency, a wing of the Foreign and Commonwealth Office (FCO) from 1970 onwards (DFID 2009b). As the 'softer' side of foreign policy, aid concerns were often trumped by more traditional concerns of diplomacy and trade, including arms sales (Porteous 2005: 281–2). An independent department, Labour argued, would allow aid to develop its own agenda and momentum, less hindered by self-interested politics (Porteous 2005: 281–2). Consequently, the Department for International Development (DFID) was established in 1997 with a mandate to: 'Lead the UK Government's fight against world poverty.'[13] As Tom Porteous notes:

> with the creation of DFID, development assistance was explicitly untied from the promotion of British commercial interests, and issues related to UK development policy in Africa got a hearing at cabinet level, a more strategic focus and a lot more cash.
>
> (Porteous 2005: 282)

DFID's influence was, for a new department, extraordinary, with a cabinet-level Secretary of State who was able to argue the Department's case at the highest levels of decision-making and thus access greater funding (Porteous 2005: 282). This funding allowed DFID to commission its own white paper, conduct large-scale recruitment and open country offices throughout Africa and the developing world (Porteous 2008: 131).

Africa had been a key and long-standing policy area for the Overseas Development Agency (Ero 2001: 54–5). However, the energies focused on Africa within the newly created DFID were unprecedented (for instance, Africa received its own Conflict Prevention Pool of funding, separate from the Global Conflict Prevention Pool). In part, this was due to the leadership of Clare Short, whose interest in the continent grew throughout her time as Secretary of State for International Development (Albrecht and Jackson 2009: 170). Short was reportedly greatly affected by her visits to Africa and was very impressed upon meeting Sierra Leonean President Kabbah, who she saw as an illegitimately ousted democratic leader with great potential (Albrecht and Jackson 2009: 170). In relation to Sierra Leone, as one UK Government source noted, Short was '...almost an elemental force ... she was very, very committed personally – she met Kabbah, and took this upon herself as a kind of personal crusade' (Garth Glentworth, quoted in Albrecht and Jackson 2009: 170). Africa was also high on DFID's agenda given the prevalence of conflict on the continent, which prompted unprecedented engagement given that the international agenda saw conflict and poverty as increasingly related, and are seen below to be central to the way the Department thought about Sierra Leone.

DFID and its place in the British civil service

In its efforts to carve out a new poverty reduction role within the UK civil service, DFID stepped on the toes of more than one government department. Porteous notes that DFID tended to:

> stray into jealously guarded areas of Whitehall outside the traditional remit of a development ministry. Inevitably, some interdepartmental frictions ensued, for example with the Treasury over who should represent

> the UK at the World Bank and IMF; with the Department of Trade and Industry over international trade; with the Ministry of Defence over its military training programmes in Africa; and with the FCO over numerous issues including the sharing of classified information, the clearing of drafts of UN Security Council Resolutions, and policy documents.
>
> (Porteous 2005: 283–4)

Through these turf battles, DFID began to develop its own identity within the civil service. This was facilitated by the clout of the Department, with a seat in cabinet, a large budget and impressive new recruits, which allowed it to take on unconventional development issues (such as conflict) and imbue them with a new approach. This approach has focused on democracy, equality and human rights in a far less nationally-interested manner than other departments, such as the FCO, Home Office and MoD, whose mandates have a stronger emphasis on the national interest. This process of setting out a clearly differentiated purpose and set of interests from other government departments helped to build, what Michael Barnett and Martha Finnemore refer to as, 'organizational autonomy' within the civil service (2004: 23). Making this clear, DFID launched a policy of 'new humanitarianism' in 1998, which attempted to ensure that the moral impulse behind aid remained central, by limiting the harm it could cause and recognizing its inherently political nature (Schümer 2008: 1). This policy was 'crucial in defining ... [DFID's] identity and was universalist, reaffirming principles and human rights' (Marriage 2006: 47). Efforts to cast DFID's work as an oasis of principles within the vast desert of otherwise unprincipled political decision-making was apparent, for instance, in the title of Clare Short's 1998 Speech, 'Principled Aid in an Unprincipled World' (Dolan 1998: 372–3). The worthy intention of the policy of new humanitarianism, to render aid more 'principled' (according to notions of human rights, liberalism and democracy), created within DFID[14] a unique identity that set it apart from the rest of government, in particular the FCO, as the former aid department (although interestingly, at this time, the FCO was also articulating an 'ethical foreign policy', demanding support for other peoples' democratic rights (Cook 1997)). As Zöe Marriage suggests, 'DFID developed a morality discourse that was seductive domestically – being ostensibly ethical, long-termist and positive-sum' (Marriage 2006: 48).

In addition to a new 'ethical' persona within the civil service, DFID's emergence meant that there were now two ministries dealing with issues such as trade, but approaching them with different goals in mind. While this has involved, as Porteous (2005: 283–4) suggests, some toe stepping, other departments were also realizing the inevitable interconnectedness of their work with DFID and others. Porteous goes on to note:

> just as DFID under Clare Short soon realised that it could not 'do' development without straying into political and military affairs, so the FCO under [Robin] Cook, and from 2001 under Jack Straw, came to

> realise that it could not 'do' foreign policy in Africa without working closely with DFID – and not just on 'pure' development issues, but also on others such as governance, security sector reform, crime, HIV, conflict and the problems of weak states. All the problems tended to merge into one.
> (Porteous 2005: 285–6)

In order to address the problem of departments doubling up on research and analysis, albeit at times with different means and goals, the Africa Conflict Prevention Pool (ACPP) and the Global Conflict Prevention Pool (GCPP) were established in 2001 (DFID, MoD and FCO 2004: 5). The Pools brought DFID, the FCO and the MoD together for 'joint analysis, financing and coordination in areas where collaboration between the three departments can add value to UK conflict prevention activities' (DFID, MoD and FCO 2004: 2). While the departments retained the integrity of their individual expertise (the FCO focusing on diplomatic initiatives; the MoD providing peace support, enforcement and training; and DFID working towards poverty reduction), the Pools were intended to maximize the impact and harmonization of UK interventions overseas and formed an integral part of the 'joined-up government' approach (DFID, MoD and FCO 2004: 4; MoD (undated)). These Pools were superseded in 2008 by the Conflict Prevention Pool (CPP), operating in the same manner and for the same purpose, but without a separate pool for Africa. The CPPs have thus allowed the three participating departments to take a looser approach to their own traditional spheres of operation and a more comprehensive approach to conflict prevention. For DFID, this has further legitimized its ability to address conflict as one of the key obstacles to poverty reduction, as understood through the security-development nexus.

Blair's influence

Tony Blair assumed office in 1997 with little experience or knowledge of African foreign policy and development concerns (Porteous 2005: 286). His father had been a lecturer in the Law Department at the University of Sierra Leone, Fourah Bay College in the 1960s, and this personal connection is said to have cultivated in Blair a particular interest and compassion for Sierra Leone (Borger 2007; Glentworth 2008).

Africa, and Sierra Leone in particular, were of interest to Blair for several reasons. The 'third way' that Blair promoted as 'an attempt to find middle ground between two diametrically opposed ideologies: old Left socialism and new Right capitalism', provided a set of values that lent themselves to a focus on Africa (Ero 2001: 52). The 'third way' implied a sense of shared responsibility for issues such as democracy, liberty and justice beyond merely our own borders (Ero 2001: 52; Abrahamsen and Williams 2001: 250). Blair perceived a lack of such qualities in many African states, demonstrated in his speech to the Labour Party Conference in 2001, in which he declared Africa to be 'a scar on the conscience of the world' (Gallagher 2009: 435–51; Blair 2001).

Blair's cooption of Africa as one of his key concerns was apparent as he pushed African issues onto the agenda at the G8 Summit in Genoa in 2001 and appointed a special advisor on Africa within Number 10 (Porteous 2005: 289). Upon re-election in 2001, Blair developed the 'New African Initiative' – a partnership between Western and African governments to 'offer greater investment, aid and debt relief for Africa' (BBC News 2001). In 2004, recognizing the need for greater local ownership, Blair launched the Commission for Africa 'to take a fresh look at Africa's past and present and the international community's role in its development path' (Commission for Africa (undated)). These initiatives indicate that the Prime Minister saw Africa as an important and legitimate field for political engagement and the continent assumed a higher profile under Blair than under any other recent administration.

Despite Blair's enthusiasm, however, Julia Gallagher notes that the terms of his African engagements meant the continent figured in moral but not political terms in British politics and this selfless approach was central in casting British involvement in Sierra Leone as an operationalization of ethical foreign policy (Gallagher 2009: 448). Sierra Leone became the real world example of many of the problems that the Labour Party and the newly-created DFID had been emphasizing. Indeed, Blair stated in the wake of the intervention in Sierra Leone, '[w]hen people say run an ethical foreign policy, I say Sierra Leone was an example of that' (Blair quoted in Wickham-Jones 2000: 29).[15] Blair's 'third way' and its evolution into an 'ethical' foreign policy that found resonance in the challenges faced by Africa, combined with a belief in interventionism to facilitate the UK's unusually strong commitment to Sierra Leone.[16] This prime ministerial commitment provided DFID with a sympathetic (and interventionist) ear in the highest echelons of decision-making.

New security and development strategies

In the late 1990s new strategies for security and development were being crafted by DFID and the MoD that attempted to confront the realities of modern conflict and underdevelopment by focusing on 'stabilization'. Sierra Leone was a prime candidate for the interventions being innovated because its diminutive geography seemed to make it an achievable theatre for operations. As a result, the Sierra Leone case offered the UK government, including DFID, the opportunity to test and showcase its new stabilization approach. As Peter Albrecht and Paul Jackson suggest:

> apart from the obvious moral imperative to aid one of the poorest countries in the world, there was also the perception that if the UK could not achieve its conflict prevention/stabilization objectives in a country such as Sierra Leone, where, then, would the instruments available to the UK Government be effective?
>
> (Albrecht and Jackson 2009: 171)

Sierra Leone offered a seemingly hospitable environment in which to implement their transforming approach to security and development through joined-up government and the rapid deployment of smaller military units (which the 1998 Strategic Defence Review advocated) (Dorman 2009: 132–3; Williams 2001: 159). As a former-DFID Senior Governance Advisor explained, 'had it been a bigger country we would have been much more intimidated because we have ended up spending proportionately a huge amount of money in Sierra Leone compared with what we would normally spend in a country with that size population and land area' (Glentworth 2008). Sierra Leone thus 'provided quite a useful test case for the new ... emerging security and development agenda' (White 2008a). It offered a geographically and financially limited theatre, while simultaneously providing a convincing moral imperative that fitted with the ethical foreign policy of New Labour and the responsible aid programme advocated by DFID.

International trends in security and development discourse brought the two fields into closer proximity and opened up the possibility for shared terrain, which would prove critical to DFID's work in Sierra Leone. Changes on the UK political scene, such as the creation of an independent DFID, promotion of an 'ethical' foreign policy, a commitment to joined-up government and a 'third way' interventionism favoured by the Prime Minister, ensured that concerns about Africa received the highest level of political consideration and that radical responses to these concerns were possible. Finally, a new stabilization approach to security and development challenges, developed by DFID and the MoD, was available to be trialled. It was in this context that greater engagement in Sierra Leone was made possible. However actual events appeared to take on a much more accidental nature. As Peter Albrecht and Paul Jackson have noted (quoting a senior DFID governance advisor and Clare Short respectively):

> 'We could not – we, being the British – could not let this fragile, but democratically elected government collapse. Now, I don't think there was much theory behind that'. Indeed, simply, as put by Clare Short, referring to this period: 'I was just doing it because it was disgraceful. No one was planning anything'.
>
> (Albrecht and Jackson 2009: 133)

While there might not have been much in the way of clearly enunciated policy to guide the manner in which the UK's intervention unfolded, the international and domestic context made such an intervention plausible. As DFID's former-Security Sector Advisor suggests, 'the geopolitical ... stars were in alignment' (White 2008a).

Britain's intervention in Sierra Leone in May 2000, initially to evacuate British and Commonwealth nationals, and later extended to buttress the weak UNAMSIL force, heralded the beginning of the UK's long engagement with the country. Michael Binyon, writing in *The Times* (2000), referred to Sierra Leone as 'Labour's expensive African albatross', where, 'in the last five years, Britain has spent more money, given more aid per head of population and been more politically engaged ... than in any other African country.' While the intervention itself played out in a rather *ad hoc* manner, the legitimacy of such a decision was embedded within an enabling political environment. This was the outcome of the interplay between a series of shifting international debates and political agendas that ensured Sierra Leone was not merely a rescue operation, but a litmus test for a new political approach involving a newly independent aid department, ethical foreign policy and a heightened proximity between security and development concerns. It was a formative context for DFID, which went on to lead the UK's response efforts in Sierra Leone. As an exploration of DFID's policies relating to Sierra Leone demonstrates, this formative context continued to have an influence and resulted in an unconventionally broad role for an aid department. This role included emphasizing poverty reduction over national interests and utilizing an ethical and interventionist foreign policy to achieve its increasingly securitized developmental aims. These influences upon DFID have been crucial in explaining how SJSR came to be seen as the appropriate solution for Sierra Leone. The following section draws upon DFID documents and interviews with staff and consultants, to examine the dominant narratives in DFID policy regarding the conflict in Sierra Leone, and how these narratives shape the programmes that DFID enacts in response to the civil war.

DFID policy on Sierra Leone

As a bureaucratic, expert agency, DFID's interpretation of problems defines the realm of possible solutions. As Michael Barnett and Martha Finnemore suggest, bureaucratic organizations:

> use frames to situate events and to interpret problems, to fashion a shared understanding of the world, to galvanize sentiments as a way to mobilize and guide social action, and to suggest possible resolutions to current plights. Events, in short, do not have an objective meaning but must be made meaningful by actors, and actors ... affix meaning to these events because doing so creates boundaries of acceptable action.
>
> (Barnett and Finnemore 2004: 33)

This section sets out how DFID has framed the causes of war in Sierra Leone, often implicitly, in a way that makes state-centred security and justice reform the appropriate response.

Uncovering the policies that guided DFID's substantial engagement in Sierra Leone reveals a lack of overarching strategy and yet a surprisingly consistent departmental approach in spite of this. In a review of the UK

Government's approach to peacebuilding, Simon Lawry-White concludes that 'the short answer to the question, "What is the UK government's strategy on peacebuilding" is that there is no overall strategy' (2003: 17). More specifically in relation to SJSR, DFID's former-Security Sector Advisor comments that 'although the British Government has a security sector reform policy brief, [which only came out in 2003], there isn't actually a comprehensive SSR policy' (White 2008a). Thus, an investigation of UK policy in relation to Sierra Leone is not as straightforward as might be imagined. The following excavation of DFID's white papers and publications from 1998 onwards in relation to Sierra Leone, Africa, conflict, governance, security and justice reform is revealing. From an analysis of these documents, as well as speeches and interviews with DFID personnel and consultants, dominant narratives emerge to explain DFID's engagement in Sierra Leone. These narratives begin with an explication of the problems that DFID perceived as needing to be addressed. The most useful document in this regard is a 2001 publication entitled, 'The Causes of Conflict in Sub-Saharan Africa'. It states that 'an effective response to African conflict requires agreement on, and understanding of, its causes. Past responses to conflict have often failed to understand the context within which conflict has operated or to address the causes' (DFID, FCO and MoD 2001: 14). It highlights the importance of understanding how a particular war came about in order to be able to effectively respond to it (DFID, FCO and MoD 2001: 3). The manner in which DFID has conceptualized the causes of war in Sierra Leone, then, has consequences for the nature of their post-conflict efforts. Their understanding of the war is demonstrated here to fit neatly with the post-conflict SJSR programme that was prescribed by the UK.

Similar to its policy on SJSR, DFID, and the UK government more broadly, has no official line on the causes of war in Sierra Leone. The intervention that was prompted there was largely *ad hoc*, with no pre-assessment of the causes of war or framework for action. This was, at least in part, due to the imperative to act quickly in response to the rapidly changing situation in Sierra Leone. Some DFID staff interviewed indicated that, given this pressure, the time-consuming processes of appraising, planning, budgeting and approving can get in the way of getting on with actually responding. Of course, there are very real concerns about the division of valuable time between planning and implementation. However, even without a rigorous planning phase to guide implementation, there will inevitably be assumptions implicit in implementation about what it is trying to address that need to be thought through. Skimming the planning in order to get on with implementation does not mean that there is an obvious consensus on the causes of war. Rather, it means that the understandings of the causes of war will be obscured and implicit in the actions being implemented. What is drawn out below is the dominant narrative of the causes of war apparent throughout DFID documents and speeches. Piecing these together assembles a coherent image of the way in which the conflict in Sierra Leone was understood by DFID, and engaged with, despite not being explicitly set out in policy terms.

State failure

The DFID publication, 'Causes of Conflict in sub-Saharan Africa', suggests that '[i]t is possible to distinguish between the root causes of conflict, the secondary causes that enable and sustain conflict and the tertiary causes, or the barriers that hinder resolution' (DFID, FCO and MoD 2001: 14). The first of the 'root causes', receiving the lengthiest explanation in the paper, is 'weak states and state collapse', with Sierra Leone specifically pinpointed as a 'failed state' (DFID, FCO and MoD 2001: 8; 14). DFID claims:

> The weakening and collapse of state institutions has caused internal and regional conflict. Collapse is rarely sudden. It arises out of a long and degenerative process ... A key part of this process is the deterioration of the security sector, which becomes unaccountable and abusive. Judicial and penal systems collapse. The state finds itself unable to provide basic social services or security to its people. The erosion of infrastructure completes the break up of the state.
>
> (DFID 2001: 14)

Sierra Leone was, in fact, pointed to explicitly as a failed state on a consistent basis in UK policy around the time of the UK intervention (DFID, MoD and FCO 2004: 3). Clare Short used this phrase to explain the causes of conflict in Africa, specifically mentioning Sierra Leone (Short 2000). In 2002, Foreign Secretary Jack Straw made a speech in the lead up to the first anniversary of 9/11, devoted to the topic of 'Failed and Failing States', in which he spoke of Sierra Leone's plight (Straw 2002). Porteous (2005: 291) notes this trend, stating that 'Sierra Leone is usually presented as the main example of successful UK intervention to rescue a collapsed state'; and that Sierra Leone is contrasted with 'weak states that have not completely failed, or have managed to overcome civil conflict and collapse' (Porteous 2005: 292). The state failure logic has been incorporated further into UK policy as an explanation for insecurity in Africa by the Africa Conflict Prevention Pool (ACPP). The Pool's 'Joint Approach to Preventing and Reducing Conflict in sub-Saharan Africa' states: '[a]s weakened authoritarian regimes lost internal control and external support, a number of states collapsed ... [and] became the focal point for wider regional instability' (DFID, MoD and FCO 2004: 3). Specific mentions of how state failure caused conflict in Sierra Leone refer to poor governance and frail state structures (Horn *et al.* 2006: 110), corruption amongst the political elite (DFID 2008: 2) and an unruly security sector (DFID, FCO and MoD 2001: 14; Vinci 2008: 298; Evans (undated)). This approach to the causes of conflict in Sierra Leone problematizes state incapacity and seeks to strengthen it in order that service delivery is improved. Such increased capacity would, in theory, alleviate discontent amongst constituents and improve the environment for investment and thus economic development (DFID, FCO and MoD 2001: 14).

The definition of a 'failed state', however, has not been entirely clear, and is often replaced by similarly obscure terms such as 'fragile', 'collapsed', or 'weak' (DFID, MoD and FCO 2001: 3; DFID 2005a: 7). Discussion of these terms focuses on poor governance, weak institutions unable or unwilling to provide services and corrupt political elites more interested in personal profit than in governing (DFID, MoD and FCO 2001: 15). Describing fragile states (as DFID later refers to them) in 2005, DFID defines them as:

> those [states] where the government cannot or will not deliver core functions to the majority of its people, including the poor. The most important functions of the state ... are territorial control, safety and security, capacity to manage public resources, delivery of basic services, and the ability to protect and support the ways in which the poorest people sustain themselves.
>
> (DFID 2005a: 7)

States fail, therefore, by ceasing to provide essential services, of which security is one of the most important. This fits with other extrapolations, such as Prime Minister Blair's Strategy Unit which stated that '[w]eak and failing states are often unable to meet the security and prosperity needs of their own people' (Centre for Development Research (undated)). By prioritizing the ability of the state to provide services, such as healthcare, education and, importantly, security, reforms centred on the state become the focus of response efforts. For instance, the 'Causes of Conflict' publication goes on to claim under 'Responses to Conflict' that restoring the legitimacy of the state through improved service delivery is crucial to addressing state failure (DFID, FCO and MoD 2001: 17) Thus, by pinpointing state failure as a central cause of conflict in Sierra Leone, attempts to address these causes legitimate intervention into the state apparatus itself (Ferguson 2006: 95; Porteous 2008: 77–8). As Porteous highlights, drawing on the Report of the Commission for Africa, the logic is that, '[i]f states could be fixed so that they 'functioned' properly in terms of delivering basic services and security, then all would be well' (2008: 66). The goal then is to strengthen and reform state institutions, of which the security services are a prime (if not *the* prime) component.

The state failure thesis, however, merely facilitates intervention into the state apparatus. While it pinpoints security provision as one of the key services which the Sierra Leonean state failed to provide, it does not in and of itself provide a justification for DFID's involvement in SJSR – a field of programming that could well have been left to the FCO or MoD. DFID's leading role in SJSR is dependent upon the second dominant narrative that emerges in DFID reports and speeches: the security-development nexus. This combines with the state failure thesis to form a coherent vision of the relationship between war and peace, security and development, legitimizing SJSR as an appropriate response by DFID to the situation in Sierra Leone.

Security-development nexus

With the abovementioned international trends pushing development and security ever closer together, DFID's poverty reduction mandate soon faced the dilemma of how to engage with the issue of conflict, which its own 1997 White Paper indicated was inhibiting development in many parts of the world, particularly in Africa (DFID 1997: 67). The International Development Act of 2002 (and its predecessor, the Overseas Development and Cooperation Act of 1980) stipulated that DFID could only spend its budget on, 'development assistance which contributes to poverty reduction' (or, in the case of the 1980 Act, that contributes to 'development'). Any programmes that engaged with conflict had to be able to demonstrate that they were simultaneously reducing poverty. DFID nested its arguments in the high correlation found between rates of poverty and incidents of conflict. As the 1997 White Paper states, '[h]alf of the world's low income countries are suffering, or have just emerged from, serious conflicts' (DFID 1997: 67). By 1998, this claim was given greater substance in a document entitled, 'Poverty and the Security Sector', claiming that '[c]oncern about insecurity is a strong concern of the poor. Evidence from participatory poverty assessments shows that wherever people's basic physical security is threatened ... dealing with this problem is seen by the poor as an overriding priority' (DFID 1998). This was supported by work done by the World Bank under their 'Voices of the Poor' project, in which 20,000 poor people at 468 sites in 23 countries were interviewed and indicated that safety, security and justice issues were of central importance to them (DFID 2000b: 3).

Here, the mutual dependence between security and development becomes crucial. The security-development nexus, as it has been termed (Duffield 2001), has provided the *modus operandi* for DFID's branching into conflict and security issues. Given that conflict and underdevelopment are often correlated, and that conflict deepens underdevelopment by destroying infrastructure, services and livelihoods and deterring investment, there is an incentive for aid departments to address conflict, to maximize the effectiveness of their aid. The high correlation between conflict and poverty in Africa made this region a key policy area (Porteous 2008: 131). From 1997 onwards, DFID cast issues of conflict and security as being firmly within its mandate.

Yet in making this move, DFID was also aware that this was new and unconventional ground for a development agency. The 'Poverty and Security Sector' document goes on to state that while 'the link between security and development has been increasingly recognized in recent years, particularly since the end of the Cold War ... few Development Ministries have until now focused directly on security sector reform' (DFID 1998). Clare Short tackled this concern in a speech at King's College London in 1999. Making the link between security and development clear, she argues:

> Twenty of the 34 poorest countries are either involved in conflict or have recently emerged from conflict. I believe that a security sector of appropriate size, properly tasked and managed is a key issue. We are therefore entering this new area of security sector reform in order to strengthen our contribution to development.
>
> (Short 1999)

Other efforts were made to show how conflict and insecurity negatively impacted on development. For instance, in 2001 DFID claimed that 'over the past twenty years Africa has lost over fifty per cent of its transport infrastructure, many of the losses due to conflict' (DFID, MoD and FCO 2001: 11). In 2004 it highlighted that 'war has led to consistent negative economic growth – at least 2% per year according to the World Bank' (DFID, MoD and FCO 2004: 3). By 2007, the importance placed on security in achieving development was even stronger, with DFID claiming that '[w]hile aid can have a considerable impact on development and reducing poverty, policies beyond aid, for example security policy, can have an even greater impact' (DFID 2007b: 168). Simon Lawry-White, reviewing UK peacebuilding approaches between 1997 and 2001, notes that the security-development nexus is an underlying principle of UK conflict prevention efforts (Lawry-Wright 2003: 20). Sierra Leone was an obvious theatre for demonstrating nexus claims, given its combined credentials of conflict and ranking at the bottom of the UN's human development index throughout the 1990s.

The state failure arguments regarding the causes of war in Sierra Leone thus paired with the security-development nexus thinking within DFID to create a neat and unifying argument about how to get from war to peace and from insecurity to development. Its rationalization suggests that as service delivery by state security services, schools, health services, and so on, broke down, the Sierra Leonean state succumbed to failure. Without a judicial system, corrupt individuals and criminal groups could not be held to account for their actions. The poorer people were, the less they were able to protect themselves and the more insecure they became. Equally, the more insecure people were, the poorer they became as they could no longer go to work, school or invest safely in their futures. In failing to provide services, the state could thus no longer protect its citizens from violence or insulate them from the spiralling costs (in both financial and safety terms) of accessing other services. Poverty and conflict therefore existed in a state of mutual dependence and where one worsened, the other similarly deteriorated. As Schümer (quoting a DFID report) explains:

> DFID maintains that 'poverty can only be eradicated through the resolution of violent conflict' and vice versa and believes that violent conflict, while indicative of a structural deficiency, is an aberration of a historical movement towards sustainable development and liberal democracy.
>
> (Schümer 2008: 61)

Thus, to reduce poverty is to help prevent conflict and to resolve conflict is to support the alleviation of poverty. Or, as Hilary Benn, former Secretary of State for International Development states: 'Development without security is impossible; security without development is only temporary' (quoted in Waddell 2006: 534).

Security sector reform

This interpretation of conflict pinpoints the state (through state failure arguments) as the epicentre of breakdown and the key cause of the war. Following this prognosis, reforms to address the causes of conflict must therefore strengthen the state by improving service delivery, including the delivery of security and justice, as principal services that can protect its citizens and create stability for investment and development (Mehler 2009: 59). As security was now perceived as being within the bounds of DFID's development work (given the international and domestic context in which DFID was established), reform of the security sector became a legitimate area of engagement. The state security sector, therefore, became the vehicle for ensuring security *and* development. Thus, SJSR represented a logical approach to addressing the causes of conflict in Sierra Leone. As the Conflict and Humanitarian Affairs Department within DFID (2002) noted:

> Security sector reform is central to DFID's mission of poverty reduction. Badly managed and bloated security forces hamper development, discourage investment, and help to perpetuate poverty. On the other hand, well-managed and effective security forces operating within institutional frameworks defined by law, can be a force for good. Security sector reform can help create stability, promote human rights, and achieve transparency and accountable security expenditure.

Strengthening the security sector feeds into a broader process of the transition from war to peace (and security to development). Following security-development nexus thinking, with the security sector functioning appropriately and effectively with the help of SJSR, development can then take place in a more conducive environment (Biddle *et al.* 1998: 1–2). Peace is enabled by means of effective and disciplined security forces. The stability provided by this secure environment paves the way for increased investment, development and prosperity for the wider population. As Adrian Horn *et al.* note, '[t]he UK government sees SSR as a foundational pre-requisite for the achievement of broad development goals' (2006: 121). SJSR then is doubly valuable, as it addresses state failure (which DFID sees as a key cause of conflict in Sierra Leone) *and* it lays the foundations upon which DFID can also achieve its goals of poverty reduction and development through security-development nexus thinking.

Having problematized the state as a cause of the war and reading state failure to be the breakdown of service delivery functions, security provision through the UK's SJSR programme has concomitantly focused predominantly upon state forces. Most notably, these include the Republic of Sierra Leone Armed Forces, the Sierra Leone Police, the Office for National Security, the Central Intelligence and Security Unit and the formal judicial system. This adheres to the reform logic that disciplined, effective and democratic security forces will be better placed to fulfil their mandate of protecting citizens, thus allowing a stable environment in which the country can develop (DFID 2002a: 7). Such development, the argument goes, will in turn improve the country's chances of remaining conflict-free, as will the presence of a reliable security force, capable of confronting threats. This state-focused SJSR response fits more broadly with international trends of operationalizing peacebuilding through statebuilding. As Volker Boege and others explain 'state-building today is seen by major donors as a central dimension of development assistance, and functioning and effective state institutions are seen as a prerequisite for sustainable development' (Boege *et al.* 2009: 16).

DFID policy revisted: A place for the informal?

While this review of DFID policy documents reveals a state-centred approach to SJSR, given the focus of this book on informal security and justice, it is important to consider those policy documents that look beyond the state. A more targeted examination of DFID documents reveals a mixed picture, with different parts of the organization recognizing the importance of informal actors at different times. In relation to security sector reform, little engagement with informal security providers was apparent prior to 2004. For instance, analysis in the 1998 'Poverty and the Security Sector' document is purely state-centric (DFID 1998). DFID's 2000 White Paper, 'Eliminating World Poverty: Making Globalization Work for the Poor', makes no reference to informal or non-state security actors, despite establishing the importance of security sector reform for poverty reduction (DFID 2000b). A 1998 Evaluation Report specifically suggests that 'DFID projects have largely ignored the presence and role of many ... traditional and communal institutions

Table 1.1 Security Actors (DFID 2002a: 7)

Core security actors	Armed forces; police; paramilitary forces; gendarmeries; presidential guards; intelligence and security services (both military and civilian); coast guards; border guards; customs authorities; reserve or local security units (civil defence forces, national guards, militias).
Security management and oversight bodies	The Executive; national security advisory bodies; legislature and legislative select committees; ministries of defence, internal affairs, foreign affairs; customary and traditional authorities; financial management bodies (finance ministers, budget offices, financial audit and planning units); and civil society organisations (civilian review boards and public complaints commissions).
Justice and law enforcement institutions	Judiciary; justice ministries; prisons; criminal investigation and prosecution services; human rights commissions and ombudsmen; customary and traditional justice systems.
Non-statutory security forces	Liberation armies; guerrilla armies; private body-guard units; private security companies; political party militias.

involved in the maintenance of social order' (Biddle *et al.* 1998: 4). By 2002, DFID policy documents employed the oft-cited list of security actors as set out by the OECD (see Table 1.1) (DFID 2002a: 7). This list includes traditional justice systems and non-statutory security forces but there is no other engagement with the role of these actors within security and justice provision, other than to suggest that they need to be brought within the legal framework of the state (DFID 2002a: 26). The first non-state security actors to receive serious attention were private security companies, in the joint DFID, FCO and MoD 'Security Sector Reform Policy Brief', in 2003 (DFID, MoD and FCO 2003: 16). Again, customary justice providers received mention, but were not dealt with in any detail (DFID, MoD and FCO 2003: 16).

It was not until 2004 that informal security actors received serious policy attention with the publication of DFID's 'Non-state Justice and Security Systems', which recognized, 'the importance of traditional and informal systems as complements to formal state systems. It notes that non-state justice and security systems may need reform in order to become fairer and more effective' (DFID 2004a: 1). The document recognizes that informal systems 'are critically important in the context of DFID's pro-poor approach to security and justice' (DFID 2004a: 1), yet also cautions that in some cases 'it may be preferable not to engage with non-state systems, or even see them dissolved' (DFID 2004a: 4).

DFID documents dealing with the justice sector, however, reveal an earlier and more extensive recognition of informal actors. In 2000, DFID produced a policy document on 'Justice and Poverty Reduction' which recognized that '[i]mproving access to justice requires that both formal and customary systems be made to work justly and equitably' (DFID 2000a: 13). The document goes on to highlight the high rates of reliance on informal justice systems and points out the human rights challenges that such actors can pose (DFID 2000a: 14–15). This was followed in 2002 by a broader policy publication on 'Safety, Security and Accessible Justice', which reiterated the importance of informal security and justice arrangements and extended the awareness of informal actors beyond justice actors to policing providers as well (DFID 2002b: 12; 26).

While an evolution in DFID's awareness of informal security and justice actors is discernible over time, with later policy showing greater recognition, and across sectors, with justice picking up on this sooner than security, this should not suggest that DFID made informal security or justice a priority between 1998 and 2011 (the timeframe of the security and justice reforms examined here).[17] Indeed, of the approximately 40 documents analysed, only eight made reference to informal actors, and just a handful of these went into more detail than simply mentioning that they exist. Shining a light on this corner of policy discourse should not exaggerate its prominence. The state clearly remains DFID's preferred vehicle for security and justice provision and engagement, with only sparing mentions of informal actors, predominantly in policy related specifically to justice reform. Alongside these sparing mentions there has also been one notable attempt during the early stages of the UK intervention in Sierra Leone to engage with Paramount Chiefs, examined below.

Paramount Chiefs' Restoration Programme

The Paramount Chiefs' Restoration Programme (PCRP), later re-named the Chiefdom Governance Reform Programme (CGRP), sought to re-empower Paramount Chiefs in order to demonstrate to citizens that order and stability were returning to Sierra Leone and encourage repatriation of the chiefs (on the assumption that their subjects would follow) (Short 2002; Glentworth 2008). In order to fill the void of political control, DFID funded the building of houses for the Paramount Chiefs and filled chieftain vacancies (following the war approximately one third of chiefs had to be replaced due to deaths and displacement) (Jackson 2006: 95–6; Short 2002). It also proposed to establish guidelines for the exercise of power by Paramount Chiefs, although this key component was never instituted (Jackson 2006: 95–6). The institution of Paramount Chieftaincy was thus restored but not reformed, in a move reminiscent of Colonial Office efforts to attain order through chiefs and indirect rule. Richard Fanthorpe, evaluating the programme, highlights the limited scope of the project:

> Fear of the consequence of a post-war power governance vacuum in rural areas prompted DFID to design a programme for restoring paramount chiefs. This was enthusiastically supported by the SLPP government, which was keen to re-establish political control over the countryside. These concerns and interests have so far overridden efforts to reform chiefdom governance in the light of grievances voiced in ... chiefdom consultations.
>
> (Quoted in Peacebuilding Support Office 2007: 4)

Problems arose when the houses being constructed resembled 'mud huts' rather than what is locally considered appropriate Paramount Chief housing (Gaima 2009). The British opted for more traditional 'sandcrete' constructions of four rooms (Gaima 2009). The Paramount Chiefs argued, however, that their houses needed to be substantially larger to accommodate their families (often made up of several wives and their children) as well as visiting guests who chiefs are obliged to house (Glentworth 2008). There was the added complication of where to build the houses within the chiefdoms. As Paramount Chiefs are derived from ruling families, and there are a few ruling families within each chiefdom residing in different locations, houses being constructed for incumbent Paramount Chiefs would not prove useful for future Paramount Chiefs who might live in a different town (Glentworth 2008). Unless houses were built in each of the towns where ruling families resided, the constructions would appear biased. State politics also interfered, with the All People's Congress (APC) opposition party (at the time) claiming that houses were being built only in chiefdoms in the South, the stronghold of the SLPP government (Glentworth 2008). In fact, it was the Southern areas that were most accessible during 1999–2001, due to ongoing rebel fighting in the North. Instability in the Northern province (the traditional stronghold of the APC) thus prevented DFID from penetrating these areas. In the end, about 50 houses were built, some of which chiefs refused to live in. After an external evaluation, and a lack of support amongst the chiefs themselves, the CGRP was terminated (Glentworth 2008; Fanthorpe 2004).

While the CGRP suggests a cognisance early on of the importance of informal actors, it was largely divorced from DFID's SJSR – residing instead in decentralization and local government work. In part, this reflected the fact that DFID did not regard the conflict as a revolt against both state and non-state governance structures, and thus did not see chiefs as an important component of reforms. The CGRP also represented, in a manner reminiscent of colonial prerogatives, a quick-fix attempt to use traditional structures to restore order and stability in provincial Sierra Leone on which other reform efforts could capitalize. The one component of the programme intended to engage with the failures of the chieftaincy system was not pursued. The CGRP thus represented a superficial flirtation with chieftaincy, revealing a lack of understanding of or engagement with the complexities of the system and treating it more as a vehicle to security and stabilization, rather than a crucial security and justice mechanism in need of long-term reforms *alongside* state systems. Critically, the CGRP did not demonstrate an understanding of how the chieftaincy system contributed to the very grievances over which the war was fought (Crawford-Garrett 2012: 112). Richard Fanthorpe (2004), in reviewing the project notes:

> It had become apparent early on that chiefdom administration in general had deep-rooted problems that no single donor programme was likely to resolve. Public consultations facilitated by the CGRP and relief agencies yielded a plethora of local complaints against chiefs of all ranks. Foremost amongs these grievances were that chiefs controlled a local judicial system regularly handing down fines that were grossly incommensurate with the offences committed, [and] that chiefs frequently compelled their subjects to work farms for them without pay.

While DFID staff are upfront about the programme's failure and the role that a lack of knowledge of the chieftaincy system played in this (Glentworth 2008; White 2008a), the lesson learned from the programme seems to have been to steer clear of informal actors, rather than to learn more and attempt to engage in a more sustained and transformative manner. Since this early attempt, DFID has not engaged directly with chiefs in their more than 15-year engagement in Sierra Leone.

Conclusion

The growing policy focus on informal actors within DFID, however minimal relative to state-focused reform policy, suggests that the organization increasingly recognizes the importance of these actors to security and justice reform. This realization appears to have taken place in different parts of the organization at different times. Certainly, the recognition of informal actors is more sustained within policy regarding justice reform, as opposed to security sector reform. Yet overall, the mentions (and the one brief programme) read as footnotes to the more dominant narrative – that state failure was the cause of conflict in Sierra Leone and that in strengthening the state so as to ensure peace and development, informal security actors *may* be taken into account. Failings within informal systems are not regarded as a cause of conflict, but rather as tangential issues that need to be considered within broader efforts to rebuild the state. This neglects the importance of failures within informal systems and the manner in which formal and informal systems bind together to create a modern security and justice matrix in Sierra Leone.

This chapter has sought to explain DFID's policy approach to Sierra Leone. It has demonstrated how DFID came into being in the midst of particular international and domestic contexts, which shaped the new aid department and the manner in which it has engaged in Sierra Leone. In the absence of an explicit policy on Sierra Leone, an excavation of DFID documents and speeches reveals a neat and cohesive explanation of the causes of war. State failure arguments regarding the causes of war justified intervention into the state apparatus, focusing initially upon the security sector as the essential coercive component of statehood. The security-development nexus complemented this state failure thinking and transformed the understanding of the causes of war into a broader and more comprehensive explanation about the causes of war, peace, security and development. This understanding shaped the UK's engagement with Sierra Leone, leading to a focus on strengthening state institutions. SJSR offered a unique opportunity to simultaneously address challenges of both security and development. State centrism prioritized the formal state organizations of security, such as the police, military and intelligence services (and later the judiciary) as the prime agents for affecting the change that would allow, comprehensively, for security, development and peace to follow. This DFID view was facilitated by international trends bringing security and development into a more proximate relationship and a domestic political scene in the UK that gave Africa unprecedented priority, promoted an ethical foreign policy and an independent aid department, and advocated intervention on humanitarian grounds.

A more targeted examination of DFID documents in relation to informal security and justice actors revealed an increasing recognition over time, occurring earlier in justice than security work. In addition, one short-lived programme, the CGRP, attempted to engage with informal actors. However, the references in policy documents and the CGRP must be understood relative to the overwhelming focus on state-centred security and justice – viewed as the vehicle to achieving security, peace and development.

In spite of having no definitive policy on SJSR or Sierra Leone, DFID appears to have maintained a surprisingly coherent image of conflict, security and development, centring upon the role of the state. But to what extent does DFID's policy approach reflect the actual experiences of on-the-ground security and justice provision and conflict causes in Sierra Leone? Chapter 2 addresses this question by providing a 'thick' account of conflict causes, security and justice in Sierra Leone, suggesting that DFID's approach might not explain as much as its coherency implies.

Notes

1 In an article in *The Times* in 2000, Michael Binyon referred to Sierra Leone as 'Labour's expensive African albatross' (Binyon 2000).

2 Taken from the title of Lansana Gberie's 2005 book, *A Dirty War in West Africa* (Gberie 2005).
3 Taylor supported the overthrow of President Momoh who had allowed the Economic Community of West African States Monitoring Group (ECOMOG) to use a Sierra Leonean airport as a base from which to launch bombers targeting NPFL territory in Liberia (Richards 1996: 4; Kargbo 2006: 15; Williams 2001: 145).
4 *The Green Book* was written by former-Libyan leader Muammar al-Qaddafi in 1975 and promotes alternative conceptions of democracy and political philosophy to Western liberal models. The books (a series of three) formed the basis of Qaddafi's Libyan Cultural Revolution and have been circulated widely throughout the developing world.
5 A significant literature has emerged on the causes of the Sierra Leonean civil war. While the well-publicized arguments offering mono-causal explanations of the war as motivated by greed or inherent barbarism have largely been discredited, debate remains over the motivations of the RUF. For an overview of the arguments see Kargbo 2006: 18–31. Key contributors to the debate include: Kaplan 1994; Collier 2001; Richards 1996; Abdullah 2004; Peters 2006; and Gberie 2005.
6 For a detailed examination of how the RUF's change of tactics led to a loss of popular support, see Richards 2006.
7 This involvement was apparently unknown to the British government at the time (although Peter Penfold, British High Commissioner to Sierra Leone from 1997–2000 and Tim Spicer, head of Sandline International, maintain the Foreign and Commonwealth Office knew about an arms deal between Sandline and the Government of Sierra Leone). This led to the 'arms to Africa' affair in the UK, as the arms deal, involving 30 tonnes of arms and ammunition, violated United Nations Security Council Resolution 1132, forbidding arms sales to any participant in the Sierra Leonean conflict. The scandal captured headlines in the UK media for several weeks and was key in raising the profile of Sierra Leone in Britain. The debacle led to internal FCO investigations and the Legg Inquiry, which absolved ministers and the FCO of breaking international law, but suggested communication channels within the FCO should have been better. Ultimately, Prime Minister Blair maintained that even if such actions *did* constitute a breach of the UN resolution, the ends of restoring a democratically elected government justified the means. For a more detailed examination of the incident, see Kargbo 2006: 277; Rawnsley 2000: 176–84; Abrahamsen and Williams 2001: 252; Kampfner 2003: 68; and Murray 2009: 19–28; 39–72.
8 This invasion was the focus of the award-winning documentary by Sorious Samura, *Cry Freetown*.
9 This was largely at the insistence of the United Nations, UK and Nigeria, who realized that the RUF could not easily be defeated militarily and that conflict might thus only be ended through a negotiated settlement (Kargbo 2006: 288). For a first-hand account of the Lomé negotiations see Murray 2009: 39–72.
10 There were, however, problems transforming troop commitments into troops on the ground. Thus, in reality, the number of troops was substantially lower than this.
11 Countless more (the number is unknown) died from their injuries (Murray 2009: 13).
12 At the beginning of the twentieth century approximately 90 per cent of war victims were soldiers. During the 1990s, an estimated 90 per cent of those killed in conflicts were civilians (Paris 2004: 1).
13 This was DFID's official slogan until late-2009 when it underwent a re-branding and the slogan was removed.
14 Or at least within some parts of DFID, such as the Conflict and Humanitarian Affairs Department, the Department within DFID that developed the policy of new humanitarianism (see Schümer 2008).

15 Tony Blair, quoted in Wickham-Jones 2000: 29.
16 Whether the 'third way' or 'ethical' foreign policy were genuine or useful guides to political conduct is another question. For discussion see Abrahamsen and Williams 2001; and Gallagher 2009.
17 In 2012, DFID launched an Access to Security and Justice Programme, which does appear to be planning a greater focus on informal, non-state or customary justice systems.

Chapter 2

'Thicker' understandings of conflict, security and governance

The understanding of the causes of war set out in Chapter 1 may present a neat and unifying picture of failure in Sierra Leone and what is required to repair it, but as this chapter demonstrates, it does not adequately reflect the complex and overlapping sites of breakdown that become apparent from a 'thicker' analysis of the antecedents to conflict. The manner in which the UK Department for International Development (DFID) has understood the civil war in Sierra Leone clearly has implications for the reforms that it delivers. If it has not sufficiently understood the causes of the war, then it is likely that its reform programmes are not addressing the full panoply of problems facing the country. In contrast to DFID's reading of the conflict set out in the previous chapter, a 'thicker' understanding of the causes of war is provided here, highlighting the importance of the failures of informal institutions alongside the state, and thus the need for an approach to security and justice sector reform (SJSR) that goes beyond the state in working towards sustainable peace.

In setting out a 'thicker' understanding of the causes of war, which engages with locally specific histories, grievances and politics, rather than abstracted logics of state failure, it is necessary to look beyond the state to the authorities that play a central role in the lives of the majority of Sierra Leoneans, and are prominent providers of security and justice services (Vincent 2012). As the below 'thick' description of the causes of war reveals, chiefs,[1] as well as the central state, are implicated in the failures that led to conflict and in providing the derisory security and justice services that require reform. It is demonstrated how the failure of these informal actors to provide equitable and just services created grievances amongst rural youth, compelling many to join the Revolutionary United Front (RUF). The nature of the administration of the chieftaincy system can thus be seen as one of the causes of civil war. In seeking to comprehensively address the causes of conflict and sustainably transform security and justice provision in Sierra Leone, therefore, reform programmes should engage with the failures of the chieftaincy system, as well as those of the state.

Adopting a state failure approach to the conflict, as DFID appears to, is not necessarily incompatible with thicker understandings of the causes of war – but failure occurred at a significantly broader level. It was not merely the state that failed, but also the institution of chieftaincy, suggesting that governance goes beyond the bureaucratic level of the state to include informal structures (Vincent 2012). Without factoring the breakdown of the chieftaincy system into its analysis, DFID misunderstands the locus of failure and sets out to reform only some of the problematic institutions and practices. In order to provide a thicker account of the causes of war in Sierra Leone, then, some historical background on the development and roles of chiefs in Sierra Leone, as well as the manner in which the chieftaincy system failed, requires elaboration.

'Thick' versus 'thin'

It is argued here that the effectiveness of DFID's security and justice sector reforms (SJSR) programmes has been limited because the understanding of the causes of war that underlies its policies is 'thin'. This is contrasted with the account of the causes of war and nature of security and justice provision set out in this chapter, which is seen to be thick. Incorporating a notion of thickness into understandings of the causes of war in Sierra Leone seeks to locate the causes within locally-specific conditions, rather than attributing them to universal abstractions (such as state failure) that may speak more to the latest development jargon than to the Sierra Leonean context. A thick understanding recognizes the deeper layers of failure that require reform in order to build a sustainably peaceful society and provides a multi-causal, rather than monocausal, explanation of the conflict.

Debates within the development field have increasingly recognized the importance of context in effective programming, with innumerable policy documents advocating an understanding of local context (for some key examples, see OECD 2007b; DFID 2002a; UN DPKO 2012). As Sue Unsworth (quoting DFID and the Netherlands Ministry of Foreign Affairs respectively) explains, 'There is increasing donor rhetoric about the importance of politics, and the need to "look behind the façade" of formal institutes to detect the "real" location of power' (2010: 6). But too often this has been operationalized as one-off context analysis at the outset of programming, focused at the national level. This is rarely continuously updated and often does not engage with detailed sub-national dynamics, where the politics of security and justice frequently play out and can change rapidly. Adrian Leftwich and Will Hout have both criticized the 'drivers of change' studies that DFID instituted as a way to integrate a better understanding of context and politics into programming, for not being consistent or thorough in seeking to understand the political economy of a given context (Leftwich 2006; Hout 2012: 410). A focus on 'context', therefore, does not necessarily achieve a thick understanding of local processes and practices. Analyses of context can still be thin if they merely describe what appears to be going on and use explanatory tools and concepts (like 'state failure' and 'fragility') that unhelpfully abstract and generalize what are distinctly local dynamics as equivalent to equally distinctive local dynamics elsewhere. Understandings of context only become thick if they aim to understand practices from within the cultural confines of the context itself.

Chiefs: The 'missing bottom' of governance in Sierra Leone[2]

The chieftaincy system in Sierra Leone is frequently pointed to as an institution that Sierra Leoneans cannot imagine living without (Members A, Promoters of Peace and Justice Freetown 2009; Member B, Promoters of Peace and Justice Freetown 2009; Fanthorpe 2004; Truth and Reconciliation Commission for Sierra Leone 2004). Despite widespread recognition of serious problems within chieftaincy, it seems few, if any Sierra Leoneans advocate abandoning this system.[3] Rather, chiefs are spoken of as 'the custodians of culture' and 'the human face of government who know their people' (Gaima 2009; Gbla 2009). Speaking of the embedded nature of chiefs in Sierra Leone, Kellie Conteh, former-Head of the Office for National Security explains:

> [O]ur people, whether you like it or not, for now seem to respect that traditional setting. No amount of education from, you know, human rights organisations, international organisations, on this sort of thing would work right now. They would listen, yes, but as soon as you leave, they go back to their tradition … This is how our people live. They live in these villages and in the village there's a town chief, they have a youth leader, a women's leader – these are structures that are there, and they respect the chief.
>
> (Quoted in Albrecht 2010: 11–12)

Indeed, many Sierra Leoneans view chiefs as more legitimate and much more accessible than the central government (Vincent 2012). Paul Jackson refers to the chiefdom as 'the basic unit of local government' (2006: 99). As their extensive functions, set out later in this chapter, demonstrate, chiefs are an integral component of governance provision in Sierra Leone and cannot be easily separated from the state, either theoretically or in practice. It is this very proximity that makes it difficult to speak of chiefs as 'non-state' or 'informal', as examined in the introduction to this book. The simultaneous centrality of chiefs to Sierra Leonean governance, and yet the absence of a definitive policy that clarifies once-and-for-all their role and position in the political system, underpin the notion of chiefs being the 'missing bottom' of governance in Sierra Leone (Gaima 2009). There have been a number of overlapping and unclear attempts to resolve this since the end of the war through the Local Government Act of 2004, the Chieftaincy Act of 2009, the Local Courts Act of 2011, and through ongoing decentralization efforts (for an examination of these processes see Broadbent 2012), yet significant ambiguity remains. Chiefs are thus ever present in practice and yet their formal position within governance processes remains strikingly unresolved. While the history of chiefs in Sierra Leone has recently become the topic of a number of academic studies (see, for instance, Broadbent 2012; Fanthorpe 2001; Richards 1996; Albrecht 2010) it is useful here to briefly examine how their modern day roles have evolved for those less familiar with the Sierra Leone context, before setting out how grievances related to the chieftaincy are integral to a full understanding of the civil war.

History of chieftaincy

The chieftaincy system in Sierra Leone arises from a mixture of cultural precedent, colonialism and patrimonialism. Prior to the arrival of colonialism, chieftaincy, as we now call it, was:

> an unstable institution founded on a not always consistent mixture of biological legitimacy, patrimonial largesse and military strength, where popular allegiances were tempered by tensions between ruling and non-ruling houses, between freemen and slaves, and between the potential advantages of going it alone and those to be had from allying with rival chiefs.
>
> (Sawyer 2008: 389)

While pre-colonial Sierra Leone possessed tribal leaders of the kingdoms that were unified through colonialism, no 'chiefs' or 'Paramount Chiefs' existed by that terminology (Conteh-Morgan and Dixon-Fyle 1999: 18–19). Reference to chiefs began when the Crown Colony of Freetown and the Western Area was established in 1808 and colonial officials began travelling upcountry to make friendship treaties with traditional leaders to facilitate trade (Kup 1975: 168–72). The terminology of 'chiefs' was formalized when the provinces of Sierra Leone became the Sierra Leone Protectorate in 1896. While the Crown Colony (Freetown and the Western Area) continued to be governed by a direct officer administration, the Protectorate (upcountry provinces) was governed through the British policy of indirect rule. As a result, the British colonizers required local leaders to implement their ordinances, collect their taxes, and control their subjects. The British used the leaders of the kingdoms and gave them the title of chiefs (common in other British African colonies) (Fyfe 1962: 136). Some chiefs claim that the previous title of 'kings' was seen by the British to compromise the supremacy of the English Monarchy and so needed to find an alternative (Tshombe Kargoi 2009; Vangahun 2009).

The concept of chiefs and Paramount Chiefs was further entrenched by the Hut Tax War of 1898. The Protectorate Ordinance, which established the Sierra Leonean Protectorate in 1896, also proposed a taxation scheme for the provinces, whereby '[e]very owner of a habitable house in the Protectorate was, from January 1 1898, to be liable henceforth to an annual tax of five shillings, and for houses of four rooms or more, ten shillings' (Newland 1916: 106–7).

Some traditional leaders refused to participate 'in what they perceived to be the demeaning exercise of tax collection for a higher political authority' and launched a rebellion that was ultimately suppressed by the British (Reno 1995: 37). Those leaders who agreed to the tax and facilitated British administration, or who 'replaced' (at British discretion) executed recalcitrant leaders, were recognized as chiefs (Peters 2006: 28). The British divided the protectorate into numerous small chiefdoms 'for organisational and administrative purposes ... each governed by a "paramount chief", with section and town chiefs under them (Peters 2006: 28).[4] Henceforth Paramount Chiefs were derived from two or three 'ruling houses' in each chiefdom (particular families, at times selected by the British) and served for life, thus making Paramount Chieftaincy a largely hereditary title (Acemoglu *et al.* 2013: 8–12; Peters 2006: 28; Fyfe 1962: 136; Fyle 1981: 57; Abraham 1978: 274). Yet, as Richard Fanthorpe explains:

> It has ... been shown that British officials' assumption that pre-colonial chiefship was a hereditary estate, owned by 'ruling families' (or 'houses'), sometimes had little historical basis. Furthermore the early British administration was not averse to promoting men – and occasionally women – to paramount chiefship on the basis of willingness to collaborate rather than previous political status.
>
> (Fanthorpe 1998: 559)

The hereditary title of chieftaincy was, in many cases, a British misunderstanding, based on customary practices of some communities, but not the majority. The idea that chieftaincy was a traditional custom derived from local precedent was also a misunderstanding and was introduced through colonialism as much as through independent cultural evolution – although it did build on pre-colonial kingdom communities (Fyfe 1962: 137; Fyle 1981: 57; Abraham 1978: 274).

The colonial experience augmented the roles and powers of chiefs in an enduring manner. During this time the administrative functions of the chiefs expanded to include new powers, such as 'preserving law and order' (in 1901) and adjudicating on customary law (in 1902) (Reno 1995: 37). Highlighting the impact of this change, William Reno notes that it 'gave chiefs explicit state approval to implement forced labour and impose sanctions against those challenging their chiefly authority', while other reforms 'allocated chiefs broad powers to enforce their decisions with little local control or accountability' (1995: 37–8). These functions were added to further throughout the 1930s so that:

> chiefs became everything from 'health authorities' (1931), to 'education officers' (1935), to enhanced 'court magistrates' (1937). Crucial for their later influence over informal diamond markets, chiefs were given greater legal powers over alienation of land, control of settlement and local immigration.
>
> (Reno 1995: 46)

Many of these colonial-era responsibilities remain in the modern chieftaincy system, as demonstrated below.

Having been administered separately, the Colony and Protectorate were united in 1951, creating what we now know as Sierra Leone, just ten years prior to independence (Kargbo 2006: 59). Yet the division between the Western Area and the provinces remained, kept in place both geographically and ethnically, with Freetown dominated by *Krios* (the Creole freed slaves who settled there), and the interior constituted by various indigenous ethnic groups, predominantly the *Mende* and *Temne*. This bifurcation has meant that the provinces have frequently been a governance afterthought, as national governments prioritize the needs and interests of the wealthier and more economically active capital and its immediate surrounds. This was most evident under President Siaka Stevens, who came to power in 1967 and increasingly centralized authority under a one-party state and abolished local government in 1972. As Jackson notes, 'the main feature of Sierra Leone's political system [since independence] has been increasing centralisation of power and resources in Freetown' (Jackson 2006: 102). Centralization resulted in government policy becoming increasingly irrelevant to the provinces, determined as it was in Freetown for Freetown concerns. As a former Revolutionary United Front (RUF) fighter I interviewed explained, the rationale of the government was that 'if Freetown has light, Sierra Leone has light' (referring to the country's intermittent power supply) (Members A, Promoters of Peace and Justice Freetown 2009). Throughout independence, the provinces were thus increasingly removed from the centre and relied more heavily upon the chieftaincy system, which was inherited by the independent Sierra Leone Republic from colonialism (Acemoglu *et al.* 2013). This, in turn, increased the relative power of the chiefs, who were left to their own devices so long as they did not interfere with the government (Zack-Williams 2002: 2). Richard Fanthorpe suggests:

> The colonial divide between colony and protectorate, and concentration of state and service activity in Freetown, has left chiefs in Sierra Leone in a stronger political position than many of their counterparts in other

> West African countries. 'Straddling' chiefdom and state politics remains the foundation of many political careers in Sierra Leone.
>
> (Fanthorpe 2005: 40)

While Freetown is now substantially more multi-ethnic, the capital-province divide remains and, as Jackson (2005: 50) notes, 'has led to a continued juxtaposition of state police and chiefdom police, magistrate's courts and customary courts, national tax and chiefdom tax, etc.' This evolution of chiefs' roles underlines their centrality to daily life in provincial Sierra Leone.

Below, the modern-day portfolio of these uniquely powerful chiefs demonstrates further their substantial areas of authority. Chiefs' most prominent roles can be divided into four key areas of responsibility: taxation; law and order; culture; and land.

Taxation

Taxation is, understandably, one of the most important powers for chiefs, as it provides the basis for their incomes and those of their staff. Chieftain authority to levy taxes has been historically contentious, with the Hut Tax War threatening these powers during colonialism and moves since the end of the civil war to curtail the relative freedom in tax collection that chiefs had exercised since independence (Broadbent 2012). With the Government of Sierra Leone's recognition that excessively centralized governance, particularly of the provinces, was a cause of conflict, it has sought to decentralize its powers to Local Councils (formerly abolished by Siaka Stevens in 1972).[5] This has resulted in chiefs and Councils operating overlapping jurisdictions, and has created tensions in relation to taxation. As Paul Jackson notes, '[l]ocal government finance has never really been a "sexy" subject. However in Sierra Leone, the financial structure of local government has become a burning issue in so far as it links traditional chiefs [and] modern local government' (2005: 49).

A new Local Government Act 2004 attempted to address the overlapping jurisdiction of chiefs and Local Councils by bringing chiefs into state revenue collection. In doing so, however, it also created space for conflict between chiefs and Councils and created more, not less, ambiguity about the role of chiefs vis-à-vis the government. As Jackson explains:

> One of the most contentious issues, which will undoubtedly lead to conflict in some areas is the collection of the local tax. This is a poll tax levied on every adult. Historically this has been set centrally at 500 Leones a year (around 20 US cents) and collected by the chiefs. Under the new law, the tax is still collected by the chiefs, but they share the tax with the local government, following the pre-1972 system. In addition the setting of the level of tax is now a district-level decision. In other words, the district

sets the tax level, the chief collects it, and then they share the proceeds (there are no guidelines about how to allocate shares in the Act).

(Jackson 2005: 56)

Thus, while the taxation system is a modern government function intended to generate revenue for the state, it relies on the traditional power of and fealty to chiefs to carry it out. This linking of chiefs and government is meant to ensure taxation is more accountable than the days when chiefs had unfettered taxing authority. Yet by splitting the taxation process, ample room is left for malpractice. For instance, Councils may set the tax rate at 500 Leones per head. Chiefs may then collect tax at a rate of 550 Leones per head, making a profit on the side. Or, as Jackson suggests, chiefs and their local headmen may under-report the local population and thus the amount due in taxes – allowing them to pocket the difference (Jackson 2005: 54). Chiefs may justify such behaviour on the basis that they are now made to share tax with the Local Councils (the central government in Freetown declared that Councils should be financially self-sustaining as of 2008) (Kargbo 2009: 17). Chiefs claim that this has decreased their funds and they are unable to pay themselves or their staff adequately. In an interview, one Paramount Chief insisted there is only enough money to pay his staff for two months of every year (Paramount Chief Tshombe Kargoi 2009). While attempts have been made to modernize tax collection, the authority to collect remains strongly vested in the chieftaincy institution.

Law and order

Linked to revenue raising activities, chiefs are also responsible for law and order within their chiefdoms (Jackson 2011). In interviews, chiefs reiterated law and order as their central purpose, alongside maintenance of culture and tradition (Paramount Chief Tshombe Kargoi 2009; Paramount Chief Vangahun 2009; Chief Ngombulango 2009; Chief Young 2012). There are several mechanisms through which they fulfil this function. Paramount Chiefs play a formal role as members of Parliament (12 seats in Parliament are reserved for a Paramount Chief from each district) and as advisors to Parliament through the National Council of Paramount Chiefs (Albrecht 2010: 7). In addition, at the chiefdom, section and town levels chiefs enforce bye-laws through influence over the Local Courts and as adjudicators of chiefdom justice themselves, oversee the chiefdom police and monitor immigration in and out of the chiefdom.

The Paramount Chief may make bye-laws through the Chiefdom Council to ensure community order, as long as such bye-laws are consistent with the Constitution of Sierra Leone (Chieftaincy Act 2009). Contravention of bye-laws is punishable through the Local Courts and so these locally crafted rules (which differ across chiefdoms) are taken seriously as laws.

Local Courts offer a more accessible form of justice to most Sierra Leoneans than the formal justice system (according to the Sierra Leone Bar Association in 2009 there were only seven lawyers in private practice outside of Freetown) (Castillejo 2009: 6). They are widely perceived to be cheaper than the formal court system, although they also have a reputation for issuing excessive fines, which have been pointed to as a key grievance of many who participated in the RUF (Castillejo 2009: 5). The Local Courts are authorized by the constitution and the Local Courts Act 2011 to hear matters of customary law and some civil cases, although there has been much confusion in the past over precise jurisdictional limits, and Local Courts frequently overstep their mandate (Castillejo 2009: 7–8).

While chiefs do not technically wield power within the Local Courts, they retain a strong influence (Magbity 2009). From 1963 until recent legislation in late-2011, Local Court Chairmen (the adjudicators in the Local Courts) were nominated by chiefs and endorsed by the Ministry for Local Government and Rural Development (Magbity 2009; Vangahun 2009). However, in practice, a 'cabinet' of the Paramount Chief and eight section chiefs 'recommended' a person to the government, and this was rarely (if ever) rejected (Vangahun 2009). Paramount Chiefs also acted as informal 'advisors', appointing four other 'court members' to advise the Local Court Chairman (Vangahun 2009; Castillejo 2009: 2). In this sense, chiefs could be seen to essentially select Court Chairmen and ensure a strong role for themselves in determining the nature of justice that the Courts delivered.

Such practices were addressed in the 2011 Local Courts Act, which puts the Local Courts under the responsibility of the judiciary. This is explicitly to address problems of politicization that the proximity of chief-chairmen relations has prompted. It remains to be seen whether the new Act will lead to changes in practice and certainly there is resistance on the part of some chiefs. One Paramount Chief, interviewed prior to the new Local Courts Act being enacted, indicated how important it was for chiefs to retain powers of Court Chairmen selection as chiefs 'know their subjects' and are able to determine which of them understands the local culture and is aware of the ancestry of the land (important in resolving land disputes), in a way that the government or judiciary cannot (Vangahun 2009). This suggests that chiefs are better positioned to determine which person will best serve the community, based upon deep local knowledge, unknown to outsiders.

Alongside the Local Court system, chiefs also operate a more arbitrary (and technically illegal) conflict resolution function. If their subjects have a dispute over a relatively minor matter – a small sum of money, an ongoing argument, fighting or other bad behaviour – the matter may be taken to the chief, rather than the Local Court (Baker 2005: 380). This process is quicker and generally less costly (depending on the resulting fine). Unlike the Local Courts, users do not have to pay for travel and accommodation for themselves and any witnesses (each village has its own chief but not necessarily a Local Court). In this instance, subjects generally only have to (literally) pay their respects – either through a small fee, food or in-kind payment (Tshombe Kargoi 2009). In one complaint I watched a tribal headman resolve, the complainant paid the equivalent of USD 5.80 for the chief to conduct a hearing and issue a summons to the accused. The chief settles the dispute after speaking to the relevant parties. Determinations are not based on fixed law or jurisdiction, but a loose customary code that differs from chiefdom to chiefdom and evolves over time (Fofanah 2009). Chief's justice generally results in a fine for one or both of the parties (Tshombe Kargoi 2009), which many have argued are unnecessarily high (Peters 2006: 34–7). Putting this complaint to chiefs, they respond that the fines need to be high in order to have their 'disciplining' and 'deterrent' effect (Tshombe Kargoi 2009). Small fines, it is argued, would not be as useful in achieving this purpose.

Chiefs are assisted in their law and order duties by chiefdom police who act as Local Court attendants, carry out the chief's business, such as issuing summonses, and conduct basic policing in places where state police are not present. One Paramount Chief claimed that the chiefdom police are 'the backbone of security in their communities' (Tshombe Kargoi 2009). Yet the chiefdom police have largely been sidelined by the government and international donors alike. While the Sierra Leone Police (SLP) have been through a comprehensive reform programme since the end of the civil war, only a small number of chiefdom police in Moyamba district received training in 2009-2010 (Awoko News 2010). Some chiefs have the impression that their police are completely disrespected, and that as the SLP have become better funded and trained, they increasingly interfere in the functions of the chiefs and chiefdom police (Vangahun 2009; Tshombe Kargoi 2009).

Finally, chiefs carry out law and order functions by controlling the movements of people through their chiefdoms. As individuals become 'strangers', that is, move outside of their own chiefdom, they are expected to inform the chief in any chiefdom they enter of their presence – although chiefs say this is increasingly rare in practice (Tshombe Kargoi 2009; Vangahun 2009). This is tied to the perception that strangers are less reliable than those indigenous to a chiefdom as their ancestry, and linked to this, their character, are unknown. Chiefs thus exercise a kind of immigration official role – maintaining order through an omnipotent knowledge of the demography of their chiefdom. This form of knowledge is interesting when contrasted to the knowledge that the state possesses. As James Scott set out in his seminal book *Seeing Like a State* (1998), the state is only able to 'know' its citizens through abstractions of the 'common man' through processes such as a national census. In contrast, chiefs have the ability to individually know each and every subject, and thus at least have the potential to contribute a unique knowledge to governance processes.

Custodians of culture

Chiefs are frequently referred to in Sierra Leone as the custodians of culture (Fofanah 2009; Gbla 2009; Macaulley 2009). This appears to be the role that most Sierra Leoneans associate with their 'traditional' leaders. They are seen as the link between the ancestors and traditional cultural practices of the past and the present. This is most clear in the chief's patronage of the two main secret societies in Sierra Leone – the *Poro* and the *Sande* (or *Bundu*)[6] – the dominant initiation societies for males and females respectively. They involve up to three months in the bush with society leaders who teach youth of adult ways of life and perform ritual ceremonies, such as clitoridectomy (female circumcision) (Ellis 1999: 224; Bledsoe 1984: 455–72). The majority of Sierra Leoneans in the provinces go through initiation practices (from a 2008 Demographic and Health Survey, it was estimated that 91 per cent of eligible females in provincial Sierra Leone undergo clitoridectomy) and the prevalence of the societies continues to be noted in the literature) (Statistics Sierra Leone and ICF Macro 2009: 13; Bledsoe 1984: 458; Alterman *et al.* 2003: 33; Manning 2009: 116; Fanthorpe 2007). However, it should also be noted that as more children go to school, and stay in school longer, initiation practices are changing. Already there are reports that the length of initiation processes is decreasing and can be as short as one week (Fanthorpe 2007: 18). Initiation is also increasingly delayed, and for those who then pursue tertiary education, training or employment in urban areas, it might not happen at all (Denney and Ibrahim 2012).

As guardians of the secret societies, chiefs preside over an important cultural institution that represents a formative aspect of many Sierra Leoneans' lives. This relationship between the chiefs and the secret societies has a long history. As Northcoate Thomas notes in his 1916 anthropological study, '[t]here is a clear relation between the chieftainship and the *Poro* society … So close is the connection that chiefs may be spoken of as … *Poro* chiefs' (1916: 143). Further, Jackson (2006: 105) highlights the important role played by chiefs in the secret societies:

> The subtleties of most secret societies are a closed door to most researchers, but their influence is a constant in Sierra Leonean politics. To stand as a paramount chief, one has to be a member, and in the *Temne*, *Loko*, *Limba*, *Susu*, *Koranko* and *Yalunka* tribes, the paramount chief is both the spiritual and the political authority over the chiefdom. It is also commonly asserted that critical governance issues have been decided by the secret societies.

The significance of the societies' teaching to many Sierra Leoneans also renders it a form of cultural education. In many instances, particularly until recent improvements in school enrolment rates, this has constituted the 'finishing school' for youths who receive only several years of primary education.

Secret societies also operate as informal justice mechanisms, resolving disputes between initiates and within the community where society laws are contravened (Jackson 2011). Drawing upon focus group discussions held throughout Sierra Leone, Magnus Jörgel and Mats Utas note that up to one third of Sierra Leoneans consider secret societies to play an important role in security provision and that the importance of the societies is increasing post-conflict (2007: 47).

The cultural estate of the chiefs is thus significant. The identities of many Sierra Leoneans are intertwined more strongly with their chiefs than with the state. As Roger Tangri noted in the late 1970s:

> The chiefdoms ... constitute the chief focus of loyalty for the vast majority of the people ... The individual is largely first and foremost a member of a chiefdom whose geographical limits are known, whose officials are often dealt with on a personal basis, and whose authority system is understood.
>
> (Tangri 1978: 165)

Key contributors to more recent debates on Sierra Leone, such as Paul Richards (2006) and Richard Fanthorpe (1998; 2005), also point to the importance of chiefdom-level politics in shaping the identities of Sierra Leoneans.

Land

Finally, chiefs are the custodians of communal land, holding it 'in trust' for the people of their chiefdom (Albrecht 2010: 7). Unlike land in the Western Area (Freetown and its surrounds), which is subject to private property rights, chiefs' legal right to the land is inalienable, meaning that no other title can remove their ownership because it belongs not just to the chief, but also to their ancestors and unborn family (except in the case of some mining rights, which can fall under national jurisdiction) (Unruh 2008: 99; 102; Jackson 2005: 53). This affords chiefs extensive powers in determining who may farm, mine or live on communal land within their chiefdom and allows them to extract payment for such privileges. Despite this, one Paramount Chief indicated in interview that chiefs are aware that they now cannot remove land from a family who have lawfully lived on it for generations (Tshombe Kargoi 2009). Their powers regarding the land now more frequently involve settling land disputes, as chiefs possess the historical knowledge of each of their subject's entitlements through ancestry (Tshombe Kargoi 2009). They can, however, still extract payment for newly acquired land, and receive royalties from non-natives of the chiefdom or mining companies operating within the chiefdom – the latter of which is becoming increasingly controversial with growing mining activity (Acemoglu *et al.* 2013: 10; Jackson 2005: 53; Collier 1970: 82; Barrows 1976: 22). Transfer of land rights must accord with both local customary laws and formal statutory law, and as chiefs have a hand in setting local customary laws, their influence over land rights is significant (Unruh 2008: 102). The ability to control land rights, determine ownership and charge for land usage represents an incredibly powerful chieftain function which has a significant impact on the people of provincial Sierra Leone and has been the basis for rent capture (Acemoglu *et al.* 2013: 11).

The four-fold chieftain functions of taxation, law and order, culture and land, set out above, demonstrate the broad powers that chiefs (at times, in collaboration with secret societies) wield. These roles ensure that chiefs' proximity to their subjects is often significantly closer than that of the state, which has historically been at a remove from the provinces (Gberie 2009: 10). This proximity and the absence of the state in provincial Sierra Leone, where the civil war began and was overwhelmingly waged, suggest that governance breakdown is likely to have been not just of the state, but also of the chiefs as central governance providers. Below, governance failures are found to reside in the actual practices of governance, security and justice, which for the majority of Sierra Leoneans includes the chieftaincy system – through which they pay their taxes and derive their cultural identity, land rights and law and order.

The manner in which these functions have been carried out by chiefs contributed to the grievances that led some to violently revolt against authority structures in Sierra Leone. In this way, the chieftaincy system (alongside the state) can be seen to have failed. At one level, it failed to provide a just social order. At another, the chieftaincy system also failed on its own terms. The chieftaincy system was instituted to govern the provinces and maintain order. Often, order was maintained through oppressive and coercive practices – and thus might be said to have worked only too well. However, by administering chiefdoms without sufficient regard for justice or equality, to the point that grievances led some to launch a rebellion, the chieftaincy system failed to fulfil its own purpose of maintaining order. These failures shall be examined here, providing a 'thicker' account of the causes of war and thus pointing to actors beyond the state as also being in need of reform. This reveals that the state-centric understanding of the causes of war, apparent in DFID policy set out in the previous chapter, provides an incomplete picture that is insufficient as a basis for reforms intended to sustainably transform security and justice provision and address the underlying causes of war.

'Thick' causes of war

Popular depictions of the causes of war in Sierra Leone centre on diamonds (Collier 2001), the inherent barbarism elicited by environmental degradation (Kaplan 1994: 44–76), and state failure (DFID 2007a: 11–12). These readings, however, are based on abstract understandings that attempt to explain conflict everywhere, not just in Sierra Leone. They also fail to resonate with particular lived experiences in Sierra Leone and with understandings of the causes of conflict that are dominant there.[7] Such abstract arguments do not grasp the 'very specific political origins' of the conflict, which are crucial in understanding the motivations and goals of the RUF (Richards 2005: 119). These political origins were consistently identified in interviews with former-RUF and civil defence force (CDF) fighters and representatives from civil society, the security and justice sectors and the civil service as issues of poor governance and injustice within the formal government of Sierra Leone, as well as within systems of traditional leadership (Members A, Promoters of Peace and Justice, Freetown 2009; Member B, Promoters of Peace and Justice, Freetown 2009; Member C, Promoters of Peace and Justice, Freetown 2009; Members D, Promoters of Peace and Justice, Bo 2009; Gaima 2009; Macaulley 2009).

Grievances against the state

The original RUF leaders were pan-Africanist, socialist-inspired 'youths',[8] attempting to topple the All Peoples' Congress (APC) government of Joseph Momoh (Peters 2006: 1). Momoh was the appointed successor of Siaka Stevens, who had ruled Sierra Leone from 1967–85 (from 1978 under one-party rule). The APC governments were widely recognized as having plundered the nation's assets and mineral wealth for personal gain, politicized the security forces to ensure regime security and, by the 1980s, given up on service delivery for the citizens they supposedly served (Smith 1997: 58; Reno 1995). In a telling example in 1980, the government spent close to the country's entire annual budget on hosting a week-long Organization for African Unity (OAU) conference in Freetown (Kandeh 1999: 352). This sort of irresponsible spending prompted labour and student union strikes which were violently (and at times lethally) suppressed by the government. Ongoing strikes throughout the 1970s and 1980s over poor work conditions and education opportunities led Momoh to claim in 1984 that '[e]ducation is a privilege, not a right' (Richards 1996: 19; 36).

Poor governance at the state level is one of the key arguments employed to explain the war by former combatants, civil servants and civil society in Sierra Leone and is largely consistent with the view taken by DFID set out in Chapter 1 (Members A, Promoters of Peace and Justice, Freetown 2009; Gbla 2009; Gaima 2009). According to one former-RUF fighter, after finishing teacher training college, he became disillusioned with the lack of job prospects and poor working conditions. Teachers were so poorly and inconsistently paid by the state that they 'became the laughing stock of this country' (Member C, Promoters of Peace and Justice, Freetown 2009). Their poverty became publicly discernible by their 'black power' footwear – sandals fashioned out of lorry tyres, and led to public ridicule (Member C, Promoters of Peace and Justice, Freetown 2009). The lack of respect teachers received, he believed, was directly attributable to the failure of the state to provide sufficient resources for education. His frustrations with the state played a key role, he said, in motivating him to join the RUF.

Alongside poor social services and inappropriate spending, the government and political elites were also accumulating vast wealth from the diamond industry in Sierra Leone (Reno 1995: 92). Systems of patrimonialism ensured that positions of power and opportunity were granted on the basis of personal connections, rather than on merit. This lack of meritocracy infected school and university placements as much as the labour workforce. As Jimmy Kandeh highlights:

> Government scholarships to attend institutions of higher learning were routinely awarded not on the basis of academic merit but on the strength of a prospective student's patronage ties and ethnic identity. It was quite common, for example, for students who were admitted at Fourah Bay College [Sierra Leone's main university] to be denied scholarships while those receiving government scholarships failed to gain admission. This anomaly of 'admission without scholarship' and 'scholarship without admission' expressed precisely the sort of injustices that alienated the vast majority of Sierra Leonean youth.
>
> (Kandeh 1999: 357)

According to interviews with former rebels, many of them had been involved in student and labour groups from an early age – often centred on a socialist, pan-African ideology drawn from Libyan leader Colonel Qaddafi's *Green Book* (Members A, Promoters of Peace and Justice, Freetown 2009). This went beyond Freetown campuses, with one former-RUF member speaking of having initiated a study group at a university in the provinces known as the 'Status Group', an offshoot of similar groups based in Freetown (Member B, Promoters of Peace and Justice, Freetown 2009). These activists-turned-rebels argued that the violent struggle of the RUF was a last resort for political change (Member B, Promoters of Peace and Justice, Freetown 2009). The military had attempted to overthrow the government in coup attempts but failed. The labour and student unions carried out strikes and riots throughout the 1970s and 1980s and had also failed. The RUF's initial intention, interviewees claimed, was to carry on this push for change through force as a last resort (Member B, Promoters of Peace and Justice, Freetown 2009). As one former-RUF fighter explained:

> Some of us took the barrel [of the gun] because we were poor. Some of us took the barrel to stand for our friends [unionists who had been killed by government forces during strikes and protests]. Some of us took the barrel because we were not represented.
>
> (Members D, Promoters of Peace and Justice, Bo 2009)

The logic, fighters say, was to deal with the government by the same means as the government had dealt with dissent – through violence (Member B, Promoters of Peace and Justice, Freetown 2009).

Grievances against the chieftaincy system

Yet failure was not only plaguing formal state structures. As a former-RUF fighter explained, failures were apparent 'from the national level down to the chiefdoms' (Member B, Promoters of Peace and Justice, Freetown 2009). Upcountry in the provinces, chiefs and 'big men' kept patrimonialism in place through often arbitrary justice systems, land ownership, marriage licences and community labour that denied substantive justice and fermented grievances that ultimately led to conflict. If a youth committed an offence (perhaps disrespecting an elder), wanted to get married or start farming his own land, an indeterminate fee had to be paid to the local chief or patron (Jackson 2005: 54). These fees were at times exorbitant, with chiefs receiving ever-less funding from the increasingly bankrupt central government (Jackson 2005: 53; Mokuwa *et al.* 2011). This meant that youths were often not able to pay the fees or fines, allowing elders and the wealthy to exploit poor youth by commuting excessive fines or land and marriage fees to labour (Richards 2006: 193–4; Mokuwa *et al.* 2011: 341–3). Caspar Fithen and Paul Richards elaborate on other forms of injustice:

> One instance was a system of imposing fines on young men (who could not afford to marry) for interfering with the wives of chiefly polygynists ('woman damage'). These fines were commuted into labour service, with the result that many young men found themselves continuing to work without wages on the farms of chiefs … In recent discussions many villagers cite heavy fines – for various torts, including 'woman damage' … as being among the main reasons why young men became 'outlaws' in the diamond fields, some later enrolling in the RUF.
>
> (Fithen and Richards 2005: 122)

The link between such injustices and participation in the conflict is explained by Joe Alie who states that in 'provincial areas especially, young men suffered at the hands of corrupt and high-handed local authorities. Some of these aggrieved young men were later to return to their communities during the civil conflict to exact revenge on their former oppressors' (Alie 2008: 126). Such injustices roused a desire for revenge on the part of those aggrieved. Importantly, grievances against chiefs are also rooted in longer histories of slavery and 'stranger' status, examined below.

Slavery

Enforced social divisions based on age, wealth and status were also steeped in a history of slavery, suggesting that these injustices, and the frustrations borne of them, were more longstanding than may first appear (Fithen and Richards 2005: 119; 122). Richards suggests that there is a correlation between the prevalence of slavery and enrolment in the RUF, as '[m]ost of those who volunteered for the movement originated in the Gola Forest region and adjacent parts of Kailahun and Pujehun Districts – precisely the chiefdoms where domestic slavery lasted longest, and slaves were most numerous in forming agrarian capital' (2006: 191).

The British Empire banned the slave trade in 1807 and slavery more broadly in 1833, but this was not formally drafted into ordinances applying to the Sierra Leone Protectorate until 1926–7, largely because colonial authorities were aware of the resistance with which abolition would be met by chiefs who relied upon unpaid labour for their wealth and status (Ferme 2001: 81). In Sierra Leone, domestic slaves were common in the provinces, with some familial relationships (such as that between a nephew and his maternal uncle) replicating slave-master hierarchies (Ferme 2001: 85). In 1928, a District Commissioner assigned to the Protectorate noted the 'calm bordering on indifference' which greeted the anti-slavery laws (quoted in Ferme 2001: 81). This, it seems, was due to the rather ingenious rebranding of slavery by slave owners in Sierra Leone. As one chief clarified, 'we don't have slaves now, we have *cousins*' (quoted in Lewis 1954: 67). Mariane Ferme explains that:

> not much had changed in the organisation of labour and social relations ... [I]n the interstices between marriage, slavery, and other relations, along the continuum of interdependence, were created spaces for the perpetuation of inequality under new guises, such as the familiar idiom of kinship that turned slaves into 'cousins'.
>
> (Ferme 2001: 81)

This new system of slavery blurred with the strong patrimonial culture in Sierra Leone whereby everyone 'stands for' somebody (Fithen and Richards 2005: 122). That is, everyone exists in a hierarchy of dependence and obligation based loosely on age, wealth, lineage and status. A client is subject to his patron and will work for, fight for, or otherwise support him (Bledsoe 1990: 75). The patron, in turn, is responsible to his clients, for example providing food, shelter or money for school fees or court fines. Fithen and Richards argue that systems of patrimonialism mirror slavery:

> Patrimonialism tried to provide a (post-slavery) framework for the incorporation of young people less inclined to challenge the values of chiefly rule. The basic idea is that of forming an orderly queue for emancipatory resources ... Patrons are vertically linked. As Mende people say 'no one stands by him or herself, everyone is behind someone' (i.e. every local person enjoys the protection of a patron higher in the system).
>
> (Fithen and Richards 2005: 122)

No relationships, it seems, escaped infiltration by patrimonial politics. Above, Ferme mentions how the 'interstices between marriage' provide room for slave-like relationships to emerge (2001: 81). It is customary for a man to pay 'bride price' to the family of the bride, which may include presents for the bride, payment of her *Sande* initiation costs,[9] work on her family's land or a percentage of the groom's own produce or profits (Richards 2006). A former-RUF conscript demonstrates this problem of excessive obligation:

> [E]lders ... force young men to marry ... as soon as we harvest our first ... palm fruits. If you refuse they cause more problems than being in the bush as a rebel. They charge you to court for smiling at a girl ... But the bride price is not reasonable. You will be required to do all sorts of physical jobs for the bride's family, like brushing [[10]] and making a farm for the family ... sharing the proceeds of your own labour, harvest or business ... You will be forced to give them seventy per cent [of your palm oil], or you will lose your wife and be taken to court ... Marriage is the same as slavery.
>
> (Quoted in Richards 2006: 194)

Consequently, the manner in which youths were often linked, through fines, labour and marriage to their elders and chiefs, is reminiscent of the slave/master relationships that saw young men unable to break free from the cycle of unpaid work. This system was at times manipulated to 'catch' young men, resulting in increased labour or fines owed to chiefs or patrons. Krijn Peters explains:

> Chiefs have at times accepted many girls as wives from poorer families, seeking patronage or preference, and ... then encouraged these girls to find young paramours as a way of increasing the labour power at their disposal through the levying of fines for *woman damage*.
>
> (Peters 2006: 36)

At other times, this system of patrimonialism essentially invented infringements in order to keep young men in check and reinstate the hierarchy in which they exist on a low rung vis-à-vis older and wealthier men. Richards argues:

> At times a charge was trumped up, because the elder needed labour, or a young man was known to have acquired some money by trading or growing a cash crop. Elders sometimes talked openly about 'squeezing dry' this or that young man for *fitiyai* ('arrogance'), resorting to some minor or imagined infringement of the customary (and unwritten) code. The fault might not be 'woman damage', but simply dressing too well, or having resources deemed inappropriate to junior status.
>
> (Richards 2006: 194)

It is not surprising, given the long history of these injustices, that young men were eager to rebel against the system. Indeed, the proclaimed slogan of the RUF was 'No more master, no more slave' (Mokuwa *et al.* 2011: 346).

'Strangers'

Youths attempting to flee these injustices, or those forced out by community elders who perceived them as troublesome or disrespectful, resulted in the migration of young and isolated individuals, often to the mining regions, where the promise of wealth lay (Richards 2006: 193). In Sierra Leone, those who come from outside a chiefdom are known as 'strangers' and accrue less rights and privileges (in terms of land, work and marriage) than those indigenous to the chiefdom (Ferme 2001: 105–6).[11] These chiefdom rights are crucial as 'the vast majority of rural Sierra Leoneans still obtain primary rights of residence, land use and political/legal representation as "natives" of chiefdoms, rather than as citizens of the state' (Fanthorpe 2003: 58). Strangers are not known to the chiefdom through their ancestry, which plays a central role in one's identity and social standing in Sierra Leone. As Kris Hardin notes:

> identity … relies on an assortment of ritual actions that actually locate individuals in particular spaces by giving them rights, as well as obligations, to others who share those spaces. Where someone is born, where they join *Sande* or *Poro*, where their ancestors are buried, where they themselves will be buried work to limit the claims to identity and the rights and statuses available through the descent and kinship system. Rituals associating the individual with particular places are performed at critical junctures. These ritual acts tie individuals to particular places and to the ancestors associated with those places. In addition to legitimising rights to resources, such public demonstrations function in ways that supersede future personal claims by making it difficult for others to forget essential parts of an individual's genealogy.
>
> (Hardin 1993: 93)

This strong linking of identity to ancestry and birthplace meant that fleeing/expelled youths were regarded as an underclass with even less access to justice and equality than they would have been entitled to within their own chiefdom. For instance, 'strangers' have traditionally not been granted the right to vote in chieftaincy elections and are unable to purchase land or marry until such a time as the chief and local elders accept the stranger into the community (Ferme 2001: 105–6). This customary system has also been held in place by national legislation, through a 1972 amendment to the Protectorate Land Ordinance of 1927, which allowed Paramount Chiefs to distinguish 'natives' of their chiefdoms from 'non-natives' (or strangers) in regard to land rights (Fanthorpe 1998: 559–60). Natives were viewed as possessing hereditary rights to local land, whereas non-natives would require leases to use chiefdom land (Fanthorpe 2001: 381). The preference for natives over non-natives also forced 'newcomers to make farms at a considerable distance from the main settlement', heightening their exclusion from the hub of community life (Fanthorpe 2001: 384). 'Stranger' status thus served to alienate migrants who were then attracted to the mining regions or urban centres, where populations were already considerably more mobile and distanced from chiefdom politics.

Thus, in the urban setting, youths were deprived of education and employment opportunities by a corrupt state. In the provinces, youths were forced to work the land of their elders, unable to cultivate their own land in order to make money to pay bride price and establish their own families or opportunities. In both instances, youth were marginalized from decision-making and positions of power and treated according to patronage rather than merit, leading to a rising discontent with the governance structures that oppressed them. As Fithen and Richards (2005: 123) lay bare:

> The contradictions between patrimonialism and meritocracy could be put no more clearly. The [RUF] movement appealed to those upon whom the brunt of patrimonial failure fell: young people in the diamond pits and failing schools ... The children of a political elite, fed by diamond wealth, enjoyed superior overseas education, while local schools fell apart and teachers remained unpaid. Cadres dreamed of a fairer, more inclusive system where hard work and ability would determine success.

The need for chieftaincy reform

Given the extreme uncertainty with which youths lived – with little or no education or employment opportunities, the prospect of long-term labour or financial commitments to elders and chiefs draining what little resources youths had and the reality of remaining locked in a system of patrimonialism where social mobility was checked by personal connections – many were looking for an alternative. This was given shape, for some, through Qaddafi's vision of democracy promoted in his *Green Book* and the study groups that formed around it on university campuses (Members A, Promoters of Peace and Justice, Freetown 2009; Richards 2005: 119). These ideologues were then able to recruit (albeit often by force) from the disenfranchised and disgruntled youth living in rural areas to whom pan-Africanist socialism appealed. Several of the former-RUF rebels interviewed as part of this research had been abducted from rural areas by the RUF in the early stages of the war. While they admitted to at first being angry or frightened, all of them claimed to have accepted the ideology and cause of the movement relatively quickly (over days or a couple of weeks at most) as it resonated with their experiences of injustice and poor governance (Members A, Promoters of Peace and Justice, Freetown 2009).

One former rebel revealed how he was kidnapped by the RUF shortly after dropping out of school (Members A, Promoters of Peace and Justice, Freetown 2009). He had been given a scholarship to complete secondary school but at the end of his first year, the principal demanded the student pay him in order to continue receiving the scholarship. The student refused (as he had no funds) and the scholarship was taken from him and given to another student, whose family was willing (and able) to pay for it. With no funds to remain in school, the former-student was travelling to Liberia to visit a cousin who had offered financial assistance when the RUF captured him. Their grievances over poor governance, corruption and injustice spoke directly to his own experiences and he became, he says, an enthusiastic recruit (Members A, Promoters of Peace and Justice Freetown 2009). These findings fit with those of Krijn Peters and Paul Richards, who have determined that '[a]bductees cooperated with the movement to save their lives, but some found the movement's analysis of the breakdown of Sierra Leonean society meaningful and accepted guerrilla training willingly' (1998: 184). Even some who fought with the Sierra Leone Army (SLA) and Civil Defence Forces (CDFs) recognize the underlying motivations of the RUF as deriving from the failure of both the state and chieftaincy system to provide education and opportunities on an equitable basis (Peters and Richards 1998: 187; 195; Members D, Promoters of Peace and Justice, Bo 2009). Moreover, they view these as legitimate frustrations (Members D, Promoters of Peace and Justice, Bo 2009).

Disillusionment with the chieftaincy system is apparent more widely within Sierra Leonean society as well. Fanthorpe notes the 'deep grievances' articulated by many rural Sierra Leoneans who support the maintenance of the chieftaincy system (Fanthorpe 2003: 59). A DFID-funded community consultation records the following summary of findings in relation to heavy fines and abuses by chiefs:

> This is an age-old problem in the community and is one of the main factors underlying the war. These heavy fines cause deep-seated grudges as well [as] force young people to flee as they are unable to pay. The chiefs in the community are not paid … therefore, they find their living from conflict and the fines that it produces. Combining this practice with other malpractices that chiefs enjoy has made chiefs a target for victimisation by armed youth, as they themselves feel victimised by the authorities.
>
> (Quoted in Fanthorpe 2003: 59)

Such concerns over the chieftaincy system are also recognized by civil society and the Government of Sierra Leone (GoSL). In a 1999 report published with the UNDP, the GoSL notes that, on the basis of community consultations '[t]he cry for reform in aspects of the institution of chieftaincy was overwhelming' (quoted in Fanthorpe 2003: 59). Similarly, local civil society groups have joined forces in an advocacy campaign that seeks to democratize aspects of chieftaincy, known as the Chieftaincy Reform Campaign (Broadbent 2012). Even the Final Report of the Truth and Reconciliation Commission (TRC 2004 Vol. 2: 27) determined that:

> Successive political elites plundered the nation's assets, including its mineral riches, at the expense of the national good ... Many Sierra Leoneans, particularly the youth, lost all sense of hope in the future. Youths became easy prey for unscrupulous forces who exploited their disenchantment to wreak vengeance against the ruling elite ... The Commission holds the political elite of successive regimes in the post-independence period responsible for creating the conditions for conflict.

Referring explicitly to the chieftaincy system, the Final Report of the TRC goes on to note:

> The overbearing attitudes and behaviour imbibed by the Chiefs from their colonial masters led to their assuming new and overwhelming powers over their subjects. Some of these measures, such as the ability to impose fines or other punishments for errant behaviour, were retained long into the post-colonial period and permanently defined the negative perceptions of Chiefs among many of their subjects. Indeed, these negative perceptions carried over into the conflict in Sierra Leone in the 1990s ... An impression spread among the people that the Chiefs had become predators on their own subjects. Such a negative perception undermined the legitimacy of the Chiefs and further alienated them from the ordinary folk ... Feelings of disenfranchisement took root quite early in the Protectorate and contributed to a diminished sense of self-esteem and perception of enforced marginalisation, especially among the youths, which became a recurring theme as a cause of conflict.
>
> (TRC 2004 Vol. 3A: 8; 11; 12)

The argument that failures of governance and justice within both state and informal structures were causes of the war is also supported by the initial tactics employed by the RUF. These included the targeting of chiefs and government personnel and property (Jackson 2005: 54; Keen 2005: 41). As James Vincent notes 'no one wanted to be identified as "the chief" as that meant you were going to die at any time there was an attack' (2012: 11). At the end of the war, one third of chiefs had to be replaced, as they had either been killed or fled the country.

The causes of the war have been demonstrated in this chapter to revolve around justice and governance issues, when explored through a 'thicker', bottom-up approach focusing on the grievances of those who fought. Specifically, the central government was perceived as culpable of failing to fund social services such as schools and healthcare and for divesting itself of responsibility for its citizens' wellbeing (Gibrill 2007: 180–2; Peters 2006: 7). The chieftaincy system supported the government and ensured that access to resources and opportunities in the provinces were regulated by wealthy elders who entangled youth into their profiteering through unpaid labour and arbitrary chieftaincy justice systems (Jackson 2006: 95–6; Powlick 2007; Richards 2006: 193). This poor governance and injustice was also rooted in longer histories of domestic slavery and patrimonialism in Sierra Leone.

Such an explanation of the RUF's motivations in no way excuses or justifies the horrific violence that they unleashed upon the Sierra Leonean population. It also does not explain the increasingly random and wanton violence that the RUF resorted to later in the war.[12] Indeed, as the war continued, the RUF became seemingly divorced from its political message of egalitarianism and systematically brutalized the very people it claimed to be fighting for.[13] Rather, the argument here aims to get to the heart of the circumstances that led to conflict being perceived as a viable option for its participants, in order that such circumstances can be addressed to prevent future violence. In doing so, it points to significantly more structural and political problems than the popular, abstract and under-specified explanations of the conflict, such as greed for diamonds, inherent barbarism, or state failure suggest.

Conclusion

DFID's approach to the causes of war in Sierra Leone revolved essentially around a state failure argument. This chapter gives greater specificity to that failure, revealing that while poor governance and injustice were key features of the breakdown, these failings were not only of the state but also of informal structures such as the chieftaincy system, which was perceived as having held in place many of the injustices that the RUF rebelled against. The problem then, is not the 'failure' aspect of DFID's understanding of the causes of war, but the 'state' component. DFID programmes have not demonstrated a thorough understanding of the causes of war because they have overlooked the multiple layers at which breakdown occurred. A former-RUF member I interviewed suggested that part of the problem with post-conflict reconstruction efforts is that Western donors take a bureaucratic approach to governance, whereas Africans take a much broader view (Member C, Promoters of Peace and Justice, Freetown 2009). His insight is apt – the grievances that instigated the war are not limited to failures of the central bureaucratic state. Rather, they are linked to and supported by failures elsewhere in the Sierra Leonean governance structure. Unless failures at this level can be addressed alongside the failures of the state, reform efforts will be of limited success as they will not engage with the manner in which security and governance *actually operate,* and deteriorate.

This speaks to the need for a thick understanding of the causes of war, that goes beyond analyses that lump together seemingly similar features of conflicts across the 'third world' to support supposedly universally explanatory concepts, such as 'failed states'. Yet the explanatory power of such concepts is relatively weak in terms of understanding what precipitated conflict in particular situations. They tell us more about why the state was unable to prevent a descent into violence from a post-hoc view, than about the locally specific conditions that triggered conflict. In order to ensure sustainable peace in Sierra Leone, development partners need to support reforms of those institutions culpable of failure. This chapter has sought to demonstrate that such failures lie not only in the state, but also in the informal structures of the chieftaincy system, which in failing to provide an equitable society fermented grievances that ultimately undermined their central purpose of maintaining social order. Understanding the failure of the chieftaincy system is crucial in ensuring sustainably better governance and security for all Sierra Leoneans, particularly those living in the provinces that rely heavily on chiefs in their daily lives.

The two case studies that follow exemplify sites of contestation between the jurisdictions of formal and informal security and justice. Of interest here is how DFID's lack of engagement (in the first case) and limited and problematic engagement (in the second case) with informal actors undermine a sustainable transformation of security and justice. Only by understanding the civil war as a violent response to wider governance, rather than merely state failure, can SJSR comprehensively address the antecedents to the conflict and build a sustainable peace.

Notes

1 Paramount Chiefs are the most senior chiefs in Sierra Leone and head up each of Sierra Leone's 149 chiefdoms (see map on at the beginning of this book). Within these chiefdoms, 5–15 smaller units (sections, villages and towns) are administered by lower level chiefs. When speaking about the chieftaincy institution as a whole, the general term 'chiefs' is used, including both Paramount Chiefs and lower level section, town and village chiefs. When speaking specifically about Paramount Chiefs, this title is used.

2 Emmanuel Gaima, previously the Coordinator of the Decentralization Secretariat and the Acting Coordinator for the Institutional Reform and Capacity Building Project, described the chieftaincy system as the 'missing bottom' of governance in Sierra Leone (Gaima 2009).

3 No interviewees (including former-RUF rebels) advocated abandoning chieftaincy, although many promoted reform. Author interviews in Sierra Leone, February–April 2009.

4 See maps provided at the beginning of this book, which depict the Northern, Southern and Eastern provinces (formerly the Protectorate) and the 149 chiefdoms.

5 There are also efforts underway within civil society to reform the chieftaincy system, most notably the Chieftaincy Reform Campaign, which brings together several local non-governmental organizations (NGOs) and is supported by Christian Aid. These organizations have lobbied for chieftaincy reform and fed into the drafting of The Chieftaincy Act 2009, which attempts to clarify the roles and limits of chieftaincy power (Broadbent 2012: 13–14).

6 Secret societies are complex spiritual sodalities which function as mechanisms of social control, carrying out initiation ceremonies and conflict resolution, as well as providing a forum for communication with the spiritual realm. Secret societies are closed to foreigners and research on them is sparse and vague. For further reading, see: Ellis 1999: 34; 220–44; Ellis and Ter Haar 2004: 77–8; and Bledsoe 1984: 455–72.

7 For a fuller critique of some of these arguments, see Richards 1996; and Peters 2006.

8 The concept of 'youth' in Sierra Leone refers to a broad age bracket of, in the case of men, those who are unmarried or otherwise perceived not yet to have taken on 'adult' responsibilities (such as through employment, ownership of land, accumulation of wealth or clients, etc.). As a result, the title 'youth' can apply to men as old as 40 who are still socially perceived to be immature within the patronage system (Jackson 2011: 222; Hoffman 2011: 131).

9 *Sande* (also existing by the name *Bondo* or *Bundu* in some parts of Sierra Leone) initiation is generally understood to provide training to girls in cooking, feminine hygiene, relations with husbands, sexual relations and childbirth. Traditional medicine and spiritual practices are involved in the training. See Ellis 1999: 34; 220–44; and Bledsoe 1984: 455–72.

10 Clearing land for planting.

11 Approximately 20–40 per cent of a village are typically classed as strangers (Peters 2006: 43; Unruh 2008: 102).

12 For an examination of RUF tactics, see Keen 2005.

13 This transformation was apparent in interviewing some former-RUF rebels, who were unable to rationalize how their brutal tactics fitted with their political goals, other than to claim that as the war went on and food shortages arose, the fighters needed to be fed in order to maintain the struggle, thus justifying the killing of civilians in order to take their food (Member C, Promoters of Peace and Justice, Freetown 2009. See also Keen 2005; and Richards 2006).

Chapter 3

A thickening blue line

Challenges of informal policing for the Family Support Units

The Family Support Units (FSUs) are one instance of security and justice sector reform (SJSR) programming in which a lack of engagement with informal actors has limited the ability of the Units to achieve their intended goals of providing improved policing to women in Sierra Leone. The FSUs combine women's rights and the rule of law in a hard-not-to-like package. They aim to confront women's vulnerability to exploitation and injustice, often worsened by the dominance of men and elders within Sierra Leonean society (Alie 2008). Women in Sierra Leone are generally excluded from decision-making or prescribed limited jurisdiction and viewed as submissive to men. Their rights are often curtailed in the name of 'culture' or 'tradition' in a manner that fortifies their subservience, thus simultaneously protecting the power of those who have historically held it (Bledsoe 1984). This inequality was clear at the end of the civil war when women who had been subjected to informal marriages during the conflict attempted to reassert their independence from their former-combatant 'husbands' (Albrecht and Jackson 2009: 39). Many women were violently prevented from leaving by their partners (Fakondo 2009). The situation led to a dramatic rise in rates of domestic violence and prompted the establishment of Family Support Units (FSUs) within the Sierra Leone Police (SLP). The Units deal exclusively with crimes involving women and children and have been hailed as one of the major success stories of UK-led SJSR. Similar initiatives have since been set up in post-conflict Liberia and the Democratic Republic of the Congo (DRC), based upon the original Sierra Leonean model (Fakondo 2009; Albrecht and Jackson 2009; Horn 2008).

But women's policing in Sierra Leone involves some far less appealing informal actors that operate outside the bounds of the FSUs. This case study provides a concrete example of how a largely successful police reform project has been limited by its focus on purely formal policing. This misses the opportunity of engaging in reforms of a much broader and more utilized set of informal policing providers, whose service quality has significantly greater repercussions for Sierra Leonean women. These informal providers include chiefs and secret societies (the focus here) as well as trade associations, community peace monitors, Mammy Queens[1] and a variety of local policing committees (see, for instance, Baker 2005). Without engaging with the broad ambit of women's policing providers, the FSUs (and by extension, DFID's goal to provide improved policing to women) will continue to be a success story limited to urban areas, Western audiences and the pages of donor reports, rather than transforming the quality of policing and justice outcomes for women in Sierra Leone, which is still overwhelmingly mediated by informal policing providers (Vincent 2012: 27).

At best, the FSUs have a limited impact in improving the quality of policing that women access. At worst, they detract attention from the need for urgent reforms to the plurality of women's policing providers. Neglecting to engage in reforms of informal actors also leaves key grievances underlying the civil war unaddressed. Yet an examination of some of the most prevalent informal policing mechanisms that women rely upon also reveals the very real challenges that donors face if they do begin to engage with the broader landscape of policing. Overcoming these challenges is the focus of Chapter 5.

DFID involvement with the Family Support Units

While the original idea for the FSUs was a local innovation, DFID has been critical in setting up, financing and rolling out the Units across the country. The first FSU (then known as the Domestic Violence Unit) was supported in its establishment and rollout by the Commonwealth Community Safety and Security Project (CCSSP), staffed and directed primarily by British personnel (Biddle 2008). The head of this deployment, retired British police detective Keith Biddle, had also at the time been appointed by the Sierra Leone Parliament as Inspector General of the Sierra Leone Police (IGP). IGP Biddle and British consultants assisted the SLP in implementing the FSU model (Albrecht and Jackson 2009: 40). Since this initial involvement, DFID has remained the primary donor to the FSUs, largely through the Justice Sector Development Programme (JSDP), which ran from 2005–11 with an overall budget of GBP 28 million, and the Access to Security and Justice Programme (ASJP), established in 2012 with a mandate until 2015 and an overall budget of GBP 20 million – although of course the FSUs were just one project supported by these facilities (Albrecht and Jackson 2009: 35; 142).

The context of police reform efforts

Reform of the SLP has occurred in the face of a dismal reputation for the force amongst the public. The police were perceived to support the oppressive regime of Siaka Stevens and, later, Joseph Momoh. The Internal Security Unit (ISU – nicknamed 'I Shoot U'), later rebranded as the Special Security Division (SSD – only to be re-nicknamed 'Siaka Stevens' Dogs'), was particularly pernicious – responsible for (at times lethal) attacks on political opponents, students and trade unions throughout the 1970s and 1980s (Member B, Promoters of Peace and Justice, Freetown 2009). Politicization of the police, including the appointment of the Inspector General as a permanent member of Parliament, led to a breakdown in command structures and efficiency, leaving no capacity (and, with salaries of approximately USD 15 per month, little incentive) to protect citizens (Gbla 2008). Police involvement in state corruption and violence against citizens meant that the SLP suffered at the hands of the RUF. Throughout the war, police were targeted by the rebels due to their history of corruption and cronyism that the RUF claimed to be fighting against. It has been estimated that approximately 900 police officers were killed and a considerable number suffered amputation – including 300 deaths during the 1999 rebel attack on Freetown alone, which left all but two police stations in the capital destroyed (Baker 2005: 175; Thompson 2002: 28). As Bruce Baker (2006b: 28) attests:

> The Truth and Reconciliation Commission describes the Police before the war as 'incompetent', 'corrupt', 'a ready tool for the perpetuation of state terror against political opponents', and as engaged in 'extortion of money' and 'the violation of basic human rights'. Predatory state policing ... [was a] contributory factor ... to the outbreak and continuance of conflict.

A small survey carried out in 1998 revealed the dismal reputation of the police, with 100 per cent of respondents viewing the police as corrupt, 83.3 per cent saying the police are generally bad, 90 per cent claiming the police victimize people and 100 per cent saying the police ask for money in police stations (Horn *et al.* 2001: 2). Initial investigations by reformers also revealed that 87 per cent of police personnel had never seen the Police Force Standing Orders, which set out official procedures (Horn *et al.* 2001: 2). The road to recovery was clearly daunting.

Set against this background, the achievements of police reform have clearly been impressive. A survey commissioned by the SLP in 2004 suggests striking progress:

> Being carried out in 4 urban areas (Freetown, Makeni, Bo, Kenema) it [the survey] gives a snapshot of urban perceptions. Importantly only 15 per cent felt that there had been 'no improvement' in SLP behaviour, whilst 46 per cent thought there had been 'a great improvement in police attitude', particularly as regards human rights and 'rudeness'.
>
> (Baker 2005: 176)

This turnaround in public perception is based not only upon good public relations campaigns, but also on improved behaviour, professionalism and service by the SLP. Their successes have also been recognized internationally with SLP officers now serving with United Nations Peacekeeping Operations in Haiti and Darfur (Fakondo 2008: 5).

Yet there are, of course, also challenges. Funding is a recurrent problem for all services in Sierra Leone, with the government remaining heavily donor reliant (Baker 2006a: 41). As security reform programmes wind down, the police have to vie with traditional development programmes in order to attract donor funds. This is no easy task, with DFID, for example, shifting its focus in Sierra Leone away from security towards human development and capacity building since early 2009 (DFID Sierra Leone staff 2009).

Despite significant progress, a 2006 survey found that 25 per cent of the public did not feel safe; a further 26 per cent said they 'just trusted in the Lord's protection', and just 3 per cent claimed to feel very safe (Baker 2006b: 31). Many people in Sierra Leone also still view the police as corrupt, and they are frequently not the first port of call for those with crimes to report, particularly outside of urban areas (Baker 2006a: 56–7). The reputation of the police must be tempered, however, by the fact that the SLP are the most visible of the security forces, and those with most contact with the public. Other parts of the security sector may merely escape such criticism because their behaviour is not on such public display. There is a danger too of unrealistic expectations. As Gordon Peake (2004: 43) highlights:

> one should not expect too much too soon from new police forces ... Police forces tend to be among the most visible symbols of the transition from conflict to peace, and are therefore almost always burdened with high expectations. It is hardly surprising that under-paid, under-equipped, under-trained and under-staffed forces almost always find such hopes difficult to fulfil. That these police forces may not live up to expectations is perhaps less a function of their own failings than a reflection of the multiplicity of demands placed upon them.

While the SLP now provide a markedly improved service to the community than they did prior to reforms, there is a need to examine this policing success story, which has received only brief analytical attention, and largely only to be singled out for praise (Albrecht and Jackson 2009: 7; Gbla 2008: 87; Stone *et al.* 2005: 18). It is these success stories that are the likely candidates to be included in future SJSR programmes and thus their challenges and lessons that are important to learn from. The FSUs, in particular, are perceived as a success story of Sierra Leonean police reform. This is evidenced by the large numbers of donors and NGOs keen to support the FSUs, at least in their initial years of operation, as well as the fact that women's police stations are now a popular strategy in numerous post-conflict countries, from Liberia to the Democratic Republic of the Congo, to Afghanistan and Nepal, to Timor-Leste (Fakondo 2009). This popularity makes it especially important that archetypal cases like Sierra Leone are sufficiently scrutinized and understood to inform programmes elsewhere.

The evolution of the Family Support Units

Women and children have been recognized since the 1990s as the most vulnerable group in conflict situations, with civilians constituting 90 per cent of conflict casualties; and women and children estimated to make up more than 70 per cent of the civilian category (Paris 2004: 1; Turpin 1998: 4). Their vulnerability also lingers into the post-war environment, when pre-war power structures, including patriarchy, seek to reassert themselves in peacetime (Schroven 2006: 9). This was apparent at the close of the conflict in Sierra Leone, particularly amongst groups of former-combatants and their dependents. The dire situation in which women often found themselves at the end of the war should not be underestimated. It is not only that women in Sierra Leone live in a highly patriarchal society but that this oppression is now taking place in a post-conflict society where the bonds that previously afforded women some form of protection have been shattered. As families were destroyed or forced apart by conflict, women became terrifyingly disaffiliated – without parents, brothers or other familial elders to monitor their treatment by husbands, in-laws and others.[2] The extreme violence that women suffered both during and after the conflict was thus facilitated by social disaffiliation and goes far beyond 'normal' levels of oppression or violence.

Kadi Fakondo has been a police officer in Sierra Leone since 1984. As a cadet she was the only female in her intake and was mocked by her male colleagues as she awkwardly scrambled in and out of police trucks in her SLP-issued skirt – as trousers were not allowed for female officers (a policy that Fakondo has now overturned, giving women the option of skirts or trousers) (Fakondo 2009). Twenty-five years later, Fakondo was the highest ranking female in the SLP, holding the rank of Assistant Inspector General. In 1999, after the rebel invasion of Freetown, the British IGP, Keith Biddle, appointed her Commander of Kissy Division. Kissy, in the east of Freetown, was a rebel stronghold throughout the RUF-occupation of the city. Since then, it has been a melting pot of former-combatants and their dependents (Fakondo 2009).

Former-combatants have struggled with the return to peacetime and the changes to their power and status that this has brought. No longer able to wield power through the gun, former-combatants risked losing the very things that power was able to bring them – respect, resources and 'wives'. Throughout the civil war in Sierra Leone, combatants from all factions entered into informal marriages, which created the category of 'bush wives'. These women were both abductees and volunteers, who joined the fighting forces and often travelled with them. While some of these unions may have been consensual, there are many reported incidences of coercion – including rape and gang rape (Keen 2005: 242). Women were thus often forced into informal marriages, or sought the relative protection of pairing with one man, to avoid assault by others (Park 2006: 327). Generally perceived as being lower down the pecking order than men, these women had less access to the limited resources of food, water and medicines. Informal marriages at times also offered a way of securing access to these valuable commodities (Keen 2005: 44). The 'marriages' were thus as much about survival as they were about choice, involving the informal pairing of men with women on the basis of mutual (although rarely equal) benefit (Park 2006: 327).

Sierra Leone's disarmament, demobilization and reintegration (DDR) process was not particularly gender-sensitive. The 'wives' of combatants did not qualify for entry into DDR and so they were not able to access the demobilization, counselling, skills training and reintegration support that combatants were able to – and that would have assisted them in reasserting their independence. This meant that an opportunity was missed for many women to leave their wartime 'marriages'. Despite this, many still sought to do so, often attempting to take their children with them. In an effort to maintain whatever resources they had left, former-combatants often violently prevented their dependents from leaving. As Fakondo explains:

> As their so-called 'wives' struggled to regain their freedom (for jungle justice was no longer applicable in the city) there was stiff resistance on the part of the ex-combatants who wanted to retain them. This precipitated a dramatic rise in domestic violence cases, which overwhelmed my personnel. I decided to create a special unit to handle them.
>
> (Fakondo 2008: 3)

Originally launched as the Domestic Violence Unit, by 2001 the Unit was transformed into the FSU and rolled out across the country with the help of IGP Biddle and UK advisors (Fakondo 2008).

The Family Support Units: Purpose and procedures

The purpose of the FSUs has evolved from providing a legal response mechanism against domestic violence to a broader focus on all crimes involving women and children (Fakondo 2008). As part of gender mainstreaming efforts within development programmes more generally, the FSUs recognize that women and children face different threats and thus require a different manner of policing to men. The FSUs thus tailor their policing style to the needs of women and children. For instance, each Unit is meant to have toys and spare clothes for children to assist in providing a safe and comfortable space for them to be interviewed. In practice, however, many Units do not have the funding to maintain these facilities (Bo FSU staff 2009). Each Unit is also meant to have a dedicated social worker, in recognition of the fact that many crimes involving women and children are characterized by trauma. However, again, as of 2007, in practice only about 30 per cent of FSUs provide a social worker, although this rises to 75 per cent in Freetown and the Western Area (Barnes *et al.* 2007: 24). This tailored policing style seeks to encourage greater reporting of crimes involving women and children, in order to end the 'culture of silence', as one Officer in Charge of an FSU termed it (Lumley FSU staff 2009). This 'culture of silence' refers to the tolerance of women and children as second class citizens within Sierra Leone and the tacit acceptance of violence (both physical and emotional) against them (Officer in Charge, Lumley Family Support Unit 2009). A case study on Sierra Leone by the United Nations Population Fund (2005: 9) found:

> The causes of domestic violence are embedded in customs and traditions and in people's attitudes and acceptance of gender inequity and inequality as the norm. Participants in ... focus-group discussions confirmed that acts such as wife-battering, sexual assault and marital rape between intimate partners or the maltreatment of children by parents or other caregivers were common.

Not only were these practices found to be commonplace, more concerning still was that many women thought such practices were acceptable. For instance, consultations with urban women between 1998 and 2000, revealed that:

> more than 60 per cent still believed that a man had the right to beat his wife if she disobeyed him. Other empirical evidence indicated that it was a wife's duty to have sex with her husband, even if she didn't want to ... Other common beliefs include the following:

- Beating one's wife or partner is a man's way of showing that he loves her;
- A married man who does not have extramarital affairs is weak and abnormal;
- A wife who speaks out about her family is a disgrace to that family;
- A good wife is expected to accept patiently whatever treatment is meted out to her by her husband and his relatives;
- A survivor of gender-based violence who reports an incident to the police is blamed for embarrassing her husband; and
- Reports made by a woman against her husband may not be addressed or validated by the police because they consider such cases to be family matters to be settled at home.

(UN Population Fund 2005: 9–10)

FSUs have attempted to confront such beliefs, often considered part of 'tradition' or 'culture'. In providing a legal avenue for reporting, investigating and prosecuting crimes against women and children, the FSUs aim to demystify beliefs about the acceptability of abuse and exploitation and create safer households and communities for women and children.

In achieving this aim, the FSUs are meant to be set up separate from police stations with staff not usually wearing uniforms and housed in a separate building (in practice, this has not always happened, and some 'FSUs' are simply dedicated staff within a police station). Numbers of staff in the Units vary from one dedicated officer in a police station, to 15 staff in the largest dedicated FSU I visited. The police officers are provided with specialist training to work in the FSUs, including awareness raising, human rights and sexual investigation (Bo FSU staff 2009). While women in particular are urged to apply there is no quota system and FSUs are still male-dominated (Bo FSU staff 2009). This reflects the sex breakdown of SLP more generally, with approximately 1,550 women in a force of 9,500, or 16 per cent (Jacob 2008: 61). Social workers are provided by the Ministry of Social Welfare, Gender and Children's Affairs (MSWGCA) and train with the police in joint investigations (Lumley and Bo FSU staff 2009). If a Unit charges a case to court (a not altogether common occurrence), this is done through the Magistrates Court under formal English law (rather than customary law). Since their countrywide roll-out in 2001, the FSUs have been actively promoted through awareness raising activities within communities and on the radio. Sensitization campaigns have also been held in order to generate understanding of the FSUs role and realization of the unacceptability of violence against women and children (UN Population Fund 2005: 18).

The FSUs have received widespread praise as a success story of Sierra Leone's SJSR programme. In fact, mentions of the FSUs are almost entirely limited to brief statements about their success, gender awareness or local innovation (Stone *et al.* 2005: 7; Albrecht and Jackson 2009: 7). There is little in-depth examination of their working procedures and even less empirical investigation of their impact upon women and children. The FSUs have been assessed as being 'particularly successful' (Gbla 2008: 87) or an example of good gender awareness (Osteria 2003). The Units seem to largely escape a critical lens, with their success rarely probed. While it seems logical that the Units represent a public good, it is important to examine *how* the FSUs improve policing for women and what their shortfalls are. It seems that by ticking the donor-friendly boxes of local innovation, gender awareness and women's and children's rights, the FSUs have largely been presumed a success.

Those limited criticisms of the FSUs that have been made constitute far from an in-depth investigation. It has been claimed, for instance, that the FSUs lack familiarity with the Gender Acts and police remain largely insensitive to gender issues (Jacob 2008: 61–2). An International Alert study on gender-based violence in Sierra Leone determines that the FSUs face substantial organizational barriers – such as insufficient office space to provide privacy for complainant interviews and lack of office supplies (Barnes *et al.* 2007: 24).

More revealingly, it also claims on the basis of conversations with women's groups in Sierra Leone that gender-based violence remains a taboo issue, in spite of FSU sensitization campaigns (Barnes *et al.* 2007: 24–5). A recent briefing on the SLP indicates that concern has arisen about the effectiveness of the Units in overcoming cultural resistance to reporting violence against women, as it was found that '96% of cases ... still were not reported to the police' (Friedman 2011: 8). Overwhelmingly, however, the small literature that mentions the FSUs does so in a positive light. Criticisms are brief and have not, to date, been sufficiently examined. Despite the rare recognition that 'the empirical success [of the FSUs] is in fact rather ambiguous,' no research down this track has as yet been pursued (Jacob 2008: 61).

The critique of the FSUs here aims to examine the very *modus operandi* (or, what is often termed the 'theory of change' in development-speak) of the Units and highlights their lack of engagement with informal policing mechanisms, such as chiefs and secret societies. Recognizing and engaging with the challenges posed by informal policing actors would not only allow the FSUs to reach their target beneficiaries more directly, it would also go some way to addressing the grievances that triggered civil war. It should be caveated, however, that while advocating for engagement with informal security actors, this is not to suggest that such engagement would have been possible or even desirable at the outset of programming. Indeed, when the Domestic Violence Unit was first set up in 1999 the conflict was ongoing in Sierra Leone, and many chiefs had fled their communities and so were not even present to be engaged. Nonetheless, the FSUs are now more than 13 years old and certainly it has been possible to engage chiefs in this time, and probably since the end of the conflict in 2002.

Challenges to the Family Support Units

The FSUs have been set up to protect the rights of women through crime response, as part of DFID's broader security reform efforts to democratize and improve security sector practices. They aim to be the primary provider of policing in this regard. Currently however, they are challenged by chiefs and secret societies who remain the primary dispensers of policing for as much as 80–90 per cent of the Sierra Leonean population, particularly relating to the subjugated categories of women and children (Barnes *et al.* 2007: 14; Baker 2005; HRW 2009; JSDP staff 2009). Kadi Fakondo explains, 'people don't go to court; they don't want to be stigmatized. They settle out of court. They give money to victims' (in Friedman 2011: 8). As a consequence of so few people *using* the police, the ability of the FSUs to achieve their aim of improved policing for women is limited and the discriminatory policing practices of chiefs and secret societies, pointed to as one of the grievances that led to conflict, continue. Thus, DFID's engagement with state security forces to the exclusion of informal security forces, limits the ability of DFID's SSR programme to achieve its aims and to address the antecedents of conflict.

Chiefs and secret societies provide significant services in terms of resolving conflict and maintaining order within their communities. This is particularly so regarding issues of domestic violence and crimes of a sexual nature, which fall within the mandate of the FSUs. The dominance of informal providers in relation to the jurisdiction also claimed by the FSUs suggests that the ability of the Units to have a lasting impact upon the rights of women requires accommodation of, or engagement with, chiefs and secret societies. This is not necessarily straightforward. The policing provided by these alternatives is strikingly different, with FSUs representing Western-style policing based upon universal human rights, and chiefs and secret societies frequently portrayed as promoting 'traditional' customs, which can oppress women. Not only do chiefs and secret societies respond, at times, inappropriately to crimes against women, they are also at times complicit in rendering women insecure, for instance through clitoridectomy (female circumcision) or through the application of customary laws that do not prioritize women's rights. This makes FSU engagement with these providers a thorny issue. Yet these informal mechanisms remain the primary policing providers due to a number of barriers in accessing FSUs, as well as a fealty to customary practices. Not engaging with them risks continuing the historical divide in Sierra Leonean policing whereby 'modern' policing pertains to those living in urban areas, while those in rural areas continue to rely upon 'traditional' policing that denies fundamental human rights. Policing reform needs to work towards overcoming this bifurcated policing system and indeed, DFID's police reform programme attempted this by making the SLP more locally-relevant, community-based and rights-respecting through a policy of 'local needs policing' (Biddle 2008; Horn 2008). Yet, in practice, the FSUs continue to face a number of access issues, set out below, and thereby do not succeed in overcoming the two-tier system of policing. Improving the rights of women in a practical, everyday sense, as the FSUs aim to do, depends upon changes to chieftaincy and secret society practices, as key providers of policing in this area. If such changes are to be sustainable they must be the outcome of a dialogue involving the problematic institutions themselves.

Physical accessibility, affordability and timeliness of FSUs

Each of the FSUs visited during fieldwork indicated that the costs of accessing the FSUs were often prohibitively expensive for complainants. There are, first of all, costs of travelling to a police station that has an FSU attached. Currently there are 44 FSUs across Sierra Leone (with 15 located in the Western Area).[3] This means that, particularly in rural areas, many communities are a reasonable distance from FSU assistance. After initially travelling to the FSU to lodge a complaint, victims reporting cases of rape or assault must obtain a medical report to file charges (Lumley FSU staff 2009). While the Sexual Offences Act 2012 states that medical reports should be provided free of charge in cases of sexual violence, this rarely happens in practice, with free reports available at just two clinics countrywide and confusion remaining as to when the reports are free and when they need to be paid for. Medical reports cost approximately 35,000 Leones (USD 8) (US Department of State 2009). If the case is charged to court, there are also costs of travelling to the nearest Magistrates' Court, which are located only in the district capitals of each of the 12 Districts (for instance, in Bo District, the Magistrate Court serves 15 chiefdoms, the closest of which is approximately 8 miles from the Court) (Bo FSU staff 2009). Currently, due to shortages within the formal legal system, there is only one Magistrate for each District, causing excessive overburdening. This shortage is compounded when a District Magistrate is unable to perform their duties. As Castillejo highlights:

> the Magistrate based in Makeni was also covering the court in Kabala, because of the lack of qualified Magistrates. Although she was supposed to visit Kabala once a week, the Magistrate had not been for almost two months because there was no money provided for her petrol. This meant that the prison was crowded with remand prisoners and struggling to cope and that the JPs [Justices of the Peace] were being forced to bail prisoners who were on remand for serious offences.
>
> (Castillejo 2009: 6–7)

The shortages and resultant overburdening of the justice system mean that delays in hearing cases are common. This adds to the costs incurred by a complainant, who must travel to court only to hear that their case has been adjourned and rescheduled. If complainants are not present when a case is called to be heard, the matter is dismissed (Bo FSU staff 2009). The financial burden of travelling to court must also be considered. Costs accrued not only involve transport to the court, but also accommodation and food for the complainant and any witnesses that they bring. There are also lost earnings over the time a complainant (and their witnesses) are absent from work. In the provinces, where many survive on subsistence agriculture, this means that lost earnings directly correlate to lost food supply.

Compounding these high costs, FSU complainants tend to come from low-socioeconomic backgrounds, in a country already dogged by severe poverty (Kenema and Lumley FSU staff 2009). In 2007, it was estimated that 75 per cent of women in Sierra Leone lived on less than USD 0.50 a day, compared to 54 per cent of men (Barnes *et al.* 2007: 16). It is therefore the target population of the FSUs that are the least likely to be able to afford their services. This means that those suffering the greatest abuses are also those most likely to have to rely upon the informal policing options of chiefs and secret societies. Many complainants who do opt to take their allegations to the FSUs subsequently drop them prior to going to court due to the high costs involved (Lumley FSU staff 2009). Women who press charges against their husbands also often settle their disputes out of court when faced with the prospect of loss of their partner's income, which has substantial follow-on effects, such as paying children's school fees (Lumley FSU staff 2009). The informal justice system of the chiefs and secret societies is perceived as being less costly than the procedures of the FSUs, and thus provides a more financially accessible service to women in Sierra Leone.

Limits of FSU justice

The costs involved with FSU procedures are also correlated to the modicum of justice achieved. For instance, those who can afford lawyers receive better representation. Those who cannot afford a lawyer must navigate the often foreign world of formal English law unaided. This is no easy task given the lack of education that has been provided to most Sierra Leonean women, amongst whom illiteracy is greater than 80 per cent (UNDP 2008). The Office of the Director of Public Prosecutions is meant to provide complainants with a legal representative where the complainant cannot afford one, but this was reported to rarely happen in practice (Lumley FSU staff 2009). As men are generally the guardians of household finances, it is usually men who can afford representation, and thus increase their chances of escaping conviction (Lumley FSU staff 2009). The FSUs do not appear to keep accurate records of convictions, but all those I spoke with suggested the rates were disappointingly low (Bo, Kenema and Lumley FSU staff and Fakondo 2009). The Lumley FSU (in the West of Freetown) indicated that in 2007 there had been only two successful convictions in the entire Western Area (Lumley FSU staff 2009). Further, a US Department of State Human Rights Report indicates that, as of October 2008, FSUs had 'reported 136 cases of child cruelty, of which only nine had been charged to court. There were no convictions' (US Department of State 2009). The Report goes on to note that of 1,186 sexual assault cases in 2008, only 437 perpetrators were charged (555 were still under investigation), with 25 cases resulting in convictions (US Department of State 2009).

FSUs also face the challenge of delivering meaningful justice to their complainants. Peter Albrecht and Helene Maria Kyed (2011: 4) comment that 'empirical evidence suggests that ... it is not likely that the kind of justice ... [that formal legal systems] provide according to rule of law principles would fulfil the justice needs of many poor and marginalized groups in the Global South.' While ensuring a perpetrator is imprisoned is important to some complainants, FSU staff suggested that the lack of financial compensation available to victims under formal, English law deters some from utilizing the FSUs (Kenema FSU staff 2009). In cases where the perpetrator is the woman's husband or otherwise known to her, women are also less likely to prosecute through the formal courts, often preferring to resolve the matter informally (Denney and Ibrahim 2012). Indeed, a survey of two districts in Sierra Leone in 2006 found that jail terms were the least satisfying form of punishment for crime victims at just 24 per cent satisfied – lower than those who were satisfied by 'dismissed with no punishment' (28 per cent satisfied) (Manning 2006: 3). It may be the case that, aside from FSUs being prohibitively expensive, the justice they have the potential to deliver might not represent the locally valued currency of justice to women in Sierra Leone. Alternatively, the justice system of the chiefs and secret societies usually results in the guilty party paying the aggrieved party. As Tanja Chopra and Deborah Isser (2011: 29) point out, 'the prospect of compensation, including medical expenses and school fees, may be far more desirable than the crippling court fees, delays and difficulties involved in taking cases to court.' Thus, while the problems of attaining justice through the FSUs may be due in part to limitations of the legal system, rather than due to FSU procedures *per se*, the costs involved in seeking justice and the kind of justice available, render the FSUs an unviable or less appealing option for many complainants.

Cultural accessibility of FSUs

There is a cultural bias against women in Sierra Leone that socializes both men and women into believing that women are inferior to their male counterparts. While attitudes are improving with relatively extensive sensitization around the three Gender Acts, passed in 2007, it will take some time for social attitudes to change. As a result, dominant community beliefs and practices lag behind formal laws. Women are often considered to be the equivalent of minors under customary law, despite formal laws, such as the Gender Acts, that set out women's legal status as equal to that of men (US Department of State 2009). They are, at times, viewed as the equivalent of children, with subsidiary rights to those males (fathers and husbands) with authority over them. Women married under customary law were legally regarded as 'chattel' in the past (Schroven 2006: 22). As the US Department of State (2009) notes in a Human Rights Report on Sierra Leone, '[a] woman was frequently perceived to be the property of her husband, to be inherited on his death with his other property.' While these attitudes are changing, the legacy of these beliefs still resonates strongly throughout the country.

More surprising perhaps than the tendency of men to fortify their powerful position by suppressing women, is the fact that many women view their position as acceptable. A 2010 survey in Sierra Leone found that 73 per cent of women between the ages of 15 and 49 think it is acceptable for a husband to beat his wife in certain circumstances (UNICEF 2013). The internalization of inferiority is not only debilitating in itself, it also results in women tolerating the injustices of the informal policing system, and not pursuing the services available to them through the FSUs. As Karen Barnes *et al.* (2007: 14) reveal:

> Many women indicate that physical violence perpetrated against them by their male partners is permissible, as they have been socialised to see this behaviour as acceptable and expected. Pursuing recourse against the perpetrators is rarely an option due to stigma, social pressure, expense, lack of awareness and generally prohibitive legal structures.

Women in Sierra Leone do not seem convinced that they should be able to press charges against their partners or men within their families or communities. This customary convention permeates even the high echelons of the Sierra Leone government. One story recounted to me told of a former Sierra Leonean Minister for Gender Affairs who explained to a group of Western women concerned about domestic violence in the country that her culture dictates that it is permissible for a man to beat his wife – even though she knows this to be morally wrong (Biddle 2008). The statement, made by a government representative with a progressive portfolio specifically mandated to promote women's rights, indicates just how prevalent such attitudes remain in Sierra Leone. Indeed, customary law in most of Sierra Leone allows for 'reasonable' use of physical force to chastise a wife (Joko Smart 1983: 152).

Further to this, women are aware that if they did choose to assert their rights against abusive men, and somehow could overcome the financial obstacles involved with FSU procedures, they would face stigmatization by their family and community. The women may be viewed as 'spoiled', if they suffer abuse prior to marriage, or else married women who report their husbands may be viewed as bad mothers, wives and daughters (Biddle 2008; UN Population Fund 2005: 9–10). Not only does such stigmatization bring disgrace upon one's family, it can also, in extreme cases, lead to expulsion from the chiefdom (Bo FSU staff 2009; US Department of State 2009).

The FSUs also represent an unknown complaints system that women are not familiar with. In contrast, informal complaints mechanisms provided by chiefs and secret societies, while far from perfect, represent a system that Sierra Leoneans know and understand. This knowledge and familiarity is particularly important when disclosing highly personal or traumatic incidents (although, this is not to suggest that chiefs and secret societies are necessarily sympathetic or supportive towards women). Such disclosures are difficult enough without the added stress of an alien environment and unfamiliar procedures and personnel. The informal system thus has the benefit of being better known to the community it serves – in terms of both the individuals who administer these systems and the processes they use. The FSUs operate predominantly in English, the official language in Sierra Leone, which, while not uncommon in Freetown, is rarely known outside of the capital, except by the educated elite. While complainant interviews may be conducted in local languages, as the formal court system that cases are prosecuted through operates in English, the majority of Sierra Leonean women are at a supreme disadvantage.

There are thus strong cultural forces working against the FSUs, making their policing service inaccessible to women in rural Sierra Leone. Women are rendered inferior to men through the legacy of discriminatory customary law, which bred a culture of oppression that women themselves have at times tacitly accepted and can play a role in reinforcing. There is also a fear of stigmatization of recalcitrant women who break cultural taboos by seeking justice against male counterparts, thus silencing women who might otherwise speak out. Finally, a cultural bias also emerges from the familiarity with informal justice procedures vis-à-vis the comparatively foreign practices of the FSUs, further inhibiting women from relying upon the latter. As the staff from the Kenema FSU (2009) told me, 'culture dies hard.' These cultural obstacles, combined with the other access issues set out above, ensure that women continue to depend overwhelmingly upon informal policing mechanisms. As Bruce Baker and Eric Scheye have noted, in support of informal policing mechanisms:

> There are many reasons for the vitality and strength of non-state service delivery, including their: physical, linguistic and cultural accessibility; legitimacy; efficacy; timeliness of decisions; low transactional costs; support for restitution and restorative justice rather than punishment and incarceration; and degree of participation afforded to disputants. For these and other reasons, in the great majority of circumstances, people look first to non-state agencies for crime protection and crime response.
>
> (Baker and Scheye 2007: 512)

The FSUs must address these obstacles if they are to improve the rights of women within policing practices in a meaningful way, as intended by DFID's SJSR programme, and address the inadequacies of informal security actors, which prompted the grievances that led to civil war.

Policing by the chiefs

Existing alongside the FSUs are alternative policing practices administered by informal security actors, such as chiefs and secret societies, complicating the image of policing for women in Sierra Leone – but also importantly providing women with policing options (albeit, not always ideal ones). Under the Local Courts Act of 1963, and reaffirmed in the updated Local Courts Act of 2011, only the Local Courts can adjudicate on customary law. While chiefs and other informal actors can arbitrate (that is, mediate without imposing penalties such as fines or prison sentences), and indeed, the Chieftaincy Act of 2009 affirms chiefs' responsibility to 'prevent the commission of offences within his chiefdom and to maintain order,' it is expressly illegal for them to adjudicate. Despite these legislative stipulations, however, in practice chiefs have traditionally adjudicated on matters of customary law, particularly in relation to family matters, debt, inheritance and property (Kent 2007: 523–4). It is to their town or village chiefs that families or communities, unable to resolve their disputes in-house, will turn to with complaints (Kent 2007: 524). Research conducted by Esther Mokuwa and others (2011) suggests that 40 per cent of all cases are settled by chiefs (with this figure rising to 45 per cent in relation to causes of 'woman damage') – the highest percentage of all dispute resolution avenues. If the chief is unable to resolve the dispute, or the disputants are not satisfied with the outcome, they can refer the dispute up the chiefdom hierarchy to the Paramount Chief, or alternatively pursue the matter through the Local Courts or the state police (Kent 2007: 524; Baker 2007: 225; Tshombe Kargoi 2009). Unless the dispute involves a serious criminal matter (and even then, not always), it will generally be referred to a chief first (Alterman *et al.* 2003: 5). This means that chiefs are the first port of call for the majority of disputes within rural Sierra Leone. As the Town Chief of Tombodou, Kono District, states:

> As local chief I deal with 70–80 per cent of the work [disputes]. I see all cases of less than 30,000 Leones [approximately USD 7]. People come to the Native Authority court because they have no respect for the [state] authorities. If people are not satisfied [with the result] they go to the police.
>
> (Quoted in Baker 2007: 225)

In resolving disputes, a chief will work through the chiefdom police who act as messengers and personal guards of the chief (Tshombe Kargoi 2009). They issue warrants, carry messages, summon subjects to the chief or Local Courts, protect the chief and enforce his dictates (Friedman 2011: 9). They are entirely separate from the state police, do not wear uniforms or carry weapons and are paid only through the chief (Friedman 2011: 9). Chiefdom police will summon the parties involved and any witnesses to speak with the chief and assist in the investigation. When questioning a woman, a male chief may request a male family member to be present with her (Vangahun 2009). Parties can also bring family or community members to 'vouch for' them, attesting to their good character (Vangahun 2009). On the basis of these discussions, the chief will come to a decision about how best to resolve the dispute, which may include issuing fines, imposing prison sentences (to be served in the chiefdom lock up), or requesting payment for their dispute resolution services. The most common result from chieftaincy policing is that one party is fined. The reasons given for such resolution speak to the role that chiefs see themselves as fulfilling in terms of maintaining peace and order within their chiefdoms. Paramount Chief Vangahun (2009) explained that if he did not fine a man for his misdemeanours, the victims of those misdemeanours would be compelled to seek revenge themselves. This would lead to increased incidents of crime and disquiet in his chiefdom. Thus, the fining system appeases the aggrieved parties and serves to keep the peace within the chiefdom (Vangahun 2009). Yet fines issued by chiefs were a central grievance of many RUF recruits, and recent research suggests that the frequency and amount of such fines has not decreased post-conflict (Boersch-Supan 2010). This leaves a potential conflict trigger unaddressed.

Furthermore, the manner in which this 'peace' is kept within the chiefdom may come at the price of substantive justice, particularly for women and young people. For instance, in an effort to 'keep the peace' chiefs often encourage women who are raped (particularly when pregnancy occurs) to marry their attackers (US Department of State 2009). This is in part justified as being for the benefit of the woman, who would otherwise be viewed as 'spoiled' within the community and thus have difficulty finding another suitor, which would, in turn, impact upon her long-term financial position and wellbeing (Lumley FSU staff 2009). It is also permissible, under customary law, for a man to 'discipline' a wife for failing to fulfil her domestic duties, providing he keeps in mind that 'she was not given to you to beat her like a drum' (quoted in Holt-Rusmore 2009: 18–19). Behaviour worthy of chastisement includes burning a meal or not having a meal ready on time, going out without a husband's permission, refusing sex, failing to care for children or the home, questioning a husband, talking back or for what is known as *woman palava*, situations when a man suspects his wife of flirting or having an affair with another man (Barnes *et al.* 2007: 4). Such permissibility 'effectively sanction[s] ... domestic violence' (Barnes *et al.* 2007: 16). In some instances, husbands and chiefs collude to make money by pressuring their wives to admit to affairs (real or imagined), which results in the adulterous male being fined, to the benefit of both the husband and chief (Peters 2006: 36). Women are forced to provide names of likely young men within the community, regardless of the truth of the affair, in order to escape or end violent treatment against them. This situation reveals the injustices towards both women and young people, the latter of whom suffer financial oppression from male elders, which in turn limits their lifestyle options (such as taking a wife of their own, buying land or undertaking skills training or further education) and have been demonstrated as lying at the heart of grievances that led to conflict. Women are also, at times, made to suffer for problems within their marriage, with reports in Kenema District of chiefs resolving domestic disputes by locking up the women (UN Population Fund 2005: 10). Joe Alie explains these injustices within husband-wife relations in writing about customary justice practices in Sierra Leone:

> The justice system is heavily tilted against women, especially in husband-wife relationships, and against young people. It is not considered in the

> best interest of the family to wrong a husband even if his guilt is clearly evident. Instead, the elders would attempt to say soothing words to the wife and later privately rebuke the husband for his misdeeds. While this may look like an injustice to the woman, there is an important social element here. The main interest is to hold the marriage together, not to create a situation where the woman will 'win the war but lose the peace'.
> (Alie 2008: 137)

The value of a solid family unit is seen as key to maintaining the community peace and order that Paramount Chief Vangahun spoke of. The value of order appears to supersede that of justice in both Alie's and the Paramount Chief's accounts, and is seen to be in the greater interests of all Sierra Leoneans. For instance, the wife in Alie's excerpt may not achieve justice against her husband for his misdemeanours, but she will ultimately be better served by respecting him and not 'causing palava' so that her marriage remains intact and she remains in a household that can support her and her children. The logic at play here clearly prioritizes community order (based upon familial peace) over the rights of women on the assumption that marriage, however tainted by abuse or adultery, is in the best interests of all. This prioritizing of community order over the individual rights of women highlights a tension between policing provided by chiefs and that provided by the FSUs. It also demonstrates the need for reforms to chiefdom policing.

Policing by secret societies

Other informal policing providers that challenge the FSUs are secret societies. Throughout Sierra Leone a number of sex-specific secret societies play a principal role in transforming initiates from children into adults and oversee rules intended to keep the spirit world appeased (Little 1948: 8; Alie 2008: 136; Fanthorpe 2007: 1). The primary female secret societies are known as *Bundu* or *Sande*, depending on the region, and 'remain a key, albeit unspoken, element in political relations between town and countryside in Sierra Leone' (Fanthorpe 2007: ii). These societies wield substantial influence within the community and particularly amongst their initiates, playing a determining role in the lives of many women in Sierra Leone. Yet due to the secrecy surrounding these groups (one rule is that initiates cannot speak about the societies to non-initiates), limited research has been carried out on their roles and functions. Secrecy continued to be a challenge in interviews – with some people flatly denying that secret societies exist. As a result, the stories of secret society practices are often anecdotal, reflecting instances recounted or reported elsewhere. Without substantial long-term ethnographic fieldwork, it is difficult to separate isolated practices from commonplace ones. What seems clear is that secret societies continue to play a central role in the lives of many Sierra Leoneans and are often intimately connected to broader chiefdom politics and justice systems (Fanthorpe 2007). Further, secret societies play a rule setting (and, in some reported instances, rule enforcing) function that can be seen to police women's behaviour. The outcome of such policing, as shall be demonstrated, is not always in the interests of women and this, combined with the prevalence of secret societies throughout the country, suggests that providing improved policing to women requires engagement with the societies.

Girls in Sierra Leone traditionally entered secret society initiation between the ages of approximately 6 and 15. Time spent in the *Sande* or *Bundu* bush (the sacred grove where initiation takes place) ranged from a few days to a few months (Bledsoe 1984: 458; Little 1948). However, as human rights awareness extends and girls stay in school for longer, the length of the initiation process has shortened and girls tend to be older. Initiation is intended to provide guidance and schooling in a range of women's experiences, including caring for a husband and children, cooking, sex, relations with co-wives and rules concerning pregnancy and childbirth (Bledsoe 1984: 457–8), with the aim of producing 'fully socialized' women (Fanthorpe 2007: 2). It also provides the occasion for clitoridectomy, 'whereby women are invested with fertility, the basis of their own long-term welfare' (Bledsoe 1984: 457–8). Upon completion of initiation, the girls have been transformed into adult women, capable of marriage and childbirth. The spiritual processes that are believed to cause this transformation are controlled by the societies, so that initiates remain beholden to the knowledge and rules set down by elders in order to maintain their 'fully socialized' status (Fanthorpe 2007: 4). Initiates are said to form a bond that links them for life in sisterly solidarity (UNHCR 2001). While it is difficult to attain accurate numbers, and although practices are constantly changing, particularly in the wake of donor and non-governmental organization (NGO) penetration into the country as well as local government decentralization linking the provinces and Freetown, it has been estimated that 94 per cent of eligible females are members of a secret society; and that 91 per cent of women between the ages of 15 and 49 have undergone clitoridectomy (BBC News 2006; Statistics Sierra Leone and ICF Macro 2009: 13). Certainly in the past 'most suitors insist[ed] that their future wives be initiated into the *Sande*, and they themselves usually contribute to the fees' (Bledsoe 1984: 457–8). There are also more recent instances of the Sierra Leonean diaspora bringing their daughters back to Sierra Leone for initiation (Fanthorpe 2007: 19).

These societies wield considerable control over women in Sierra Leone through their law and order functions (Fanthorpe 2007: 4). As Anita Schroven explains:

> Throughout a woman's life, *Sande* rules and leading members exert a large amount of control due to 'secret knowledge' of fertility and child birth and the power to implement social regulations, fines or other punishments. This is part of a larger network controlling especially young women due to their productive and reproductive capacities, first exploited

> by their family of origin, later by their husband's family, and starting from the beginning of their initiation also by leaders of the local *Sande* society. This control network, intertwined with values and beliefs, is able to keep women submissive to any figure of authority.
>
> (Schroven 2006: 24)

Through their venerated knowledge of secret society rules and conduct, *Sande* elders are able to police women's behaviour. Some suggest that this 'policing' is limited to setting rules for social behaviour, which are then enforced through customary law. Other accounts portray the societies as also being involved in enforcing rules or behavioural standards, for instance through rituals surrounding childbirth, which, at least until the introduction of free maternal healthcare in 2010, happened largely under female secret society supervision. Fertility and easy childbirth are taken as symbols of a woman's good behaviour and long or complicated births can be blamed on bad behaviour by the labouring woman (Carlson 2009; Bash-Taqi 2012). Secret society midwives sometimes beat labouring women in order to hasten delivery if adulterous or other unsanctioned behaviour is suspected (Bledsoe 1984: 460; Bash-Taqi 2012). Caroline Bledsoe (1984: 460) highlights that society midwives 'use such times of extreme dependence upon them to extract money from women, threatening to expose adulterous affairs to their husbands unless compensated.' The fear of suffering such treatment has the simultaneous effect of policing women's behaviour. The horrific irony is that secret society practices that at times surround childbirth, such as pushing on a woman's stomach or rolling a log down her body, can complicate and lengthen childbirth (Carlson 2009; Bash-Taqi 2012). So too can the practice of clitoridectomy, as 'after a girl has been cut, scar tissue can form and skin that has lost its natural elasticity can tear during labour, leading to excessive bleeding' (Bowers 2007). Traditional birth practices can thus contribute to the difficult labour conditions which secret societies at times punish on the basis of assumed contraventions of society laws. Such punishments and threats, regardless of the veracity of the crimes they are punishing, serve to reinforce the power of society codes of conduct and the ability of society elders to police women's behaviour.

Secret societies also wield substantial powers in enforcing society codes of conduct and prescribed behaviours. Contraventions of such codes are punishable by fines and offenders also risk spiritual punishments that society elders are capable of causing due to their secret knowledge of traditional medicine (Alie 2008). Such power is demonstrated through Caroline Bledsoe's example of *Sande* elders pursuing a case of abuse of one of their members, not for the woman's benefit, but for their own. The example suggests that the secret societies operate not so much in support of 'sisterly solidarity' or justice for their members, but of traditional elders. Bledsoe explains:

> I witnessed a major public event in Sierra Leone in which the leaders of the Sande sued a Mende man in court for violating a Sande law by

> 'abusing' a young woman – he made insulting allusions to her sexual organs – in the heat of a bitter quarrel. Everyone agreed that the man would lose, and many people worried about what the Sande might do to him or to anyone who dared to support him. Even the male secular chiefs who adjudicated the case seemed submissive to Sande wishes, and in the end they fined him the equivalent of about US $180. The notion that Sande members maintain a consistent female solidarity against men, even in Sande affairs, is difficult to support. In the court case the male chiefs were in league with the leaders of the local Sande. Although the head of the Sande publicly expressed moral outrage that she said was shared by all women when the man broke this Sande law, she gloated privately to me about the large fine that the Sande leadership and the male chiefs would share when the man was sued. The 'abused' woman actually got very little money from the fine.
>
> (Bledsoe 1984: 459)

The justice achieved by the aggrieved woman appears secondary to the financial potential the case provided to *Sande* elders and the power it demonstrated to the community. This suggests that leaders of the secret societies are at least not only interested in protecting the rights of their initiates, but also value the economic and power incentives of their privileged position. This is further supported by Bledsoe's (1984: 459) account that 'leaders exact heavy tolls of labour from those whom they initiate. Initiates commonly work on leaders' farms, increasing the leaders' wealth.' While secret societies are at times seen as mechanisms of female cohesiveness or solidarity, they have also been demonstrated to more commonly reinforce class, age and lineage divides, with elders collaborating with elite men in the community vis-à-vis subordinate women and men (Bledsoe 1984; Fanthorpe 2007: 10).

The societies also maintain a powerful political influence, as Zainab Bangura (the sole female presidential candidate in 2002) attests:

> A woman from Freetown and the Western Area [where *Sande* initiation is less common] would get no chance to be a successful politician if she were not part of a secret society. Those of us who joined the society are expected to support it – we cannot stand out and criticise it, otherwise you will be sidelined by the family.
>
> (Quoted in Baker 2006b: 31–2)

The political power of the secret societies has also been reinforced during Presidential elections. In an attempt to sway undecided voters in the 1996 election the First Lady, Patricia Kabbah, sponsored initiation costs of 1,500 young girls, suggesting that secret society participation is a vote-winner in Sierra Leone (IRIN News 2007a). Other politicians also organized smaller-scale initiation sponsorship to boost their support in almost every district of the country (IRIN News 2007a). Even the Minister of Social Welfare, Gender and Women's Affairs from 1998–2007 threatened to 'sew up the mouths' of those who preached against secret society clitoridectomy (IRIN News 2005). More broadly, as Richard Fanthorpe explains:

> Men and women winning seats in Parliament and jobs in government are expected to remain loyal to their home communities and direct state resources towards these communities. The secret societies remain a fundamental, if unspoken, factor in these informal political pacts. Few politicians that were not initiated in the localities they wish to represent can expect to win elections and once in office they are expected to provide job opportunities for fellow initiations ... They are also expected to send their children back to rural areas for initiation and to serve as patrons of these and other local ceremonies in honour of their hereditary culture.
>
> (Fanthorpe 2007: 7)

If these forces hold sway within the country in terms of policing women's behaviour, the FSUs face an uphill struggle in terms of promoting improved policing for women without engaging with these informal sites of resistance.

The above illustration reveals the diverse roles that secret societies play in policing the behaviour of women in Sierra Leone and how society elders may manipulate their leadership positions to encourage fealty to society rules. Ultimately, secret societies are influential not so much because of the actual rules they promote, but because of their teachings of obedience to those rules. As Bledsoe suggests:

> Although Sande leaders may teach their initiates a few techniques for their future lives, the most important lesson they learn is that the leaders ultimately control the esoteric medicines and ritual techniques that can benefit or harm them. Such outcomes are contingent on proper obedience and respect from the initiates, and on appropriate payments.
>
> (Bledsoe 1984: 460–1)

This is supported by Danny Hoffman, who highlights that the power of secret societies is based not so much on the content of the secrets they protect, but rather the division of people into those who possess knowledge of the 'secrets' and those who do not (2011: 77–8). The operation of such forms of policing without inclusion in reform programmes drastically limits the ability of the FSUs to improve the quality of policing provided to women in Sierra Leone.

Despite the practices of chiefs and secret societies having adverse consequences for women, their position as the primary providers of policing regarding women's behaviour and crimes involving them render them an essential component of the policing puzzle in Sierra Leone. Efforts to address the causes of conflict and to improve the policing services for women must take these informal mechanisms into account. Given the geographic, financial and cultural obstacles preventing the FSUs from accessing rural women, efforts need to be focused on engaging with chiefs and secret societies in order to ensure that the services most available to women do not cause them harm. This means confronting undesirable practices within informal policing mechanisms that are often couched in terms of culture and tradition (and are often genuinely understood in this way).

Interactions between the policing systems

To date, the interaction between the FSUs and chiefs and secret societies has been minimal. There was initially funding for sensitization programmes, which some FSUs claim were successful in improving relations, with chiefs even referring complaints to the FSUs in some instances (Lumley FSU staff 2009). These sensitization programmes have not taken place since the first few years of FSU establishment (interviewees reported since about 2004) (Bo FSU staff 2009). The chieftaincy system is not entirely supportive of the new policing provided by the FSUs. As one Paramount Chief told me in relation to the SLP, 'they are taking our job' (Tshombe Kargoi 2009). As chiefs make money from their policing role they are thus unlikely to be eager to give it up, particularly given their reduction in funding since having to share collected taxes with Local Councils (Castillejo 2009: 5). Staff at one FSU reported that chiefs have even threatened to evict subjects from their chiefdoms if they complain to the FSUs (Bo FSU staff 2009). That being said, evolutions in Sierra Leonean law, with the 2007 Gender Acts and the 2012 Sexual Offences Act, have at least begun to create a division of labour between formal and informal policing. It is increasingly accepted that chiefs (and other informal policing providers) refer cases of sexual assault or rape to the police, even if this does not always occur in practice.

There are reported instances of secret societies forcibly initiating people who they feel are speaking out against the societies (Fanthorpe 2007: 15). There have also been reports, of FSU staff 'rescuing' girls from the *Sande* bush, to prevent them undergoing clitoridectomy as part of their secret society initiation (Kenema FSU staff 2009). This has, at times, fostered a confrontational relationship between the FSUs and the secret societies and chiefs who support them. It has also positioned the debate about policing and women's rights along a false binary, between the 'modern' policing system of the FSUs and the 'traditional' policing provided by the chiefs and secret societies. It is this false (but historically perceptible) binary that policing reform needs to overcome in order to provide accessible and democratic policing for all *and* to comprehensively address the causes of the civil war that go beyond just state failure.

Understanding policing options in a simplistic, 'modern-versus-traditional' manner is not a fruitful way of winning over the majority of rural women, who are socialized in local customs and often feel uncomfortable with the unknown and foreign environment and procedures of the FSUs. Arguments about the modern and traditional are invoked as legitimating claims by both the SLP and chiefs to justify their practices, yet both contain aspects that cater more and less effectively to the needs of women. Given the importance of tradition in the lives of many, particularly rural, Sierra Leoneans, the FSUs should be careful not to align themselves 'against' tradition by refusing to cooperate with chiefs and secret societies, as this may risk pushing women into a further dependence upon unreformed informal policing providers.

Given the not-always-pleasant reality of chiefs and secret societies as policing providers, the argument is likely to be made that efforts should focus on strengthening the state police service in order to overtake the informal as the primary provider. A thorough rebuttal of arguments against engagement with informal actors is dealt with in Chapter 5, but it is important to note here that progress towards improving the rights of women within traditional practices has already begun, supporting arguments that 'culture' is not fixed but malleable. The Sierra Leone Parliament passed the Gender Acts in 2007, covering issues of domestic violence, intestate succession and registration of customary marriages and provide women with rights that were either denied or ambiguous under customary, Islamic and previous formal laws (Teale 2007a, 2007b; Mannah 2007). A Sexual Offences Act was also passed in 2012. The government of Ernest Bai Koroma, elected in 2007 (and re-elected in 2012), pledged to outlaw clitoridectomy in Sierra Leone, but has yet to do so (AFP 2008). In 2009, however, clitoridectomy before the age of 18 was banned in Kambia District, in the Northern Province, although it is not clear that this is enforced in practice (IRIN News 2009). Nonetheless, chiefs, *soweis*[4] and community members signed an agreement that protects the cultural value of the practice, whilst making it optional and giving adult women a choice. More broadly, voices speaking out against secret society practices are on the increase from human rights groups, and Christians and Muslims who feel animist elements of society teachings are against their religion (Fanthorpe 2007: 18). Further, as girls stay in school for longer, society initiation is increasingly delayed so that women reach the age of consent and can choose whether or not to take part. Change may also be assisted by the new breed of chiefs that have been elected since the end of the war. Many of these new chiefs are relatively young and literate, with some well-travelled and foreign educated (Jackson 2006: 106). These new chiefs may offer a unique opportunity for updating customary policing practices that older stalwarts may feel compelled to defend.

Conclusion

A lack of engagement with the informal, demonstrated through the FSU case study, leaves harmful policing practices unreformed. Such practices instituted by informal actors in the past created grievances and inequalities that prompted some to join the RUF. In order to sustainably transform policing for women and to address the causes of conflict at both formal and informal levels, policing reforms need to engage with informal actors beyond the state, such as chiefs and secret societies who are the dominant providers of policing to poor women. This dominance is due in part to accessibility issues faced by the FSUs, but also to a fealty amongst Sierra Leoneans who value the role of the tradition and culture that pervade informal institutions. Yet these informal policing actors also present challenges and do not always provide policing services that are supportive of women's rights. Without engaging with these providers, poor quality policing will continue and the FSUs will limit their improved service to urban, wealthy or educated women. This means that those most at risk will continue to rely upon policing provided by chiefs and secret societies. DFID's new Access to Security and Justice Programme (ASJP) has the opportunity to set the terms of engagement between state and informal policing differently, recognizing traditional practices as evolving forces with the potential for change. Such recognition would help to address failures within the informal, as well as state, system that led to the breakdown in Sierra Leone.

Notes

1 Mammy Queens are respected female elders within the community who provide advice to women who seek it. They are often related to the chief but not in all cases.
2 This is not to suggest that women were always treated admirably in pre-war times. However, it was possible for women to complain to their families about violent treatment by their husbands (which served no-one's interests given the importance of women's productive and reproductive qualities to families and communities). In such circumstances women were sometimes able to return to the familial home, in exchange for the return of the bride price.
3 Although it should be noted that what constitutes an FSU differs substantially amongst the 44. While some are fully fledged Units, physically separate from police stations with their own staff, others constitute just one dedicated police officer sitting within a station.
4 The women who conduct clitoridectomy in Sierra Leone.

Chapter 4

Courting local justice

DFID's Justice Sector Development Programme

Injustice has consistently been pointed to as a cause of the civil war in Sierra Leone. Efforts to rebuild the justice system, so that more equitable and rights-respecting justice is provided, are therefore crucial to ensuring a sustainable post-conflict peace. Critically, any efforts to do so need to address the injustices perpetrated at both the state and informal levels of justice provision, as set out in Chapter 2. This chapter examines DFID's Justice Sector Development Programme (JSDP), in order to determine whether it demonstrated engagement with informal justice actors. Whereas in the case study of the Family Support Units in Chapter 3, DFID's reform programmes were shown to have failed to engage with informal security actors, an examination of DFID's justice reforms reveals greater acknowledgement of the role of informal actors. However, operationalization of this insight has been limited due to continued prioritization of the formal justice system, engagement with only a limited range of informal actors and a focus on formalizing the informal. As a result, the JSDP's reforms have demonstrated a somewhat thicker understanding of the causes of conflict – recognizing that injustice in both formal and customary legal systems contributed to grievances that triggered the civil war – but have not sufficiently operationalized this insight.

This chapter first examines the role of justice reform within security and justice sector reform (SJSR) and the current popularity of rule of law programmes. Second, the overwhelming focus of justice programmes in Sierra Leone on high level, international legal procedures (as opposed to local law reforms that are more relevant to the majority of the population) is spotlighted, followed by a history of the judicial system in Sierra Leone, highlighting the central role played by informal justice systems and how these have functioned. Finally, JSDP's primary justice programmes will be detailed, before analysing the effectiveness and challenges of engagement with informal justice mechanisms.

Rule of law reform – 'like apple pie and ice-cream'

Justice, or rule of law reform, as it is also known, has emerged as a key component of SJSR and statebuilding more broadly. As Thomas Carothers noted

15 years ago, '[a]ssistance in [the rule of law] field has mushroomed in recent years, becoming a major category of international aid' (1998: 103). Since the mid-1980s, aid agencies have spent more than a billion dollars trying to build the rule of law in transitioning countries (Kleinfeld 2005: 5). Just as development practitioners focused on economic and governance reforms respectively in the 1980s and 1990s, legal reform is now a key component of statebuilding, the latest panacea for the global south (Carothers 1998: 95).[1] While Carothers is sceptical of this latest trend, highlighting the common but erroneous presumption that law is non-ideological and technocratic (1998: 99), there are also more optimistic readings of the 'rule of law orthodoxy', as Stephen Golub (2003) has termed it.

The rule of law is seen as central to sustainable development, with strong legal institutions supporting a just social order that minimizes physical conflict by providing peaceful avenues for the resolution of disputes and thus contributing to economic growth (Decker *et al.* 2005: 68; North 1981; Acemoglu *et al.* 2013; Varvaloucas *et al.* 2012: 1). This conflict-minimizing benefit of justice – both procedural and substantive – is described in the UN Secretary General's Report on the Rule of Law and Transitional Justice in Conflict and Post-Conflict Societies. It states that peace cannot be sustained unless 'the population is confident that redress for grievances can be obtained through legitimate structures for the peaceful settlement of disputes and the fair administration of justice' (quoted in Sannerholm 2007: 68). Pierre Englebert (2000: 18) suggests that 'the prevalence of the rule of law has a more significant positive impact on growth than the quality of public administration', due to investor concerns regarding stability, as while investment is possible under highly illiberal political systems, it is less possible without an operable rule of law (such a model of stability within illiberal settings has been seen to exist in some parts of East Asia) (Golub 2006: 110). The rule of law thus contributes to sustainable peace, which in turn, following the logic of the dominant international donor agencies, provides fertile ground for the investment necessary for economic growth and development (Golub 2006: 110; Viner 2009). This seeming consensus on justice reform has led some commentators to remark that the rule of law is like apple pie and ice-cream – something no one can dislike (Sannerholm 2007: 66). This supposedly universally likeable quality is supported by the emergence of justice reform initiatives on the project lists of many international donors including DFID, USAID, the UN and World Bank (Decker *et al.* 2005: 1). Recognizing the connection between conflict and injustice, these agencies are attempting to re-link justice and peace in the aftermath of conflict (Mani 2002: 5). This has particular resonance in the case of Sierra Leone where injustice is recognized as having been a principal cause of conflict (Castillejo 2009: 2; Alterman *et al.* 2003: 3; Park 2008: 539).

The Final Report of Sierra Leone's Truth and Reconciliation Commission (TRC) (2004: 90–3) concluded that the judicial system was culpable of contributing to the permissive culture of impunity that facilitated civil war. It went on to recommend that resources be devoted to improving the justice system in order to ensure conflict is not rekindled (TRC Final Report 2004: 122). Taking on this challenge, the Government of Sierra Leone (GoSL) has accepted that 'the long term decline of the justice system preceded and even facilitated the on-set of the conflict' and that 11 years of civil war further deteriorated the judiciary (GoSL 2006: 1). On this basis it recognizes that 'addressing these consequences [of the deteriorated justice system] are also crucial for the permanent restoration of state authority' (GoSL 2006: 1). This recognition that justice is central to sustainable peace is not limited to the corridors of state political power, but also discernible within local politics. As a villager in rural central Sierra Leone expressed to researchers Steven Archibald and Paul Richards (2002: 346), 'through injustice we have turned our young people to rebels.' This acknowledgement was evident in many of the interviews conducted during fieldwork, across a broad spectrum of respondents – from former-rebels, to civil society representatives, to members of the judiciary (Members B and D, Promoters of Peace and Justice Freetown and Bo 2009; Koroma 2009; Fofanah 2009). There is thus a unique convergence between development policy trends and the realities of the civil war in Sierra Leone that has provided an opportunity for justice reform. Yet reforms have only happened at some levels at which justice is accessed in Sierra Leone.

Justice initiatives in Sierra Leone: The Special Court and the TRC

While substantial donor funds have been directed to justice-related programmes in Sierra Leone, the vast majority of these resources have been mobilized for high-level, international law efforts, rather than local-level initiatives (Hoffman 2008: 130; Chirayath *et al.* 2005: 1). This is most obviously reflected in the Special Court for Sierra Leone, established by agreement between the UN and GoSL to prosecute those deemed most responsible for the atrocities of the civil war. While the Special Court has undoubtedly had an impact on the post-conflict landscape in Sierra Leone, its short-term nature, limited scope and overwhelming 'foreignness' have rendered it less consequential than reforms to Sierra Leone's legal system – which will remain long after the white four wheel drives and international staff depart. The incredible costs of the Special Court in relation to the Sierra Leonean judiciary are most stark in highlighting the divergence in assistance. The Special Court, established in 2002, has cost over USD 200 million to prosecute nine individuals from the Revolutionary United Front (RUF), Civil Defence Forces (CDFs) and Armed Forces Revolutionary Council (AFRC) (Bowcott and Mark 2012).[2] In 2002, the year the Special Court was established, the total payroll of Sierra Leone's judiciary was approximately USD 215,000 (Thompson 2002: 39). In 2007, the entire budget for the Government of Sierra Leone was USD 414 million, of which less than one per cent was spent on the judiciary – less than USD 4 million (IRIN News 2007b). Even now the GoSL spends just USD 8–10 million annually – less than 1 per cent of its annual budget – on the prisons, police, and courts combined (Varvaloucas *et al.* 2012: 7–8). As Niobe Thompson (2002: 39) suggested at the outset of the Special Court's mandate, '[t]o those working in Sierra Leone's own judiciary, this operation will likely seem like an extraterrestrial visit, so disproportionate will be the conditions of work of its staff in comparison to its own.'

Despite the Court's laudable aims of seeking to extend international law by securing conviction precedents for the recruitment of child soldiers and acts of sexual violence, it has failed to resonate with the lives of many Sierra Leoneans (Hoffman 2008: 129–41; Penfold 2009). Outside the Special Court compound, post-conflict lives have had to adapt to living side-by-side with the majority of perpetrators and finding reconciliation through alternative means (Penfold 2009; Keen 2005: 300–1). In this regard, the TRC should have provided a more locally meaningful contribution to substantive justice by documenting people's experiences and seeking to heal communities. Yet the TRC was viewed as primarily UN, rather than GoSL, driven and the mandates of the TRC and Special Court, operating in the country at the same time, created confusion about whether justice was restorative or punitive and deterred many from coming forward to testify. The TRC also did not engage with the enduring legal system in Sierra Leone that will determine whether justice becomes fairer, more accessible and reliable in future, or whether disputes will be settled by more violent means (Hoffman 2008: 131). This more pressing need to engage with local justice practices, which would address the country's history of grievance and violent conflict and provide a long-term legacy of justice (both procedural and substantive), has often been neglected (IRIN News 2007b).

Of the more limited donor engagements that have happened with the Sierra Leone justice systems, these have focused primarily on the formal justice system and not the customary justice system which is dominant in Sierra Leone. Engagement with informal actors is not only advocated here because they are the dominant justice providers (indeed, a 2006 survey noted that 85 per cent of crimes looked at in the survey were reported first to village level traditional leaders) (Manning 2006: 2).[3] Engagement is also necessary because failures in the informal justice system were a key cause of the civil war, as set out in Chapter 2, and therefore must be resolved if peace is to be sustained. Recognizing the importance of both formal and informal justice practices, DFID embarked upon a wide-ranging justice reform programme in Sierra Leone, the Justice Sector Development Programme (JSDP), engaging directly with Sierra Leone's justice systems. Most impressively, this engagement has extended beyond the formal judiciary to encompass parts of the customary legal system as well (what the JSDP termed 'primary justice'). This breadth of programming is necessary in Sierra Leone and reflects the fact that informal justice providers are 'the predominant method by which the public goods of justice and safety are delivered' (Scheye 2008: 64; see also Castillejo 2009; Manning 2009; Albrecht 2010; Jackson 2011). The longevity and embeddedness of customary legal systems in Sierra Leone's history is set out below.

History of the justice system

Prior to colonialism, the law in Sierra Leone was particular to specific regions and varied from kingdom to kingdom, presided over by cultural leaders who were considered knowledgeable in local affairs (Kane *et al.* 2005: 16). They were assisted by secret societies in ensuring the maintenance of customary law and behaviour (Little 1967: 255; Fyfe 1962: 3–4; 22–3). Law was not fixed and, as Kristin Mann and Richard Roberts highlight (1991: 4), 'there was no single, unchanging tradition. There were, instead, contested and continuously reconstituted traditions, best understood as clusters of rules, moralities, expectations, and conflicts, which gave rise to changing regulatory practices.'

Under colonialism

Through colonialism a three-tiered system of formal, customary and Islamic law emerged that endures in Sierra Leone today.[4] Under the policy of indirect rule, formal English law was to apply to Europeans and consenting Africans, while customary law applied to matters involving Africans. District Commissioners administered justice for Europeans in rural Sierra Leone (where the formal courts of Freetown were absent), while Native Courts resolved disputes amongst Africans according to customary practice (Jearey 1960: 409–10; Denzer 1971). Requiring local representatives to administer customary law, Britain relied upon community leaders, henceforth termed Paramount Chiefs, section chiefs or town chiefs (in descending order of seniority) (see Chapter 2 for further details on the history of chieftaincy).

The logic of the British colonizers was to create a neat social order that would be predictable and reliable (Kup 1975: 198), facilitating commerce between the provinces and the Freetown colony (Alldridge 1970 [1910]: 295). Customary law was used by colonizers to maintain this order and thus served an explicitly administrative purpose. British colonizers viewed the law as the harbinger of order, and thus of peace, which would facilitate commerce, in turn improving the situation of rural Sierra Leoneans, while simultaneously creating wealth for the empire (Fyfe 1962: 135).[5] The administrative function of customary law was apparent in the appeals process, in which appeals from the Native Courts went to a colonial administrative officer, rather than the formal English Courts, so that the judicial powers of customary law were capped by administrative power (Fyfe 1962: 135; Ghai 1987: 752–3). This underscores the point that customary law was not necessarily intended to provide substantive justice, but rather to maintain social order.

Often regarded by Europeans as indigenous law, customary law was in fact invented by Africans and Europeans (Mann and Roberts 1991: 8). While intended to ensure continuity with past indigenous practice, customary law created new rules that drew upon indigenous custom but did not always replicate it (Mann and Roberts 1991: 8). This was due to a combination of factors – including an insufficient consideration on the part of the colonizers of the biased manner in which 'custom' was discerned, as well as the non-static nature of custom (Alldridge 1970 [1910]). As Mann and Roberts explain:

> When questions arose about custom, officials turned for answers to chiefs and others they regarded as repositories of local knowledge and upholders of local authority. Such persons were always men and usually elders. The reliance of officials on particular individuals or groups to define tradition gave them [chiefs and elders] new advantages in the competition for resources and labour and it augmented their power.
>
> (Mann and Roberts 1991: 22)

Customary law was thus produced by overlapping power struggles between men and women, elders and youth, rulers and ruled, and land owners and slaves (Mann and Roberts 1991; Mamdani 1996: 122). Not always cognisant of, or concerned with, these struggles, colonizers crystallized the versions of customary law as reported to them by the powerful, thus enforcing a highly particular version of 'custom'. This 'solidified fluid cultural and legal ideas and relationships into reproducible ones' (Mann and Roberts 1991: 4). New conceptions of 'custom' thus altered rights, duties and relationships (Finnegan and Murray 1970: 417).

Stretching 'custom' even further, colonizers also forcibly changed custom to suit their interests. As Arthur Abraham notes, 'eager to create a neat system out of pre-colonial dynamics, [colonial officials] insisted on or invented principles that were not altogether indigenous' (1978: 274). Similarly, where local leaders were not willing to perform the tasks assigned to them by the colonizers, the British simply created new, more pliable leaders, and imbued them with 'customary' right (Fullerton Joireman 2001: 579). Law thus became an instrument for social change, whether that change was biased, invented or imposed (Mann and Roberts 1991: 6). Rather than being reproduced through social practice, custom became enforced by a legal order, backed up by the coercive colonial state.

The manner in which custom was interpreted has had long-term impacts on configurations of justice in Sierra Leone. Although British District Commissioners curtailed the jurisdiction of chiefs, allowing them to arbitrate only on issues of land, marriage, divorce and petty offences, chiefs' powers within these realms increased, as they had greater purview for determining what constituted 'custom' within their jurisdiction (Kup 1975: 181–2; Jearey 1960: 409). As Finnegan and Murray suggest, this meant that 'a new definitive power was introduced where before a ruler had to rely on persuasion and diplomacy' (1970: 417). As noted in Chapter 2, these powers have been contentious within Sierra Leone, with abuses by chiefs pointed to as a cause of the war, and the jurisdiction of chiefs being re-examined as a result.

Chiefly abuse in administering customary law was a problem even under colonialism, prompting action by the Colonial government who feared that oppressive behaviour might incite public disorder. In an effort to check chiefs' powers, Tribal Authorities (representing taxpayers) were established within chiefdoms in 1937, requiring that chiefs consult with them on judicial matters (Finnegan and Murray 1970: 421). Modernization plans became more frequent as independence approached, recognizing that while chiefs had been useful under indirect rule, they were not necessarily suited to independent government (Ghai 1987: 751–3). District Councils were established in 1947, reducing the formal role of chiefs. Yet despite the administrative changes, little was altered in practice. As Finnegan and Murray explain:

> The chiefs still combined judicial, tax assessing and collecting, and local administrative roles, as well as filling an office of considerable prestige. In the execution of their powers they were not subjected to close supervision, and the Commission into the disturbances in the Provinces in 1956 [a revolt against chiefs] revealed the manner in which the chiefs were able to use their powers: using the tax assessment committees to impose fines, arranging the judicial bench to suit their interests, using the power to assess taxes to distribute favours and punishments, imposing unlawful levies and tributes, selective summoning of persons to Tribal Authority meetings, incarcerating on their own authority, and so on.
>
> (Finnegan and Murray 1970: 428)

Throughout independence

Independence in 1961 saw a continued reliance on customary law, despite European assumptions that this would wane with modernization (Wambura Kimathi 2005: 7–8; Aryeetey 1996: 119). Predictions that the former-colonies would reject the colonially imposed formal English law also proved incorrect (Fullerton Joireman 2001: 576). Instead, rather than streamlining its multiple justice systems, independent Sierra Leone embraced a complex array of legal institutions, maintaining formal and customary law (as well as Islamic law in relation to Muslim marriages) (Kabbah 2006). Yet independence was to prove as rocky a road as the colonial encounter, with both formal and informal justice systems implicated in abuses.

Within the formal legal system, the judiciary quickly succumbed to politicization and legislation curtailing individual rights was introduced throughout the 1960s (African Human Security Initiative 2009: 61;

Thompson 2002: 5). Niobe Thompson sums up the general perception of the post-independence judiciary:

> Judges and magistrates ... [were] widely perceived as corrupt and the justice system came to be seen as an instrument of state power and wealthy interests. A reservoir of resentment developed towards the judiciary among those who ... received unfair treatment at its hands.
>
> (2002: 10)

While formal Magistrates Courts, dispensing English law, were present in the provinces from 1965, they were not nearly as popular or common as their customary law counterparts. By the 1980s, the formal judiciary was virtually non-existent in provincial Sierra Leone as state resources dried up (Thompson 2002: 16; Malan 2003). Customary law, however, continued to operate.

In 1963 Local Courts replaced Native Courts in adjudicating customary law. The 1963 Local Courts Act defined customary law as '[a]ny rule ... having the force of law in any chiefdom of the provinces ... and conforms with natural justice and equity' (quoted in Joko Smart 1980: 88). Breaking with the practice of the Native Courts, chiefs were replaced by Court Chairmen as adjudicators within the new Local Courts (Manning 2009: 133; Kabbah 2006; Joko Smart 1980: 88; Sierra Leone Court Monitoring Programme 2006). This ostensibly removed chiefs from the Local Courts and afforded greater judicial independence. However, in practice, chiefs continued to adjudicate illegally on many matters. Furthermore, Court Chairmen were largely selected by chiefs and therefore influenced by them, so that the system did not necessarily curtail the abuses it was intended to (Thompson 2002: 48). For instance, Ryann Manning (2009: 131) notes that 'in a Bombali chiefdom, a previous court chairman was alleged to have consulted the Paramount Chief on all cases before ruling.'

Local Courts were integrated into the formal legal system through the appeals process, but certain procedures remained unique. For instance, Local Courts barred lawyers from representing clients within the Court, although users could draw upon persons knowledgeable in customary law to build their case (Sierra Leone Court Monitoring Programme 2006). This was important as customary law is unwritten, and people are not always certain of the content of the law. Appeals from Local Courts were to the District Appeals Court, the Local Appeals Division of the High Court, the Court of Appeal, and finally the Supreme Court (Sierra Leone Court Monitoring Programme 2006). However, while the appeals process integrated the Local Courts into the formal system, in deciding cases in the formal appeals courts, judges apply customary law, which requires the presence of customary law expert assessors in an advisory capacity to provide knowledge of the laws, as judges in the formal system are not necessarily trained in its application or many forms. Local Courts were also, in theory, meant to be supervised by customary law officers from the Attorney General's Office to ensure decisions adhered to natural justice and equity, but these did not function throughout the civil war, and in 2007, there were only three in the entire country to supervise the estimated 288 Local Courts (Thompson 2002: 18; Koroma 2007: 8).

While the appeals process through the formal legal system suggests that the Local Courts were at the bottom of the justice chain, in practice, Local Courts also represented the highest body of appeal within chiefdoms, where customary law is usually first administered by other informal actors, such as chiefs (Alterman *et al.* 2003: 4). Despite the changes to the customary law system since independence and integration of its courts with the formal legal system through appeals, in practice, most people in the provinces continued to take disputes to their local chiefs, elders, workplace associations or secret societies first, and only to the Local Courts if the matter remained unresolved (Sierra Leone Court Monitoring Programme 2006; Baker 2005: 371–90). Such customs were further facilitated by the contraction of state revenues and the allocation of the majority of resources towards the capital, ensuring that services for provincial Sierra Leone remained an afterthought. Justice in the provinces thus continued to function largely according to its own logic. As a result, practices such as chiefs' adjudications continued to occur with little outside scrutiny (Rennie 2006: 22).

Throughout the war, oversight of provincial justice, where a 'system' of any kind was even in place, was even rarer still. Crime rates increased as police stations and courthouses were destroyed (Varvaloucas *et al.* 2012: 4). Eleven years of conflict left courts and records destroyed, judicial staff unpaid, Local Courts exacting hefty fines to meet costs, and a huge backlog of cases.

Post-conflict legal system

The failures of the Sierra Leonean justice system to both administer judicial processes and to provide substantive justice cannot be underestimated. The formal court system suffers from chronic understaffing, a lack of funding and a paucity of resources, which ultimately deprive provincial Sierra Leoneans more than those in the Western Area, where limited resources are concentrated. In 2000, there were only 15 magistrates and 20 judges in the entire country, with the vast majority of these Freetown-based, serving approximately 20 per cent of the population (Thompson 2002: 4). No Magistrate Court was operable in the Northern Province, with a temporary court set up to carry out its functions (Thompson 2002: 4). At the end of 2001 there were approximately 100 lawyers in the country, 92 of them were Freetown-based, eight served the regions around Bo and Kenema, while there were no practising lawyers in the Northern Province (Dale 2008: 7–8). By 2008, this situation had not improved, with the Sierra Leone Bar Association reporting approximately 100 lawyers nationwide, yet only seven outside Freetown (Castillejo 2009: 6). The Director of Public Prosecutions informed researchers in 2008 that there were ten state prosecutors nationwide, with seven based in Freetown and three allocated to the Provinces – meaning that prosecutions are usually carried out by police prosecutors, who are poorly trained (Castillejo 2009: 2). Rent-seeking behaviour by court personnel is common, deterring many from utilizing the Magistrates' Courts, which are already perceived as being more expensive than Local Courts (Castillejo 2009: 5). One lawyer interviewed by Alterman *et al.* (2003: 15) notes that 'corruption is more open and shameless than in the past.' This is not surprising when one considers that in Moyamba town, JSDP staff reported in 2008 that court clerks had not been paid for 28 months (Castillejo 2009: 7). Staff shortages have meant excessive workloads within the courts and a backlog of cases overwhelming staff. In 2002, it was reported that Freetown Magistrates heard up to 50 cases per day and that at the High Court level, the backlog had caused delays for several years, with a number of active cases dating back to 1993 (Thompson 2002: 11).

While failures to provide both order and equitable justice in the formal system should not be underestimated, it is failures in the customary legal system that are more relevant to the majority of Sierra Leoneans. Pamela Dale (2008: 8) notes that in the provinces '[t]he limited number of functioning magistrates courts are based in district headquarter towns, which are far away (both physically and mentally) from residents of many remote – and even not-so-remote – villages.' People thus more commonly rely upon the Local Courts. There are between one and five Local Courts in each chiefdom, with an estimated 288 countrywide, making these Courts substantially more accessible (Dale 2008: 8; JSCO 2008: 29). Yet this accessibility has meant little in terms of improving access to substantive justice. In fact, the conditions in the Local Courts led Castillejo to suggest:

> While there is undoubtedly discrimination in the formal justice system, the most serious concerns relate to inequality in the customary justice system, where the laws are set and the procedures managed by senior men, with little oversight from other authorities and often in contradiction with the rights of marginalised groups.
>
> (Castillejo 2009: 9)

The legacy of the Local Courts is one of gerontocratic abuse of power vis-à-vis youth, 'strangers', women and other marginalized categories within Sierra Leone (Jackson 2011). Local Court Chairmen are rarely trained, meaning that sentencing can be inconsistent and disproportionate – exacerbated by the fact that decisions are rarely recorded so it is difficult to hold them accountable to past decisions (Varvaloucas *et al.* 2012: 20–1). The jurisdictional limits of the Local Courts have also been unclear, with Castillejo noting that '[a] number of local court chairmen and officers interviewed were unaware of the legal limits of their jurisdiction. For example, one local court officer in Koidu town reported that his court could hear cases that carry fines of up to 1 million Leones' (2009: 7–8). This uncertainty has now been clarified by the new Local Courts Act, passed in 2011, which limits the jurisdiction of the Local Courts to civil cases and criminal cases in which punishments are less than six months imprisonment or less than 50,000 Leones (approximately USD 11.50) (Sierra Leone Court Monitoring Programme 2006; Jonnie 2006).

As the hub of local elites, chiefs exercise substantial power over all local political and justice processes (Jackson 2011: 218). This influence is heightened by kinship networks, which mean that those staffing the Local Courts are often relatives of chiefs (Manning 2009; Jackson 2011). While the Local Courts are meant to provide a justice service to communities, they are often inhospitable environments in which community members are poorly treated. As Gabriel Jonnie (2006) explains:

> The conduct of proceedings at the Native Authority courts [Local Courts] is often held in an unfriendly atmosphere characterised by fear and intimidation. Court officials are notorious for intimidating parties by frequently shouting at them, thereby creating panic. Litigants, therefore, find it difficult to compose themselves well when giving evidence.

Disproportionate fines are issued for sometimes invented offences. Vivek Maru (2005: 20) illustrates a scenario he witnessed in a Local Court, where two fines of 10,000 Leones (USD 2.30) were levied against a witness as punishment for the witness speaking 'a one-word answer to a question asked of him before the court clerk had finished recording the question in his languid handwriting.' As Maru notes, the irony of this situation is that the witness was 'someone who was in principle assisting the court in its work' (2005: 20). Those unable to pay fines can be imprisoned, made to work off the fine through labour, or forced to leave the chiefdom (Jackson 2011). Castillejo notes that these fines:

> appear to be becoming increasingly important as the new local councils now take a proportion of the tax that previously went entirely to the chiefdom. It was widely reported that fines levied by local courts bear less relation to the offence than to the current financial needs of the court and chief.
>
> (Castillejo 2009: 5)

These excessive fines mean that one of the prime benefits of the customary system – its financial accessibility – is potentially a perception rather than reality and that grievances over injustices that led to civil war in the past remain unaddressed.

This depiction of Sierra Leone's justice system provides ample justification for the 'rule of law orthodoxy' that has become increasingly popular amongst development agencies (Golub 2003). In Sierra Leone, DFID, in particular, has recognized the importance of engaging the justice sector as part of broader efforts to build a sustainable peace:

> Where there is poor governance and lack of belief in a rule of law ... then grievances, social exclusion and competition for resources are more likely to become violent. This can result in insecurity and conflict. Therefore, an important means of conflict prevention is for a country to have an effective state which provides free and fair justice.
>
> (DFID 2009a)

The efforts by DFID to create 'free and fair justice' through primary justice reform projects are the focus of the remainder of this chapter.

DFID's justice reform programmes

While UK support to Sierra Leone focused initially on security reforms of the military and police, it was soon realized that gains in these areas depended on related improvements in the justice sector (Howlett-Bolton 2008: 5; Albrecht and Jackson 2009: 41). Further, international justice efforts, such as the TRC, pointed to injustice as a central cause of the civil war, providing evidence of the need for justice reform to ensure post-conflict peace (TRC Final Report 2004). While a small DFID-sponsored Law Development Project commenced in 2001, it was not until 2003–4 that the extent of breakdown within the legal system was fully realized (Jackson 2011). Around this time initial preparatory planning was being done for Sierra Leone's Poverty Reduction Strategy Paper (PRSP), in which the rule of law, human rights and due process were highlighted as fundamental to economic growth (World Bank 2005: 44; 59; 84; DFID 2004b). Commitment to a sector-wide justice reform programme was indicated in the 'Long-Term Partnership for Development', agreed between the governments of the UK and Sierra Leone in 2003 (DFID 2003). A 'broad programme of support' for the justice sector was also flagged as one of the UK's indicators of progress within the Poverty Reduction Framework Agreement between the UK and Sierra Leone (DFID 2004b). As justice was increasingly recognized as being important for both security (in support of policing functions and providing people with an effective non-violent conflict resolution mechanism) and development (by maintaining the rule of law and due process that would attract investors), DFID's work in this area duly expanded.

The JSDP was launched in 2005, funded by DFID and managed by the British Council. Its five-year mandate (later extended to 2011) was to establish safety, security and access to justice for the people of Sierra Leone, in particular the poor, vulnerable and marginalized (Rennie 2006: 2; Park 2008: 543; Viner 2009). The JSDP took a broad, multi-sector approach to justice, working with 'all stakeholders who have a part to play in delivering justice, both within government and within civil society' (Rennie 2006: 2). They involved the judiciary (the formal and parts of the customary systems), Ministry of Internal Affairs, police, prisons service and civil society in an attempt to create a fairer and more effective justice system (DFID 2004a: 1). This joined-up approach represented an important shift away from conceiving of institutions in isolated reform packages, as tended to occur with early policing and military reform programmes (Albrecht and Jackson 2009: 134). The JSDP became regarded as 'the first Sierra Leone experience of a broad sector-wide programme' (quoted in Albrecht and Jackson 2009: 134), with the programme regarded as 'the most ambitious and far-reaching of reform efforts' (Sriram 2009: 12). While the JSDP undertook substantial reforms of the formal justice sector, it is their efforts to engage with the customary system that are of interest here.

Informal justice reforms

As Stephen Golub notes (2007: 48–9), DFID 'has … played a trailblazing role in studying customary and other non-state justice systems, which the poor employ far more than their societies' less affordable, accessible and comprehensible judiciaries.' Given that dissatisfaction with the justice system in Sierra Leone has been noted as a cause of the conflict, and given the greater reliance upon informal justice practices than on the formal judiciary, such engagement and reform is crucial to building a sustainable peace.

The JSDP assisted the GoSL in developing a Justice Sector Reform Strategy and Investment Plan (2007), which sets a goal of providing improved justice at the community level, as 'with a formal legal system that is inaccessible to 70% of our people, we need to make sure that alternative systems for delivering justice (including through chiefdoms) are functioning properly and fairly' (GoSL 2007). According to the JSDP, primary justice is where justice intersects with communities and becomes meaningful at the local level (Magbity 2009). Primary justice projects within the JSDP focused predominantly on efforts to reform the Local Court system that administers customary law and to codify customary law. Pilots of these projects were carried out in Moyamba District (the JSDP's pilot location) (Magbity 2009). These two projects demonstrate that while the JSDP made headway engaging with informal justice actors, their approach to doing so was also problematic, engaging with only some informal actors and attempting to formalize them. Ultimately this represented a 'thin' understanding of informal justice, overlooking the ways in which failures of informal justice contributed to the grievances that triggered civil war. What is more, the targeting of pilot projects in Moyamba district has meant that the JSDP's impact on security and justice outside of Moyamba has been limited (Albrecht 2010: 14).

Codification of customary law

The JSDP embarked on a project to codify customary law in the Moyamba pilot district to test the viability of codification more broadly across Sierra Leone's 149 chiefdoms, which each operate according to their own version of customary law. Customary law in Sierra Leone is not written, and interpretations of the law within Local Courts are based upon the memory of community leaders, and differ markedly across the country (Fofanah 2009). The unwritten status of customary law has created difficulties in determining precedents and in affording citizens knowledge of the law. Such inexactitudes have meant that the law as applied by the Local Courts is often unclear, with citizens not knowing what behaviours constitute a crime and what the punishments for contraventions might be (Magbity 2009). This lack of clarity has also allowed the Courts to pass judgments that are unlawful (according to statutes limiting their jurisdiction) as well as unjust. It is recognized within the Sierra Leonean legal system that such injustices contributed to the dissatisfactions that led to conflict, and customary law therefore needs to be rendered more transparent in order to avoid injustice in future (Magbity 2009). The logic underlying the JSDP's codification project was to reduce the arbitrariness of customary law by recording it and turning that record into fixed legislation that could be consistently applied.

Codification, as understood by Justice Fofanah of the High Court of Sierra Leone tasked with the project, involves three stages – restatement, unification and codification. Only the first stage was ultimately completed within Moyamba District (one of 12 districts in Sierra Leone), containing 14 chiefdoms (Fofanah 2009). Justice Fofanah took just under 12 months to complete the process. Restatement involves compiling a description of all laws of the communities within a district, drawing upon interviews with community elders, written works, court records, District Council reports and chiefdom bye-laws (Fofanah 2009). The restatement is thus a 'systematic description of all laws of various tribes as they exist in an approved, simplified and coherent manner' (Fofanah 2009). The JSDP initially estimated that restatement within each district will take approximately six months (despite the fact that the Moyamba pilot project took nearly double this time) (Magbity 2009). They aimed to have several teams working on restatements in different districts at one time, so as to complete the process before the JSDP's 2011 pull-out date. In theory, once the restatements were completed, unification would be undertaken, attempting to harmonize the laws through legal integration. Where contradictions in laws arose, a determination of the 'greatest good for the greatest number' would be used to resolve discrepancies (Fofanah 2009). Some locally specific regulations that do not contradict the codified version of customary law would be maintained in chiefdom bye-laws, applying only to a specific chiefdom, however overwhelmingly customary law would become general in nature (Magbity 2009). Finally, the unified statement of customary law across Sierra Leone would be enacted into legislation, becoming prescriptive and legally binding on all Local Courts across the country (Fofanah 2009). Application of laws outside of or contradictory to this code would be illegal. With a general and prescriptive customary legal code in place, Sierra Leoneans would be able to know the legal implications of their actions, and Local Courts would be limited in their ability to make arbitrary or unfair judgments. Yet in practice, the challenges of codifying 149 unique sets of laws into one version became apparent after restatement and an attempt at unification in Moyamba was drafted (which was not taken further).

Local Court reform

As the only *legal* informal administrator of customary law in Sierra Leone, the Local Courts represent potentially the most promising judicial institution in the country (Alterman *et al.* 2003: 4). As Alterman *et al.* explain:

> The local court has more potential for transparency than any other legal mechanism in Sierra Leone. Its adjudications are open to the public, its rulings are generally recorded, and the customary procedure and law is familiar and accessible to the public. The local court seems to be the most accepted and best understood ... legal institution in the provinces. It can therefore be strategically the single most important element of reform.
>
> (Alterman *et al.* 2003: 21)

Yet despite such potential, a 2007 perception survey of these Courts revealed that 80 per cent of respondents agreed that there were barriers to accessing them, 50 per cent of respondents felt that Local Court officials had unfavourable attitudes, and only 26.8 per cent believed that the Local Courts Act bound Court procedures (Koroma 2007). As the most popular *legal* channel for resolving disputes (chiefs and other community-level informal actors remain the more utilized institution but are legally not allowed to act in a judicial capacity), the Local Courts were pinpointed by the JSDP as a key target for reform if the injustices of the past were to be ended.

Reform of the Local Courts has been extensive and, given the dire state of Sierra Leone's legal system at the end of the war, had to start from the basics. Training was a key focus as the last time training had been provided to Local Court staff was in the early 1980s (Viner 2009). Given the tense relationship between youths and the customary justice system, and the role that this played in triggering conflict, efforts were also made to improve communication between the two. In the JSDP's pilot district of Moyamba efforts were made to sensitize Local Court staff to youth rights issues, as well as more broadly to jurisdictional limits and independence (Castillejo 2009: 10). Reports following up these projects attest that 'JSDP's work with local courts had resulted in these courts levying more appropriate fines' (Castillejo 2009: 5). Further to this, Castillejo notes:

> The Moyamba Youth Movement reported that ... [sensitisation on youth rights] has resulted in improvements in the relationship between young people and police and that young people are now more willing to take disputes to local courts, rather than seeking to resolve them through violence, as they are receiving fairer hearings and verdicts from the local courts.
>
> (Castillejo 2009: 9)

The primary focus of Local Court reforms has been placed on amending the Local Courts Act 1963. A new Act, passed in 2011, clarifies the jurisdiction of the Local Courts, which had been a matter of confusion since the 1963 Act. The new Act also grants more power to the judiciary, for instance by shifting the power to elect Local Court Chairmen from the Ministry of Local Government and Rural Development (MLGRD) to the Chief Justice, and puts limits on the influence of chiefs and elders within Local Court processes (Viner 2009; Local Courts Act 2011). By so doing, the Act reinforces the independence of the judiciary as the best placed body for ensuring due process within the justice system, both formal and customary. In placing the Local Courts under the supervision of the judiciary (rather than the MLGRD, where they were formerly housed), the new Local Courts Act also links the formal and customary legal systems in an unprecedented manner, 'enabling closer supervision, and hopefully strengthening the emphasis on judicial standards and human and constitutional rights in the local courts' (Castillejo 2009: 14). This closer proximity between the two legal systems aims to overcome the justice divide between rural and urban Sierra Leone by harmonizing the formal and informal.

Judging primary justice reforms

While reforms of the formal legal system still predominate, the JSDP reforms have been the most extensive within the DFID-led SJSR programme in Sierra Leone in engaging with informal processes. Yet JSDP reform efforts are also limited by the manner in which they have understood informal justice and sought to engage with it. In assessing JSDP primary justice reforms, three key observations are made. First, engagements with the informal are still a footnote to the much more extensive engagements with the formal justice system. Second, where the informal *has* been engaged, the JSDP worked only with *some* customary justice actors, overlooking the dominant providers. Third, engagements with the limited customary justice actors that JSDP *has* worked with generally sought to formalize informal practices, misunderstanding the perceived benefits of customary law in important ways. As a result, the JSDP was not always able to transfer the level of detail of its knowledge in policy and amongst staff into projects on the ground. The manner in which the JSDP engaged with the informal therefore slightly detracts from the otherwise laudable fact that the programme tried to address failures beyond the state security and justice apparatus. It seems that while the JSDP recognized the important role played by informal justice actors, its engagements were constrained by a 'thin' understanding of customary law and how it operates in Sierra Leone.

Engagements remain overwhelmingly state-centric

First, while the JSDP demonstrated an increased recognition of and engagement with customary justice systems, this should not be overstated. Engagements with the formal legal system still overwhelmingly predominated. Despite the JSDP's claim to focus on justice for the poor and marginalized, engagement with customary justice was limited to the Local Courts, excluding key customary justice providers. Although a primary justice sector coordinator was appointed by JSDP, they remained based in Freetown and projects did not extend beyond Moyamba district (Albrecht 2010: 6). As Castillejo points out, JSDP:

> strategy actually focuses far more on reform of the formal system than the customary system, and the majority of customary justice personnel and chiefs interviewed during this research were unaware of the strategy's existence, despite apparently being its main targets. Moreover, the vast majority of donor support to the justice sector is focused on formal institutions, with only the JSDP pilot in Moyamba doing any significant work with customary institutions. This gap between the recognition of the importance of the customary sector and the limited plans to address it highlights the challenges of working with customary justice institutions, and the importance of finding new ways to do this.
>
> (Castillejo 2009: 20)

As a result, the JSDP did not constitute a fundamental reorientation of programming, but rather grafted some limited (although undoubtedly important) engagements with the informal system onto a broader programme of work with the formal system.

Selective definition of the 'informal'

Second, where the JSDP *did* engage with informal justice systems, they worked with only *some* of the relevant actors (namely, the Local Courts). This overlooks the other informal actors, including chiefs and secret societies, which are the most commonly relied upon providers of customary justice in the country. While DFID policy documents recognize the predominant roles played by chiefs, elders and secret societies within customary justice practices, the JSDP's engagement with these actors has been negligible (DFID 2004a). Rather, the JSDP engaged with the Local Courts, which represent the only *legal* informal adjudicators of customary law (according to the Local Courts Act 2011 and the Constitution of Sierra Leone). Outside of the Local Courts, the more utilized illegal informal adjudicators – predominantly chiefs, elders and secret societies – continue to arbitrate without interference from SJSR. As Alterman *et al.* note:

> While customary law is most institutionalised in the form of local courts, the public tends to consider the chief's audience the initial formal forum of customary law adjudication. Even where local courts are accessible and operational, the people turn to the chief in their disputes when their informal mediations or arbitrations in auxiliary social groups fail. This is true even though district officers and Freetown officials speak against the practice and official government laws to not recognise chief's adjudications ... people and chiefs rally behind chief adjudications. Such popular support may cause any attempts to circumvent this mechanism to fail. While the chief does not necessarily guarantee a fair and objective adjudication, he is honoured as the head of the community, knowledgeable of the community ways, customary law, and tribal justice.
>
> (Alterman *et al.* 2003: 23–4; 29)

While the JSDP's unprecedented engagement with informal justice actors should be applauded, their willingness to engage with only *some* of these actors, to the exclusion of those most utilized, still limits the effectiveness of justice reforms. Moreover, a 2006 survey of two districts in Sierra Leone found that both Magistrates and Local Courts had a user satisfaction rate of just 20 per cent – the lowest of all conflict resolution channels, including chiefs (Manning 2006: 2).

Focusing reform efforts on improving legal customary channels suggests an assumption that an improved legal justice service will deter people from relying on illegal customary channels. Yet this approach also risks alienating reform efforts from the actual manner in which justice in Sierra Leone is practised, especially given that a 2007 Institutional Reform and Capacity Building Project (IRCBP) survey indicated that 'respondents tended to trust customary bodies more than formal bodies, specifically chiefdom officials more than central government officials' (Varvaloucas *et al.* 2012: 16). The JSDP *might* be able to attract users who would otherwise have relied upon the chiefs and secret societies, but structuring reforms around this assumption might also lead to the creation of a thin upper layer to the Sierra Leone justice system that operates in an effective manner for the minority of people who rely upon it. Cracking that surface is risky, but potentially crucial in ensuring sustained reforms of the justice system that will provide substantive justice to its users.

The option of engaging with the full gambit of informal actors, both legal and illegal does, of course, risk being seen (not least by the Sierra Leone government) to support an illegal and arbitrary justice system. Interviews during fieldwork revealed that resistance to engaging with informal justice actors is evident on the part of the GoSL and the formal justice system. This can be traced to the historic divide between Freetown and the indigenous inhabitants of the provinces. Some Freetonians, particularly the dominant *Krio* settler population, considered the provinces 'traditional' or backward and resistant to the benefits of modernization (Collier 1970: 55; Pham 2006). Historically there has been, at times, a sense of embarrassment on the part of the urban *Krio* population that their country should encourage reliance upon what they perceive to be distinctly un-modern justice or governance systems (Collier 1970: 55; Pham 2006). This is exacerbated by historical legal legacies, apparent for instance in the Constitution of Sierra Leone (1991) in which customary law is put at the bottom of the hierarchy of laws (Varvaloucas *et al.* 2012: 25).

In addition, the state may be opposed to interfering in the functions of chiefs given the political support that some politicians receive from chiefs in their constituencies. Chiefs are regularly reported to 'deliver' votes to politicians in return for favourable support from politicians by directing their subjects who to vote for, although some research suggests this influence is waning (Fanthorpe *et al.* 2011; Manson 2007). This has led to a hands-off approach to the chieftaincy system in the past, with the MLGRD (who oversaw the Local Courts until new legislation in 2011) seeing chiefs as self-regulated, and not providing any meaningful oversight (Albrecht 2010: 15).

Of course, the realms of possibility of donor operations in-country are not boundless and will be determined to a great extent by relations with the host government (more on this in the final chapter). Yet it is arguably these very arbitrary systems that are most in need of reform from an end-user perspective. Policing and justice consultant, Piet Biesheuvel (2008), notes the need to engage with unappealing characters in both the formal and informal settings:

> There has been this debate, not just in DFID ... about whether you should engage with unsavoury people or not ... Do you say 'we can't possibly have anything to do with it', or do you try and engage and change? I mean, it is the same debate ... about police reform. A lot of the police services worldwide are pretty foul regimes but if you never engage with them, you are not going to be able to change them are you? So I think engagement is absolutely right ... I don't pretend ... [the customary system] is perfect. It's far from it ... But I don't think that should stop us from engaging with it – in fact exactly the opposite.

The entire SJSR process is predicated on engaging with less than desirable security and justice actors in order to reform them. The illegal informal, in this sense, is no different from formal security and justice forces also in need of reform. A lack of reform in both instances leads to poor quality justice outcomes for those Sierra Leoneans who rely upon them. Moreover, donors can take some cover from any pushback from the state through GoSL planning documents, like the Justice Sector Reform Strategy and Investment Plan, which includes efforts to 'improve public satisfaction levels with Local Courts, Paramount and Local Chiefs' as one of its six targets (GoSL 2007: v).

Formalizing the informal

Third, even where the JSDP *has* engaged with some customary justice actors, their engagements have sought to formalize the informal. This is apparent in both the Local Court reform and codification projects. Doing so fundamentally misunderstands the nature of customary law, and how it is often the very differences between customary and formal law that lead people to take their disputes to informal providers.

The law, as understood in legal-rational terms, is impersonal and process-oriented, with an emphasis on the individual rights of the parties involved (Kleinfeld 2005; Lubkemann *et al.* 2011). Application of these principles is assumed to lead to the most just outcome. JSDP primary justice programmes can be seen to push towards these kinds of legal principles, for instance through making Local Court Chairmen more objectively selected and independent from chiefdom politics. Further, reforming Local Court processes has the aim of ensuring that evidence presented in the Courts is admissible or that the individual rights of parties before the court are upheld (Magbity 2009). Similarly, ensuring that customary laws are recorded firms up the law in a way that allows citizens to know what behaviours are legal or illegal. Such reforms are often presumed by Western reformers to constitute 'goods', as our own legal cultures suggest that legal-rational principles like impersonality and due process are important for ensuring justice. However, customary law is founded on a different set of principles that also hold justice as the ultimate goal, but see this as being achieved through fundamentally different processes. People do not necessarily just rely upon the customary legal system because the formal system does not function as it ideally should, but also because the nature of justice obtained through the customary system is sometimes preferred. As Lubkemann *et al.* note from their research in Liberia:

> One of the most striking findings ... is that most Liberians would still be unsatisfied with the justice meted out by the formal system even if it could perform well. This is because the core principles of justice that underlie the formal system differ considerably from those valued by most Liberians.
>
> (Lubkemann *et al.* 2011: 217)

A key difference between formal and customary laws is that while the latter is focused on processes, customary law is decidedly focused on outcomes. Whereas in legal-rational models is it assumed that by adhering to certain impersonal *processes*, a just outcome will be achieved, customary law sees the outcome as what determines best process. As Deborah Isser notes in relation to customary law in Liberia, the idea that someone accused of a crime could be excused because of a procedural technicality or lack of due process is itself considered fundamentally unjust (2011: 335).

Similarly, customary law sees the impersonality of legal-rational approaches to the law as impeding, rather than facilitating a just outcome. In Sierra Leone, it is considered vitally important that the person adjudicating a case knows the parties involved and their family histories, place in the community, and so on. It is these very subjective and personal attributes that allow an adjudicator to determine who is trustworthy, what the interests of the disputing parties might be, and what repercussions decisions will have on broader community order. In part, the importance placed on 'knowing people' derives both from chiefdom politics and the experience of civil war. This is apparent in the 'stranger' phenomenon in Sierra Leone. 'Strangers', those who move outside of their chiefdom of origin, accrue less rights vis-à-vis those indigenous to a chiefdom, suggesting that who you are – your age, birthplace, sex, lineage, and so on – determines to a large extent the rights to which you are entitled (Fanthorpe 2003: 58; Ferme 2001: 105–6). The better known you are to a community, the more rights you are capable of accruing, because you are more trusted. The experience of civil war has elevated the importance of 'knowing' people, as trust broke down within communities and even families, so that suspicions were substantially heightened. Young men, the most mobile demographic in the country, were particularly feared and it remains common for Sierra Leoneans to warn you of young men not known to them who are not to be trusted. These histories mean that adjudication of crimes through customary law is perceived to require knowledge of the community, the individuals and their histories and relationships in a way that defies the impersonality or objectivity of legal-rational approaches to the law.

Another important difference between formal and customary approaches to justice is that while legal-rational laws are interested in protecting the individual rights of parties involved, customary law places significantly more emphasis on the importance of social order and harmony (Isser 2011: 335; Alie 2008). As a result, a decision which might be in the interests of the individual rights of the wronged party may still be considered unjust in Sierra Leone if it is perceived not to contribute to the broader social good. In relation to cases of domestic violence, for instance, while it may be in the interests of the female victim's individual rights to have a guilty partner sentenced to prison, this would not necessarily result in improved social harmony, including for the victim – the woman would lose the financial support of her husband resulting in her children being unable to attend school, for example. The bride price that the husband's family paid at the time of marriage may need to be returned, creating financial difficulties for the husband's family and potentially leading to further disputes within the community. As a result, such cases are often mediated and can result in the husband paying compensation to his wife and her family. At times, women themselves prefer such outcomes in comparison to the financial and social consequences of an imprisoned husband (Maguire 2012). It should be noted, however, that some attempts to protect individual rights are gaining ground in Sierra Leone, with cases of murder, rape and repeated assault increasingly being taken to the police to be dealt with through the formal legal system, and chiefs supporting this process (Denney and Ibrahim 2012: 14–16). Yet reforms to the customary legal system that focus on promoting individual rights may miss the central purpose of customary laws – which are not solely to protect individuals, but to protect community harmony. Lubkemann *et al.* (2011: 234) note in relation to customary justice in Liberia, 'in a country still struggling with social tensions and war-generated animosities, an emphasis of social reconciliation may be a better guarantor of peace and stability than an adversarial, winner-takes-all approach to justice.' In a post-conflict context, a focus on community harmony might not be wholly negative.

Problems with a thin understanding of the law

The JSDP's efforts to reform informal justice therefore seem to have operated with a 'thin' understanding of how it actually works (Jackson 2011) – without realizing that the alterations it attempted to make contradicted some of the key features that potentially make customary law so valued to those who use it. This suggests that while the JSDP recognized failures at the informal level, and thus engaged with some informal actors to reform them, these engagements have been limited by a 'thin' understanding of customary law. This thin understanding risks creating three problems: customary law becomes frozen; practices flout laws because reforms outstrip attitudinal change; and people are pushed to rely upon the 'informal informal'.

Customary law becomes frozen

Much has been written on the problems of codifying customary law,[6] and in fact, even DFID guidance demonstrates an awareness of the challenges:

> Governments may request help with writing down customary law. Past experience with restatement and other codification projects suggests that there is a danger that law will become 'frozen' and that judges and lawyers will start formally applying customary law without taking into account the particular context. It is more useful to work with multidisciplinary teams, including anthropologists, to understand the norms and

> principles of non-state systems and assess options for collaborating between state and non-state systems.
>
> (DFID guidance 2004a: 14)

Yet despite these acknowledged concerns, codification or 'ascertainment' of customary law has undergone a resurgence, with donors supporting such processes as part of rule of law reforms, most recently in South Sudan, for instance (Chopra and Isser 2011: 31). By writing down and fixing what is otherwise a flexible and adaptive system of law, codification risks 'freezing' the law at one particular point in time, thus shutting down the possibility of it evolving with social attitudes. This results in formalizing social relations in favour those who currently hold power (Chopra and Isser 2011: 31). Furthermore, codification can also shut down the ability of citizens to find, within customary laws, opportunities for evolution and articulation of rights. As Chopra and Isser note:

> In practice, the flexible and negotiated nature of customary law provides considerable space for contestation and adaptation, including for women, who have been adept at using these spaces to advance their rights. In the name of predictability and equal application, codification is likely to reduce these constructive spaces of contestation and with it, the practical options available to women to define and redefine norms as their rights consciousness grows.
>
> (Chopra and Isser 2011: 32)

Thus while JSDP's codification efforts were intended to improve the quality of customary justice, they overlooked the possibility that this would close down the space for flexible interpretations and contestation that provide users, particularly the marginalized, with room for manoeuvre.

Practices flout laws because reforms outstrip attitudinal change

A further risk is that JSDP reforms, by attempting to formalize customary law and accelerate its modernization, may fail simply because the pace of reforms outstrips attitudinal change and practice. A disjuncture between laws and practice will always exist to some extent, but the gap is particularly wide where legal reforms are conducted in a manner that is disconnected from the attitudes and practices of the communities they are meant to apply to (Isser 2011: 348). Stephen Ellis and Gerrie Ter Haar highlight the longevity of this disjuncture in Africa:

> Colonial officials were in practice often frustrated to find that people in villages persisted in doing things in ways that did not accord with the

> monographs on ethnic tradition that were being printed on the basis of expert research, and that chiefs often did not apply the customary laws that had been identified. Rather, chiefs and others were constantly updating custom in light of new circumstances. Even in postcolonial Africa, the same process continues, as officials of some central governments continue to uphold a bureaucratic notion of proper customary law that differs from what people actually do, or what might be called 'living' law.
>
> (Ellis and Ter Haar 2004: 145)

A contemporary example of the disjuncture between formal rules and practice in customary justice in Sierra Leone demonstrating this point can be found in the removal of judicial powers from chiefs in 1963, whereupon this power was bestowed upon the judiciary (African Human Security Initiative 2009: 109). Yet to this day many chiefs are unaware of this law, or choose to flout it, and continue to exercise judicial power (also, at times, under pressure from members of the community (African Human Security Initiative 2009: 109; Lubkemann *et al.* 2011: 221). Most Sierra Leoneans also believe that such power is legal (African Human Security Initiative 2009: 109). By law, chiefs actually wield incredibly limited powers but this is not reflected in practice, studies of which suggest that provincial Sierra Leoneans use the conflict resolution mechanisms of chiefs more frequently than any other forum (Koroma 2007: 6; Sierra Leone Court Monitoring Programme 2006).

Both the JSDP's codification and Local Court reform projects operated on the assumption that changing the laws governing Local Court practice would lead to changes in behaviour. The JSDP's codification process took a top-down approach to resolving the interaction of various laws in Sierra Leone, rooted in how these laws *should,* according to legal-rationalism, be harmonized (Fofanah 2009). Responding to questions about how a unified and generally applicable customary code would be enforced, it was suggested that Local Courts would enforce the new code because the new code would be the law (Fofanah 2009). This does not show a great deal of correlation to how the Local Courts or informal justice have in fact been practising to date. This approach to codification means that the process was highly ambitious, potentially overlooking the tactile problems of enforcing adherence to legislation *in practice.* The danger is that by focusing efforts on formalizing informal practices, reforms will outstrip social attitudes and practices, and therefore be largely redundant. This would be a missed opportunity in terms of genuinely improving justice practices in Sierra Leone.

The disconnect between formal laws and practice suggests that there is little reason to expect that further formal reforms to the legal code will be meaningful for how informal justice in fact functions (Jensen 2008: 119; Kleinfeld 2005: 15). While, at law, formal English law overrides customary, and thus legislative changes should 'trickle down', it would be a mistake to believe that this hierarchy always plays out in practice (Jensen 2008: 119). Rather, reforms need to engage with practical regulation, instead of words on paper written in Freetown in a language most of the population cannot understand. For instance, people from the provinces need to be familiarized with the formal court system and the manner in which the two justice systems interact (not only through the rule-based operation of courts set out in legislation, but also through assisted visits to courts, to see where they are, how they operate and who does what). Various impediments to building such a relationship in practice exist, such as the geographic and financial barriers to travelling to formal courts, the legal formalism ('legalese') adopted in the formal courts and the use of English as the language of operation. It is reforms to address these impediments, more than amendments to legislation, that will bring the customary and formal legal systems closer together in practice.

In part, the failure to carry out in practice what is formally law on paper is due to understaffing, resource shortages and a lack of training, all of which make the application of the law prone to inefficiencies and difficulties. Reformers might hope, then, that formal laws will take hold with a strengthened capacity. However, neglect of formal laws has its roots in more than just capacity and resource scarcities. There is a sense in which the formal courts and legislation of Freetown are distant more than merely geographically from provincial practices (Dale 2008: 8). The hinterland separating Freetown from the provinces also represents a divide in lifestyle, culture and authority structures that must be understood if reforms hope to alter practices in the provinces (Jackson 2011). Whereas the rule of law in Freetown is derived from an (increasingly) independent judiciary and 'modern' policing functions of the SLP, the provinces have conventionally derived order from more localized, customary authority structures, such as chiefs, elders and secret societies. As research by Alterman *et al.* discerned:

> Customary law encompasses a crucial dimension of the people's identity and sense of community belonging. Customary law is perceived as a link between the past where the law has been minted by ancestors. Thus, obedience to the law is validation of belonging. The people adhere to customary law more loyally than to common law, which is often poorly known and perceived as 'coming from Freetown'.
>
> (Alterman *et al.* 2003: 10)

This underscores some of the problems in attempting to create a formalized and generally applicable version of customary law for the provinces. Citizenship in Sierra Leone is chiefdom-specific, with individuals becoming 'strangers' when they leave their original chiefdoms (Jackson 2011: 222). Key aspects that differentiate chiefdoms from one another are the rules and customs that apply within their boundaries. For example, customary law in the predominantly Islamic Northern province of Sierra Leone does not allow women to be elected as chiefs, whereas this is permissible in the more Christian South. Changing the laws either way in those regions will not only be a question of law, but also one of politics, religion and culture. Attempts to apply a generally applicable, formalized version of customary law would mask these important, identity-enforcing differences in rules and customs that make each chiefdom unique and bestow identity. The challenges that provincial identity constructions pose to formal law and to formalized versions of customary law thus need to be considered in greater depth.

Erik Jensen suggests that laws are ultimately most powerful and effective when they are broadly compatible with previously existing practices (2008: 136). It is these existing practices which are most 'thickly' (and thus most easily) enforced – not merely through 'thin' legislation, but also through custom and convention. Jensen explains in more detail:

> Law (or rules) is just one potential mechanism by which behaviour is ordered, and often not the most robust mechanism, especially in postconflict situations. Custom and convention play predominant roles in ordering behaviour, even in rule-based societies, and an overwhelming role in statebuilding contexts where formal institutions are often weak.
>
> (Jensen 2008: 121)

Promoting change through alterations to the law is a top-down and 'thin' approach to change. It expects behaviours to alter on the basis of decree. Yet unless such decrees are embedded in a 'thick' understanding of the practices of the community they wish to change, they will remain superficial and most likely be ignored by those they attempt to regulate. Tanja Chopra and Deborah Isser note this tension between legal and social change. They argue that justice processes are a reflection of the underlying cultural, political and social dynamics of a society, and that legal reforms must connect to these underlying dynamics if they are to have any hope of impacting practice (2011: 24).

Furthermore, even the threat of enforcement has its limitations. As Max Weber points out, 'legal coercion ... where it opposes custom, frequently fails in the attempt to influence actual conduct ... Only a limited measure of success can be attained through the threat of coercion supporting the legal order' (1978: 320; 334). In other words, the potential for the law to transform practices is limited. Recognizing that the interaction of the formal rules with actual practice is not as straightforward as reformers' models of change would suggest is key to enhancing their ability to promote long-term transformations. Incremental changes that have greater resonance with actual practices will ultimately be more meaningful and sustainable after reform programmes end, even though this might not suit development agencies' results frameworks and short- to medium-term timeframes.

The 'informal informal'?

Efforts to formalize primary justice in Sierra Leone also risk discouraging users from the Local Courts and pushing them to rely, instead, on other unreformed informal justice providers. As Simeon Koroma, Director of TIMAP for Justice (a Sierra Leonean NGO that trains paralegals) points out, even if reformers' attempts to formalize and modernize the customary legal system were successful, that is, if the Local Courts did implement the reformed Local Courts Act and codified version of customary law, this would not ensure that people would continue to use this form of the customary legal system. Rather, people may instead take their disputes to chiefs and secret societies, who, having not undergone reforms, continue to arbitrate on the basis of localized customary law and thus continue to provide the important identity link to culture, custom and ancestry. As Isser notes, the 'state's attempts to ban certain customary practices may merely drive them underground and out of the realm of potential state influence' (2011: 342).

Again, this point emphasizes the proximity of customary law to the people of the provinces, whose identities are linked to their ancestors by custom, and thus also to custom by their ancestors (Koroma 2009). As Koroma suggests, 'if we formalise the informal system, people will go down to the informal informal system' (Koroma 2009). That is, those informal justice actors existing outside the legal realm which the JSDP is engaging with that are derided for providing even more arbitrary justice than Local Courts. Thus, if the Local Court system ceases to provide justice outcomes that are commensurate with Sierra Leoneans' own understandings of justice, there is a danger that rather than modernizing the justice that provincial Sierra Leoneans rely upon, it will merely lead to such people relying upon customary justice as applied by alternative informal sources.

Conclusion

Despite focusing overwhelmingly on the formal legal system, DFID's JSDP demonstrated a substantially broader engagement with informal actors than was evident in other aspects of reform. However, limitations remain and the JSDP was not able to operationalize a 'thick' understanding of customary justice that engaged with the law as it is, rather than it should be. The programme engaged predominantly with only the legal informal justice institutions and not the illegal informal who remain the dominant providers of justice to the majority of rural Sierra Leone. This risks further marginalizing this majority by leaving their principal justice providers unreformed and thus not improving the quality of justice that they choose to, or are forced to, rely upon. Moreover, where the JSDP did engage with the customary justice system, efforts were focused on formalizing the informal, which risks freezing customary law, legal norms outpacing social norms so that the former carry little weight, and forcing people to rely upon the unregulated 'informal informal'. JSDP primary justice projects appear not to have adequately considered the lack of correlation between formalized rules and practice in the history of Sierra Leone's customary legal system. It thus remains dubious as to whether formalizing rules and creating further legislation will have a sustainable impact upon the actual functioning of the customary justice system.

These limitations should not suggest that DFID or JSDP staff were unaware of the importance of the issues raised in this chapter. Indeed, it is precisely because of the impressively nuanced staff knowledge that the inability to translate 'thick' understandings of primary justice into programming is so interesting. This puzzle of *why* DFID programmes have been unable to transform their knowledge of the importance of working with informal security and justice actors into programmes on the ground, and what can be done about it, is the focus of the final chapter.

Notes

1 This is not to suggest that justice reform is new, however. In the 1960s, the law and development movement also saw aid programmes focused on rule of law issues. Yet this experience is often largely forgotten in the current enthusiasm for justice reform.

2 For more on the exorbitant costs of the Special Court, see Penfold 2009 and Hoffman 2008: 130.

3 Surveys were undertaken in two districts, covering 2,799 households. They do not claim to be nationally representative.

4 The recognition of Islamic law refers to the Muslim Marriage Ordinance, which recognizes Islamic law in relation to marriage, divorce and intestate succession. However, Islamic law is generally subservient to customary law and is encapsulated within it in predominantly Islamic chiefdoms (Joko Smart 1980: 87–102).

5 Note the similarities to the logic of current 'rule of law orthodoxy', which views the law as creating stability to attract investment, which will lead to development and thus a more sustainable peace.

6 See for instance, Fenrich *et al.* 2011; Ubink and McInerney 2011; and Chopra and Isser 2011.

Chapter 5

Security and justice reform

Political and bureaucratic constraints

This chapter answers some of the looming 'whys' that have emerged throughout this book: why won't state-centred security and justice reforms lead to the decline of informal actors?; why has there been more engagement with informal actors in justice reforms than in security reforms?; and, ultimately, why do donors seemingly find it so hard to engage with informal security and justice actors? On the basis of the answers to these questions, the conclusion will draw out the implications for donors' work in security and justice programming more broadly, and make recommendations about what donors can do about the reasons for their lack of engagement with informal security and justice actors.

The problematic set out in this book revolves around the overly state-centric approach that the UK's Department for International Development (DFID) has adopted towards understanding the conflict in Sierra Leone and the resultant lack of engagement with informal security and justice actors in its reforms. These informal actors have been highlighted as key to a more comprehensive understanding of the causes of conflict in Sierra Leone, as well as being central to the matrix of security and justice provision. The case studies yielded somewhat divergent findings as to whether engagement has occurred in practice. In the case of police reform, negligible engagement with informal actors was discerned, limiting the effectiveness of reforms to improve the dominant policing providers. In the case of the Justice Sector Development Programme (JSDP), greater engagement was apparent at the level of primary justice, although the nature of the engagement was also problematic, dwarfed by state-centred reforms, limited to only some (and not the most pervasive) informal actors, and attempting to formalize the informal.

Following a rebuttal of arguments that the informal will disappear as the state develops, this chapter seeks to explain the differences between the two case studies, as well as to address the larger question that the chapters combined point to: Why has DFID been seemingly unable to engage with informal security actors? In answering this larger question, the chapter examines the bureaucratic and political aspects of DFID, revealing how a state-focused agenda within the organization emerges to limit its programmatic engagements. This is coupled with a revealed state bias within the concept of security and justice reform itself, as it has historically developed. As a result, the ability of donors to engage with informal actors in security and justice programming may be seriously constrained.

Why the informal won't simply disappear

Much of the logic underpinning security and justice sector reforms (SJSR), and development more broadly is a remnant of modernization theory (and neo-modernization theory) that suggests that building an effective state that governs capably will decrease the need for citizens in 'modernizing' or 'developing' countries to rely upon often illiberal informal actors (Huntington 1971; Harrison 1988; Inglehart and Baker 2000). This was the thinking around independence, when former colonies and many African governments both assumed traditional authorities who had been vested with administrative powers under colonial rule would simply dissolve as modern government took hold (Ubink 2008: 10–11). Theories around statebuilding can be seen to internalize this logic in suggesting that the prevalence of informal security and justice actors is due to weak state capacity or 'the absence of functioning institutions' (Smits and Wright 2012: 1; Rotberg 2003). Some Africanists and policing specialists also indicate that traditional authorities have retained their strength due primarily to state weakness (Marks and Goldsmith 2006: 139; Herbst 2000; Chabal and Daloz 1999; Forrest 1998). Helene Maria Kyed and Lars Buur explain:

> The idea that traditional leaders have filled the 'gap' left by fragile states and continued to contest the monopoly of state authority in primarily rural areas has influenced much rethinking on their role ... [Scholars argue that] 'failed' or 'hollowed out' African states that have been reduced, institutionally speaking, to a mere shell have led to the dominance of modern informal governance.
>
> (Kyed and Buur 2007: 4)

By focusing on state weakness as the primary reason for the existence or continuation of informal practices, these approaches imply that as the state becomes more dominant, informal mechanisms will eventually become redundant. Yet this argument ignores the important role that traditional authorities continue to play in many *strong* African states, which suggests that a reliance on chiefs does not merely happen in the absence of state strength. Englebert (2005: 42–4) points out that Sierra Leone is one of only a few examples (alongside Somalia) where a resurgence of 'indigenous authority structures' has occurred in a weak or failed state context. The vast majority of countries that have relatively strong traditional authorities and have undergone the furthest-reaching restorations of traditional authorities are, in fact, strong states, such as South Africa, Uganda and Nigeria, indicating that the strength of traditional authorities is not linked to the weakness of state institutions (Englebert 2005: 42–3). This suggests that informal governance providers are likely to be around in Sierra Leone for some time to come, even with a stronger state delivery of security and justice. This trend may result from the greater confidence that strong states have in their own institutions and are less likely, therefore, to feel threatened by alternative providers (2005: 44–5). Weak states, in contrast, may react in a more hostile manner to traditional authorities or informal actors, as they are more likely to be protective of their fragile hold on power.

In addition to this Africa-wide perspective highlighting the prevalence of informal actors in strong states, there are three pragmatic reasons why it is unlikely that informal actors will recede as the state strengthens in Sierra Leone: the durability and adaptability of informal actors over time; the interconnectedness of the formal and informal; and the identity-producing role that informal actors play in the lives of many Sierra Leoneans. These are discussed respectively below.

First, it is unrealistic to assume that long-standing informal mechanisms will simply wither away in the face of a fortified state. These mechanisms are substantially more durable and intrinsic to the Sierra Leonean state than is often acknowledged and are no strangers to change. As Eric Scheye and Gordon Peake note:

> In many societies … non-institutional and non-formal regulatory mechanisms have strong roots, long histories and proven effectiveness in mitigating the invasiveness of the formal security sector … Initiatives to alter the police, military and/or court system may be unable to erase or substitute for that reality. Thus there may be much more local adherence and fealty to alternative security providers and little enthusiasm to alter current power relations within civil society, resistances that could undermine reform efforts regardless of the will of national authorities and their 'ownership' of the process.
>
> (Quoted in Baker 2006b: 38)

Chiefs and secret societies have survived dramatic episodes in Sierra Leone's past – including the arrival and departure of colonialism, independence, military coups, civil war, and now donor (and increasingly private sector) infusions. It is unrealistic to assume that these informal providers will simply disappear with the onslaught of 'modern' state security and justice given their proven durability and adaptiveness in the face of change. This longevity of informal practices – however 'invented' or at times contested – has meant that they remain a very real component of Sierra Leone's political configuration (Fanthorpe 2001; Sawyer 2008).

In order to have remained relevant in the face of such change, informal actors have had to adapt. Chiefs and secret societies are often ascribed to the category of 'tradition' (viewed in opposition to 'modernity') in a manner that denies malleability. The 'informal', 'traditional', 'cultural' or 'customary', are seen to possess a static identity, enforcing the status quo, rather than adapting to change. Much has been written to invalidate this position (see, for instance, Hobsbawm and Ranger 1983; Vaughan 2005; Mustapha and Larbi Jones 2005; Ubink 2008). Regarding traditional authorities, Abdul Raufu Mustapha and Emily Larbi Jones (2005: 253) note that '[c]hieftaincy is not a fixed traditional or religious institution, whose core content remains consistent. This is often the erroneous view conveyed when chiefs are described, or describe themselves, as "custodians" of culture and tradition ... [Rather] the very essence of their institution changes.'

This process of continuity through change is apparent in all societies. Eric Hobsbawm (1983: 5) points to the example of the Catholic Church, which has successfully adapted its practices over time while the general tradition and purpose of the church have remained constant. It is incorrect to cast chiefs and secret societies, often described as 'customary' or 'traditional', as immutable and unchanging. This mistakes their resilience and durability for being static and unchanging. These practices are clearly resilient, but in order to be so they have had to adapt to the changing circumstances around them, in a way that in fact lends itself to engagement in reform processes. As Olufemi Vaughan notes, 'rapidly changing social, political and economic environments present adaptive and resilient indigenous political institutions as important domains where communal values are profoundly expressed' (Vaughan 2005: 2). Informal actors thus seem well placed to adapt to donor-supported reforms of the state security and justice sectors.

Second, arguments that a strengthened state will obviate the need for informal providers of security and justice also fail to take account of the interwoven nature of informal actors and the state. As Ryann Manning (2009: 110–1) notes, 'modern' and 'traditional' governance mechanisms 'are actually integrated, interdependent, and even fused.' This is due both to functional relationships between chiefs and political leaders throughout Sierra Leone's history and the manner in which many Sierra Leoneans, including formal security and justice sector staff, view the informal as a constituent part of the broader security and justice system.

Functional relationships have existed between politicians and chiefs throughout Sierra Leone's history that have made the two interdependent and not easily separated. British colonial officials granted positions of power to 'chiefs' in exchange for peace that facilitated commerce in the provinces; and mining companies allowed small-scale illicit diamond mining to continue in exchange for chiefs maintaining social order (Reno 1995: 22). During times of austerity, from the 1980s and throughout the civil war, politicians also relied upon 'big men' to gain access to services and resources that were not available on the formal market (Reno 1995: 22). Politicians are often seen to rely on chiefs to deliver votes from their subjects (whom chiefs often hold sway over), in return for favourable treatment once the politician is in office (Broadbent 2012). The powers of these informal actors have ensured that chiefs have remained useful and thus relevant not just to their subjects, but also to the state's political elite. This has meant that the state itself has not necessarily opposed the power of informal actors and that practices like chieftaincy have fundamentally shaped the Sierra Leonean state in ways that need to be taken into account when seeking to reform the state exogenously (Reno 1995: 15; Zack-Williams 2002: 2).

A neat segregation of the formal and informal justice and security systems also does not reflect the manner in which Sierra Leoneans, as the 'end users', perceive provision. Rather, chiefs, secret societies, heads of trade associations, community elders, police, Local Courts, paralegals – and so on – are all perceived as various parts of one response system (Denney and Ibrahim 2012). People accessing security or justice often move between the formal and informal components – with chiefs at times referring complainants to the police (for instance, in cases of sexual violence) and some Magistrates Courts referring minor disputes back to chiefs. The idea, then, that reforms of some parts of the security and justice system will lead to others dissolving, ignores the extensive interactions between these components in practice.

In addition, arguments about the informal receding as the state becomes stronger fail to recognize that those who make up the formal security and justice sectors are themselves steeped in informal culture and social practices. That is, the formal security and justice sectors are not outside of the culture or tradition that pervades Sierra Leonean society more broadly. The Sierra Leone Police, for instance, may resemble a 'modern' organization, but it is staffed by individuals who are, at the same time, woven into cultural fabrics. With the 2008 Demographic and Health Survey findings that 91 per cent of women between the ages of 15 and 49 in the provinces have undergone clitoridectomy (Statistics Sierra Leone and ICF Macro 2009: 13), it is almost certain that female police officers, for instance, and the daughters of police officers participate in secret society initiation. The formal security sector is not apart from society and their informal security and justice practices. To assume the informal will simply wither away as state security and justice strengthen overlooks how even those who constitute the state police and justice system also help to sustain informal practices.

Third, as this book has tried to demonstrate, chiefs and secret societies are valued because of the identity-producing role they provide to their subjects and communities and the link they provide to ancestral history, not simply because of state weakness. This identity-producing power is in part shaped by the rights that chiefdom belonging carries. Land ownership, marriage prospects and labour rights continue to depend, albeit to varying degrees, upon one's status as an indigene in Sierra Leonean chiefdoms (Labonte 2008: 72). These rights, combined with more ephemeral connections to ancestors, communities and place, are still strongly mediated by chiefs and secret societies, rendering chiefdom-level politics a determining factor in policing and justice in the lives of many Sierra Leoneans.

This identity-producing role of informal actors is especially important in the Sierra Leonean context, where the state has often distinctly failed to fulfil this role – where, indeed, the state has often been seen as 'the enemy' of the population (Englebert 2009: 1; Stepputat, Andersen and Møller 2007: 8–9). While this may now be shifting in peacetime democracy, historic divides (both geographical and relational) between the *Krio* and indigenous populations, and between the *Mende* and *Temne* (as the primary ethnic groups and, increasingly, the respective heartlands of the two major political parties), makes the formation of a state identity difficult. If it is to traditional authorities that a large number of Sierra Leoneans look for part of their identity, any efforts to suppress these authorities risk being widely unpopular and perceived as an assault on identity.

For these reasons, the assumption that strengthening the state will result in the decline of informal actors does not connect to the reality of informal security and justice practices in Sierra Leone – their longevity and malleability, their interdependence with the formal system, and their identity-producing nature. Security and justice reforms that do not include informal actors, and are based instead on building a Weberian-style state derived from Western experience, must concede that the outcome will be 'thin' (Geertz 1975). That is, where reforms bear only limited relevance to actual experiences of security and justice in Sierra Leone, the resulting outcomes will not engage with the deep politics of how security and justice get delivered through complex and interdependent chains of formal and informal providers – and the ongoing contestations of who can legitimately provide these services. Reforms thus risk creating a formal security and justice sector that sits precariously and without foundations upon a much more complex web of informal governance mechanisms. The newly built security and justice sector, however ideal in design, will not easily grow roots in a system where alternative practices, boasting greater longevity and fealty, are entrenched unless these alternative practices are explicitly engaged. Social roots cannot be socially engineered; they must be grounded in practical experience (Scott 1998). In order to retain the possibility of fundamentally transforming security and justice to ensure that the causes of conflict are comprehensively addressed, engagement must be at the level at which security and justice happens on a daily basis and where it is 'thick', in the sense of being locally understood and legitimated (Geertz 1975). This might mean letting go of the assumption that the Weberian approach to the state will be the best governance mechanism across time and space. Many in the West have largely succumbed to the belief that the state, as it is known there, is a natural entity (Migdal 1988: 15–16; Unsworth 2010). Yet, as Lisa Anderson demonstrates:

> Human history is full of complex and orderly communities, tribes, chivalric orders, churches, empires, trade federations, aristocracies, religious brotherhoods and other expressions of human ingenuity ... Yet, for most citizens of established states, particularly in Europe and North America, these alternatives to the state have been dispatched to the curiosity shops of history or relegated to the private lives of citizens ... However they served for millennia as vehicles for regulating societal interaction, fortifying human bonds, organising economic production and exchange and assuring security in the absence of what we know as the state – and in many places they still do.
>
> (Anderson 2004: 3)

Engaging overwhelmingly with state actors incorporates into programming only one dimension – a thin dimension – of the security and justice matrix in Sierra Leone, ignoring the fact that the state there shares authority with a number of informal actors central to security and justice functions. This state-centred response emerges from an equally state-centred understanding of the causes of war, as set out in Chapter 1. Yet this understanding is largely ahistorical, neglecting both the thicker causes of war and experience of shared authority between state and informal actors. Security and justice reform programmes implemented through this state-centred logic reify the state as a natural object in a manner that is discordant with *actual practices* of security and justice provision. Calls to recalibrate reforms to engage with governance as it happens in practice have been widespread in academia (Ellis 2007; Stepputat *et al.* 2007: 6; Migdal 1988; Chazan 1988: 121–3; Herbst 2000: 270). It follows that if DFID wants to make a real impact on the quality of security and justice that Sierra Leoneans receive, they need to be prepared to engage with authority structures as they exist, not as they would like them to be. In order to better reform security and justice provision and comprehensively address the causes of the war, DFID needs to build into programmes 'thick' understandings that are locally grounded and historically informed, and which reveal a fuller understanding of the nature of the state and security and justice architectures in Sierra Leone.

We cannot, therefore, simply ignore the informal, in the hope that, as development assists in the modernization process, informal security and justice actors will become redundant. Instead, in seeking to improve people's access to and quality of security and justice, these informal actors must be engaged in reforms, alongside state actors. Below, reasons are provided as to why greater engagement with informal security and justice actors was apparent in DFID justice programming, as opposed to its police programming.

Explaing the divergence in case studies

The empirical case studies in Chapters 3 and 4 reveal a more extensive engagement with informal actors (relatively speaking) in DFID's justice reform programme than its police reform programme. While it should be pointed out that neither programme exhibited extensive engagement with informal actors and both remained overwhelmingly state-centric, a perceptible difference between the two programmes is discernible. Any answer as to why DFID has found it difficult to engage with informal security and justice actors must, therefore, be able to account for the variation in levels of engagement across the policing and justice sectors.

Perhaps the most obvious reason for the different levels of engagement in the two case studies is one of institutional learning. Given that DFID's police reform programme occurred in the early stages of its involvement in Sierra Leone and SJSR (1998–2005), the programme could not benefit from lessons learned in the same way that the justice programme, coming later (2004–10), could. As DFID's involvement in Sierra Leone and in SJSR more broadly continues, it is likely that more will be learnt about both the country context and causes of the war, as well as about processes of security and justice reform. According to this logic, later programmes can benefit from this accrued knowledge and at least have the potential to learn from earlier mistakes. This explanation is supported by evolutions within DFID policy documents, detailed in Chapter 1, which suggest that an understanding of the importance of informal actors developed more fully over time, and especially from 2004 onwards.

Connected to this issue of institutional learning, it might be that the political environment in which the earlier police reform programme was operating was not amenable to engagement with informal actors and that the space for such engagements became more possible as the country progressed out of conflict. As Keith Biddle, former British Inspector General of the Sierra Leone Police (IGP SLP) notes:

> In Sierra Leone 1998–2003 the concept [of engaging with informal actors] would not have been permitted by the people, as many had been under the 'policing' of the RUF, the CDU and the CDF. They suffered violence, suppression of expression, forcible conscription to fighting arms – all took children into their fighting units – and women and girls were subjected to extreme sexual violence with many being taken as 'Bush Wives'. For the GoSL or the IGP SLP to have gone for the non-state actor approach would have resulted in failure if not a reigniting of the conflict ... I would opine that by 2008 the situation was very different from 1998 and the NSA [nonstate actor] approach then had more validity.
>
> (Biddle 2013)

Rather than simply institutional learning, therefore, the difference in levels of engagement with informal actors in policing as opposed to justice reforms might also be explained by the political room for manoeuvre available at different stages of the post-conflict process. Given that early emphasis in Sierra Leone was on strengthening the legitimacy of the state, external support focused overwhelmingly on formal security systems. However, while this may explain why there was no engagement with informal security and justice actors in the early stages of police reform, DFID support to the FSUs has been ongoing and the sequencing argument therefore does not explain why engagement with informal actors on issues of women's policing has not happened in later programming.

It is also possible that the divergence in case studies results from the different personalities leading the police and justice reform programmes. While the British Inspector General of the Sierra Leone Police, Keith Biddle (2008), maintained that engagement with informal actors was 'a lot of woolly thinking', the JSDP Programme Manager, Peter Viner (2009), claimed that the JSDP was 'only too keen' to engage with informal justice actors. Undoubtedly, the leadership of the programmes had a strong impact on what was and was not included in programming. Yet the relative consistency with which DFID's policy on justice sector reform has recognized the importance of engaging with informal actors (albeit in a limited manner), contrasted with the policy approach taken to the rest of the security sector, also suggests that the different treatment might be more systematic than institutional learning, sequencing or personalities alone can account for. Therefore, while the divergence in findings between the two case studies might suggest a process of learning from previous programmes, sequencing appropriate to the political environment, or personal preferences of the programme leaders, it also hints at importantly different standards within policing and justice programmes when it comes to informal engagement.

Dominant SJSR policy suggests that security and justice are programmatically compatible concepts that should be 'coordinated', 'joined up', 'holistic', or 'integrated'. The most notable policy documents on SSR are the OECD DAC's 2005 and 2007 guidelines and handbook on SSR, which Paul Jackson suggests 'form the current "orthodoxy" on security and justice interventions' (2011: 208). The handbook suggests that a '[h]olistic and comprehensive reform – or a system-wide approach – is SSR's overarching objective' (2007b: 29). Similarly, the UN Secretary-General's 2008 report on SSR calls for a 'coherent' and 'holistic' approach to the constituent parts of the security sector. The *OECD/DAC Handbook* clarifies these terms slightly, noting that:

> The terms holistic, comprehensive and integrated are frequently used interchangeably, but it is important to be clear about the core objective. If not carefully designed, implemented and monitored, efforts for an apparent comprehensive reform can in practice result in a 'stovepiped' approach, with separate projects developed for different institutions and sectors. A strategically integrated approach based on a clear

> understanding of these interrelationships is more likely to lead to successful outcomes and focus reform activities where they are most needed and desired.
>
> (OECD 2007b: 67)

The 'SSR orthodoxy' thus warns against siloed approaches to programming. While it is, of course, important that multiple reform processes are broadly coordinated, the emphasis on 'joined up' and 'integrated' approaches to reforms can also have the effect of downplaying important differences between military, policing and justice functions (and interestingly, tensions between military and police are much better documented than tensions between security and justice: see, for instance, Stone *et al.* 2005). This uncertain relationship between security and justice is evident, to some extent, in DFID policy and suggests the need to further interrogate the relationship between security and justice, and to ensure that efforts aimed at coordinating programming do not overshadow the importance of also recognizing the different political functions of security and justice.

There are indications that despite promoting a 'joined-up' approach to security and justice, DFID sees the two fields as overlapping but not integrated (Howlett-Bolton 2008: 5). A DFID Explanatory Note on Security and Access to Justice (2007c: 11) notes that '[c]onceptually and institutionally, the security and justice sectors are closely connected, and overlapping, but are not identical.' It goes on to claim that the principle of the separation of powers needs to be instituted in countries undergoing reforms, requiring a strengthening of judicial independence away from the influence of the executive, as well as the security forces, including the military, police and intelligence actors (DFID 2007c). The Explanatory Note reinforces that security actors are not one and the same with the judiciary, but rather are subject to judicial oversight. As a result, distance between the security and justice sectors is suggested. The document goes on to point out that the goals of security and justice are not always complementary and, in particular, that security threats may in some circumstances justify curtailments of individual rights – an act that is not necessarily in the interests of justice (DFID 2007c). Thus, the understanding of the relationship between security and justice that DFID ultimately promotes appears to be one of 'coherence' and 'coordination', recognizing some overlap and complementary goals, but not of unproblematic integration (DFID 2007c; Howlett-Bolton 2008: 5–6). This approach recognizes the importance of the role that justice can play in attaining sustainable security, but does not see justice and security goals as always being one and the same.

On the ground, this nuanced DFID messaging around security and justice was most challenging in relation to the police, as an institution that performs both justice and security functions. With the establishment of the JSDP, funding for the SLP was split between the JSDP and the ongoing

SSR programme, whereby the former funded the justice aspects of policing, and the latter funded its security functions. As Albrecht and Jackson conclude:

> It became clear that having two separate programmes with separate funding within a single organisation was difficult to coordinate and almost impossible to manage coherently. In addition, it nurtured an impression in the MoD that the SLP had an 'unfair advantage' in access to DFID funding, since, in effect, the SLP had two pools of funding. Equally, within the SLP, it was not very clear how, as it was by far the greatest beneficiary of CCSSP [Commonwealth Community Safety and Security Project], it should be part of JSDP, precisely because of the latter's much broader focus.
>
> (Albrecht and Jackson 2009: 140)

The splitting of security and justice functions of the police across two programmes has been seen as stymieing an integrated approach to police reform in Sierra Leone and delaying justice reforms (Howlett-Bolton 2008: 5). However, the tensions that emerged in supporting the different components of policing are also the unsurprising, and perhaps healthy, result of a programming approach that emphasizes the importance of coordination and coherence; while at the same time recognizing the need to hold security and justice functions apart in certain respects. The explanation for DFID's seemingly increased ability to engage with informal actors in relation to justice reform, as separate from policing reform, might thus be explained by important differences between the concepts of security and justice themselves. If this is the case, then a distinction is being made by DFID between justice and the rest of the security sector about the centrality of the state to these functions. This speaks to the important and insufficiently interrogated assumptions about the respective roles and functions of justice and security within the state and society and how these fit together – in ways that are both mutually supportive but also in tension.

To fulfil its intended purpose of holding actors, including the powerful, to account for breaches of accepted legal frameworks, justice importantly needs some degree of separation and independence from the state. Security, on the other hand, has a much more intrinsic relationship to the state, at least in Western political thought. Whereas police services, like armed forces, fit with conventional Western understandings of security that narrowly focus on the monopoly of force, the justice sector, despite possessing coercive powers (such as imposing fines and prison sentences) does not fit comfortably within this strict security purview (Hänggi 2004: 3). Because courts do not wield the ultimate coercive implements of physical violence, a multiplicity of actors involved in justice does not necessarily threaten the essence of statehood in the same way that giving up the monopoly of violence does.

In articulating one of the most significant definitions of the modern state, Max Weber emphasized two crucial characteristics: territoriality and violence (1972: 78). David Held, explaining this model, contends that '[t]he state's web of agencies and institutions finds its ultimate sanction in the claim of the monopoly of coercion, and a political order is only, in the last instance, vulnerable to crisis when this monopoly erodes' (2006: 130). While Weber (1972) goes on to explain that, of course, other characteristics also inform the modern state, territoriality and a monopoly of violence are his pre-eminent conditions. A more intrinsic relationship can therefore be seen to exist between the state and security forces wielding physical force than between the state and its other functions. Informal justice actors making arbitrary judgments, while not necessarily desirable, do not tend to elicit the same degree of panic or threat amongst the public and executive as the image of informal soldiers or police brandishing weapons or locking people up. This is a particularly sensitive issue in Sierra Leone given its recent history of the Revolutionary United Front (RUF) – perhaps a textbook example of the dangers of an armed informal group. Because the justice sector does *not* wield physical force, which is intimately bound up with statehood, the legitimacy of informal actors within this sector is, perhaps, more acceptable than in the case of the police. The reason for the variance in engagement with informal actors seen in the two case studies might, therefore, be explained by the tension between the very concepts of security and justice that are coupled together in SJSR in a manner that can be misleading as to their similarities and differences.

This sense of justice being 'sort-of-but-not-quite' akin to security raises important questions about the role of justice within security sector reforms more broadly. While there are, of course, important linkages between reforms to policing and reforms to the justice system – most often articulated by the problem created when a reformed police service begins to arrest more people due to growing capacity but the courts are too weak to prosecute them – it is not clear that this implies that the category of SSR is usefully conceptually expanded so that it includes everything that can be fitted within the concept of justice becoming SJSR. A pertinent example was raised by Piet Biesheuvel, a consultant on policing and justice in Sierra Leone, in relation to primary justice programmes, such as long-term education campaigns to raise awareness of human rights, which might not be upheld under customary law. As Biesheuvel (2008) noted, such programmes are certainly part of justice reform – in that they aim to improve the substantive justice provided by primary justice mechanisms. Yet it is not clear as to whether such long-term education campaigns can be conceived of as part of SSR. As Biesheuvel (2008) reasoned:

> Is it security sector reform? Well *maybe* it is, but it certainly is justice reform, isn't it? It's ... a sub-set of SSR. We come back to the definition of

> the problem ... I don't think it is SSR, although SSR gurus would say 'well it's a component part of it', but nearly everything is a component part of SSR, frankly. I think it's pure justice work.

The language of SJSR and its attempts to address the constituent parts of the security and justice apparatuses as a coherent sector in a joined-up manner, disguise underlying differences that make engaging with informal actors potentially more problematic in relation to the security sector than the justice sector. The variance detected in DFID's level of engagement with informal actors across reform programmes suggests that while it is clearly important to have a coordinated approach to security and justice reforms, this may still require that the unique needs of each are protected. The importance of coordination should not be mistaken for squeezing a vast array of importantly different projects and approaches under the single banner of increasingly integrated and joined-up SJSR. Donors could probably do more to clarify the relationship between security and justice and how precisely they can be 'coordinated' and 'coherent', while still maintaining the conceptual integrity needed to fulfil their respective functions on the ground. Yet it is clear that expecting a seamless packaging of security and justice programming denies the tensions that characterize the practices and allow them to fulfil their respective political functions.

While it is important to explain the divergent findings of the case studies and what these suggest about DFID's understanding of security and justice, in both cases DFID's engagement with informal security actors was not straightforward. Either, in the case of police reform, it did not occur, or, in the case of justice reform, it did so only in a limited and problematic manner. Aside from looking to explain the variation in levels of engagement in each case study then, this chapter also seeks to explain the difficulty that DFID has in engaging informal security and justice actors across the board.

Explaining DFID's lack of engagement with the informal

Against the lack of engagement with informal actors in security and justice programming, DFID staff and more recent policy documents seem acutely aware of the importance of informal actors and the roles they play in the lives of many Sierra Leoneans. There has been a growing recognition in DFID's policy documents (as well as those of other major donors and SJSR actors) of the importance of acknowledging informal security and justice actors, indicative of the significance of these actors in SJSR processes (Stepputat *et al.* 2007: 14; DFID 2004a). Yet despite this recognition, at least in the Sierra Leone case, the transformation into practice has been limited. It is one thing to recognize the importance of informal actors, but quite another to be able to turn this into practice. Homage to informal actors in DFID policy thus risks becoming a vacant concept with little practical meaning, rather than flagging concerted organizational attempts to recalibrate the manner in which it conducts SJSR. What explains this emerging disjuncture between policy and practice?

The seeming inability of DFID to engage with informal security actors in practice belies important features of the organization itself. DFID does not (only) overlook engagement with informal security actors because it lacks awareness or understanding of their importance, as their later policy positions and interviews with DFID staff attest. It is keenly aware of the challenges posed by informal actors within the Sierra Leonean context. All DFID staff interviewed demonstrated a clear understanding of such challenges and the central role that informal actors play in Sierra Leonean life. Mark White, DFID's former-Programme Manager for Sierra Leone and former-Security Sector Advisor, notes that 'there remains a clear gap between the policy and the practice … as evidenced by the fact that 80 percent of the population in sub-Saharan Africa get their security and justice services from non-state actors' (White 2009: 110). More than many other international organizations and donors, DFID is also known for its reflexive approach and willingness to be critical of itself, though of course, institutional learning is not so straightforward (Schümer 2008: 142). Its lack of practical engagement with informal security and justice actors, then, suggests something more intrinsic to DFID itself. Partly the policy-practice disjuncture can be explained by bureaucratic inertia, whereby changes in practices lag behind 'eureka moments' at the policy level (not least due to funding cycles and project planning) (Peters 2001: 225). It can take some time for an idea to be developed, incorporated into programming, funded and equipped (with lengthy procurement processes, for instance), staffed and finally implemented. But beyond this and more importantly, DFID's bureaucratic and political nature also curtails its programmatic practices and results in overwhelmingly statist engagements. The effects of these characteristics are set out below.

DFID as a bureaucratic organization

While perhaps a mundane observation, an important starting point for understanding DFID's behaviour is to recognize that DFID is first and foremost a bureaucratic organization, rooted in legal-rational processes. As Michael Barnett and Martha Finnemore explain, organizations 'are constituted as bureaucracies, and that bureaucratic character profoundly shapes the way they behave' (Barnett and Finnemore 2004: 16). DFID's bureaucratic nature legitimizes certain kinds of knowledge that in turn creates rules that, while intended to enforce the values of the bureaucracy, also result in 'red tape'.

Organizations like DFID exhibit bureaucratic decision-making and administrative processes, which are rooted in particular values, most comprehensively set out in the work of Max Weber (1968). These bureaucratic processes are centred on impersonal, neutral rules enforced by experts (Weber 1968: 958; Peters 2001: 39). Experts are hired on the basis of their capacity to do a specific job, and their loyalty is to the purpose of their office, not to a higher ranking person (as opposed, for instance, to patrimonialism where loyalty is to one's patron and the hierarchy in which they stand) (Weber 1968: 959). This commitment to the office and the impersonality of the rules ensures, in principle, their rational, dispassionate and thus consistent application, which is in turn monitored by equally impersonal accountability structures (Peters 2001: 39; Barnett and Finnemore 2004: 17–18). Rules are based upon legal-rationalism and are general, abstract and universalisable. Their rationality derives from their 'objectiveness', which Weber defines as 'the discharge of business according to calculable rules and "without regard for persons"' (1968: 975). He goes on to suggest that his ideal type[1] of bureaucracy 'develops more perfectly, the more it is "dehumanised", the more completely it succeeds in eliminating from official business love, hatred, and all purely personal, irrational, and emotional elements which escape calculation' (1968: 975). Weber proposed that an organization with these bureaucratic attributes possessed a 'technical superiority over any other form of organization', given its heightened efficiency (1968: 973). This belief has been internalized (albeit imperfectly) by most large organizations operating in contemporary Western societies, and DFID is no exception. Bureaucratic politics are now 'demanded by law as well as by "modern" conceptions of fairness and justice' (Peters 2001: 39). The stringencies of bureaucratic legal requirements were mentioned in interviews with DFID staff, particularly in relation to cumbersome procurement procedures.

These bureaucratic rules, internal to DFID, act upon the organization and help to forge its behaviour by delimiting the manner in which 'bureaucrats see the world and perceive the problems they face' (Barnett and Finnemore 2004: 18). Communities of practice, such as development practitioners, brought together by a shared aim, develop particular worldviews that legitimate certain forms of knowledge over others (Douglas 1986: 75). For DFID, this worldview is given substantial shape by bureaucratic principles that promote legal-rational decision-making. This kind of decision-making, and the rules and procedures put in place for facilitating it, aim to achieve ordered and consistent solutions to common problems (Eyben 2005: 99). Bureaucratic processes do not lend themselves to complex problems that require detailed knowledge of the anomalies of each context – they seek to 'flatten diversity because they are supposed to generate universal rules and categories that are by design inattentive to contextual and particularistic concerns' (Barnett and Finnemore 2004: 39). While DFID staff, as individuals, may be able to see beyond the institutional bureaucratic worldview, acting beyond its bounds is problematic, and even the analytical tools needed to come up with this knowledge in the first place are limited by the bureaucratic confines that donors must work within. For instance, rules about DFID's development partner obligations (including accounting and reporting requirements, procurement procedures, and so on), result in only a certain kind of, overwhelmingly legal-rational, partner making the cut. Informal security and justice actors struggle to meet the cumbersome bureaucratic requirements of donors (not least because many are likely to be illiterate or innumerate), making them problematic partners. Engagement with the broad spectrum of providers, needed to improve security and justice for marginalized and vulnerable groups and to comprehensively address the causes of conflict, thus might not be possible, given these constraints that focus the donor viewfinder on a legal-rational world, that leaves the informal blurred in the background.

Informal security actors in Sierra Leone often do not display legal-rational decision-making. They do not operate according to impersonal rules, are not expertise-oriented, or accountable in any impersonal sense. Rather, they act in a highly personalized manner with one's identity being a key determinant in the outcome of particular, often arbitrary, decisions (Richards 1996: 34; Bøås 2001: 698). The 'rules' vary depending on who they are being applied to and one's position in a hierarchy is often not based upon dispassionate expertise but lineage, wealth, age, sex, personal connections or birthplace. Informal security and justice actors, therefore, do not fit with DFID's legal-rational worldview, but are more representative of Weber's patrimonial model of administration (a model made increasingly relevant to the Sierra Leonean context by neopatrimonialism, most convincingly set out by William Reno) (Weber 1968: 1010–41; Reno 1995; 1998).

Bureaucratic influence filters down to staff, for instance through the ways they are incentivized, which can have perverse effects on programming. This means that what is in the interests of individual staff is often not suited to engaging with informal security and justice actors. For instance, as Will Hout explains:

> The focus of incentives for staff of aid bureaucracies on observable outputs such as disbursement activity, management and written work, brings about an orientation of staff to the technical aspects of their work, as their advancement within the organisation depends on assessments of their performance in financial and project or programme management. Overall, there seem to be very few incentives for staff to learn from past activities and gain an in-depth knowledge about the country they are working in.
>
> (Hout 2012: 408)

Staff are more likely to be rewarded for agreeing a new loan facility, or coming up with a new policy approach, rather than achieving developmental results that benefit intended ultimate beneficiaries (Easterly 2002: 7). Yet these individual incentives are not necessarily aligned with the kinds of engagement necessary for working with informal actors. The focus on 'moving money' has led to large, multi-year security and justice programmes, rather than the kinds of small and flexible forms of engagement needed in working with informal actors (see, for instance, Scheye 2009b: 42–3). This has played out in Sierra Leone, with big, five-year security and justice programmes the norm for DFID engagement (there have been three stages of DFID support to security and justice in Sierra Leone, each of which have involved five-year programmes). Donor staff that are 'hard pressed to meet targets, spend budgets and show signs of progress', are also not incentivized to develop programming that is small-scale and only likely to yield results in the long-term (Mosse 2004: 652).

In addition to this, because donor staff are recruited and promoted on the basis of their ability to fulfil bureaucratic functions (like moving money, managing projects, writing reports, etc.); there is a tendency to prefer either technical sectoral knowledge or generalist expertise, with experience within a bureaucracy, for instance, over specific knowledge of a particular country or region (Unsworth 2009: 889). This can be seen in DFID, and other donors, increasingly hiring civil servants from other government agencies, rather than development or country experts. This is compounded by short stints (often two to three years) in country offices, which are inevitably based in capital cities – meaning that many staff do not achieve in-depth knowledge of the country in which they are working – to say nothing of learning local languages (Marriage 2006: 202; De Haan and Everest-Phillips 2007; Easterly 2002: 27; Berg 2000). This is not to suggest that no DFID staff achieve this kind of knowledge, but they do so *in spite* of bureaucratic processes, not because of them.

Andrew Natsios (2010) has written about the counter-developmental impacts of this over-bureaucratization, which he calls the 'counter-bureaucracy'. He argues that in the US, the compliance side of development has become more important than the programmatic side, with disastrous consequences for development (2010: 1–7). A growing focus on accounting, reporting, rigid procurement procedures, etc., means that more and more time and energy must be devoted to these tasks, rather than the work that is meant to be the content of development. One USAID former mission director revealed that almost eight months of every year were dominated by reporting and budget processes (Natsios 2010: 43). Similarly, Ron Kerr critiques the manner in which management techniques, such as the 'logframe' (logical framework), have been adopted by the development industry in a manner that makes bureaucratic tasks ends in themselves, alienated from their (at least initially) intended purpose (2008: 105). This seems to represent the 'irrationality of rationalisation' that Weber feared, wherein bureaucratic rules become an end in themselves rather than a means to some higher purpose (Barnett and Finnemore 2004: 39). While Natsios' work is specific to the US, the creep of the compliance side has also been felt in European development agencies, including that of the UK, particularly with greater fiscal austerity due to the global financial crisis. As Will Hout explains:

> Concerns about the effectiveness of development assistance policies, coupled with a general move to enhanced 'accountability' of government agencies, have led to the introduction of monitoring and evaluation tools deriving from New Public Management. So-called 'new development management' spurred the adoption of techniques that aim to minimise risk and control the behaviour of public servants. Examples of this trend are the mushrooming of evaluations ... and the introduction of new accountability instruments such as the Public Service Agreements for international development in the UK ... The techniques of 'new development management' enhance the inherently technocratic orientation of development agencies, as a larger part of their resources needs to be devoted to establishing the measurable results of their work.
>
> (Hout 2012: 408)

This has made demonstrating results in short time frames more important, again denying the possibility of meaningful engagement with informal security and justice actors that represent risky, long-term engagements with an unclear results dividend.

The weight of bureaucracy within development should not suggest, however, that DFID lacks normative values, despite such values often being overlooked in political science because bureaucracies are seen to be neutral (Meier and O'Toole 2006: 137). Rather, as Barnett and Finnemore argue, 'bureaucracies always serve some social purpose or set of cultural values, even when they are shrouded in myths of impartiality or value-neutral technocracy' (2004: 21). Therefore while DFID is bounded in part by the bureaucratic processes internal to it, it is also bounded by a commitment to a particular political mandate, defining the organization's purpose, to reduce global poverty.

DFID as a political entity

Aside from its bureaucratic nature, as part of a liberal democratic Western state, DFID is also a political entity with a mandate to reduce global poverty. This 'politicalness' has a significant impact on the realm of the possible, in terms of what DFID does and who it partners with. DFID's programmatic choices are not unbounded – they are in fact stringently curtailed by the various audiences and political commitments the organization must serve.

DFID, like most organizations, must perform to various constituencies which shape their actions – in this case, the British public, the government and the rest of the British civil service, and its donor recipients, such as Sierra Leone (Peters 2001: 182–5; 220; Barnett and Finnemore 2004: 35–6).

As government agencies are given only minimal direct authority through legislation (in the case of DFID this is primarily through the 2002 International Development Act), the remainder is based upon delegated authority from government and legitimacy (Peters 2001: 237). Delegated authority and legitimacy are, of course, intimately connected, with the extent of delegated authority granted to a government agency, at least to some degree, reliant on the agency's ability to accrue legitimacy amongst the public and the rest of government. The role of legitimacy thus means that DFID's activities must be defensible to its various constituencies, but particularly the British government and public, from whom it ultimately derives its funds. DFID maintains this legitimacy through its professionalism and expertise, but also by relying on ethical politics, advocating human rights, good governance and sustainable development to assist those living in poverty (Marriage 2006: 47–8). This ideology grants it legitimacy in the eyes of much of the public (although arguably, this is waning in the current fiscal climate), and also provides DFID with a discrete identity within the British civil service. The latter is particularly important to DFID given its relatively recent devolution in 1997 from the Foreign and Commonwealth Office (FCO) (Porteous 2008: 20–1). Differentiation from the FCO's main task of diplomacy in the name of British interests has thus been important for the younger organization in marking out its sphere of influence and creating a public profile (Porteous 2008: 20–1). As Guy Peters notes, 'bureaucracies develop *agency ideologies* as a means of justifying their actions. These ideologies are important weapons in the struggle over influence' (Peters 2001: 236, emphasis in original). Having the authority, for example, to establish aid spending priorities, represent the government in bilateral negotiations and implement SJSR programmes, relies upon DFID successfully attaining the legitimacy to do so.

Thus even if engagement with informal security and justice actors was deemed appropriate or necessary in the Sierra Leonean context by DFID, the British public might not be satisfied that engaging with secret societies and chiefs to improve security and justice provision to in turn reduce poverty, is the best way to spend their tax payer money. In 1998, British newspapers created a publicity nightmare for the FCO and its supposedly 'ethical' foreign policy with the exposure of the 'arms to Africa' affair, in which a British private security company (allegedly with the knowledge of some in the FCO) provided weapons to forces supporting President Kabbah – perceived internationally as the more legitimate side of the war in Sierra Leone. The potential outcry were news headlines to read: 'Despotic chiefs receive DFID funding' or 'DFID makes FGM safe' is not difficult to imagine! Given its commitment to human rights and the British public's perception of DFID as a rights protecting organization, illiberal development partners can pose a challenge for DFID. However, arguments about the poor human rights record of informal security and justice actors are not very convincing given that the state actors that DFID routinely engage with often do not have a much better record. If the human rights abuses of states can supposedly be transformed, why not also those of informal actors? Given that both are culpable of human rights abuses, the same logic should be applied (Scheye 2008: 67).

Zöe Marriage has problematized DFID's engagement with state actors in Sierra Leone on the basis that they represent 'good governance' (2006: 48–9). As Marriage points out, DFID claims to support good governance in its aid commitments and partnerships, often leading it to engage with states, but it is unclear what 'good' means:

> Empirically 'good' reveals little, and governance supported by DFID was compatible with violence and destitution. In Sierra Leone Kabbah was elected when the country was divided and people were facing death to vote in a system they had little reason to trust; when ousted he was reinstated by foreign military intervention. Asked whether there had been questions about the government's legitimacy, DFID's First Secretary in Freetown replied, 'Not so far. It's the democratically elected government of Sierra Leone. If it postponed the election for an indefinite period, let's say one year, I think everyone would have to question it.' Elections took place over a year later in May 2002, but nobody questioned it.
>
> (Marriage 2006: 48–9)

Thus while the iniquities of the state are deemed to be legitimate targets for reform, the iniquities of informal security actors are not. As Eric Scheye and Louise Andersen note, the illiberal nature of non-state security providers does not:

> set them apart from the state systems. In fragile states, the security provided by both state and nonstate systems is unequal and 'patchy' and provides varying levels of service (if any) to different community members … The donor's choice is not between supporting a human-rights-respecting state system and an illiberal nonstate system. If only that were the case, the choice would be simple. The complexity and the predicament arise when faced with a state system that provides very few … services and a nonstate system that does provide some – albeit in a less than perfect manner.
>
> (Scheye and Andersen 2007: 233)

The human rights concerns around engagement with informal security and justice actors thus seem to be more of a political concern than a substantive issue, again speaking to the influence of political perceptions and repercussions in development decision-making. Bill Easterly, writing about the perverse incentives that render the good intentions of the aid industry futile, explains:

> The aid agency must satisfy a lot of extraneous political objectives of the rich country government as well as try to reduce poverty ... Probability of

> failure is high. The aid agency is in the unenviable position of being blamed for a likely bad outcome. There is an asymmetry of information in that bureaucratic mistakes – an indigenous group displaced or environment ruined by an aid agency dam or road – are likely to be more observable than successes with diffuse benefits for many.
>
> (Easterly 2002: 30)

These 'extraneous political objectives' are not to be underestimated in terms of their ability to dictate how donors go about development work and who they engage with in doing so.

Donors are clearly aware of the tensions between what good development practice might require and what political expediency demands. As the OECD DAC Network on Governance (2005) highlights:

> Tensions are emerging between corporate objectives and the implications of power and DOC (drivers of change) analysis, which emphasise the prime importance of local political process and incremental change, in the face of pressures on donors to meet short term spending targets, and to be accountable to their own taxpayers.

The illiberal character of some of the organizations that informal engagement would bring DFID into contact with does not fit with their broader political agenda (Scheye and Andersen 2007: 241). While Britain's Colonial Office was able to justify using chiefs as administrators through indirect rule because this facilitated order and stability, DFID's political mandate is importantly different, requiring that its engagements fit with its liberal, democratic goals (principles that the Colonial Office was less bound by because their authority depended upon other interests). Difficult decisions thus need to be made not only about how best to provide security, but also about how best to build the kinds of security that will support equality, justice and broader human rights concerns. In making such decisions, DFID does not operate in its own vacuum of expertise, but rather within a political context in which it must also balance public perceptions and those within government. As David Mosse concludes, 'the operational control which bureaucracies or NGOs have over events and practices in development is always constrained and often quite limited' (2004: 646).

In addition to balancing commitments to serve the government and the UK public, DFID's organizational mandate to reduce global poverty also creates particular internal agency ideologies that do not always sit comfortably with engaging with illiberal actors. As Will Hout argues (2012: 407), development practitioners form an '"epistemic community" that is motivated by the common endeavour of reducing or eradicating poverty and empowering the poorest parts of the population in developing countries.' As a result, this 'commitment to "making poverty history" and to improving the quality of life of people in developing countries' creates a kind of 'institutional ethos' or a shared set of values about the good of development (Hout 2012: 407). This institutional ethos (or agency ideology or organizational culture) unites DFID staff through a shared vision of their *raison d'etre,* which conventionally focuses on promoting liberal values, such as openness and human rights, and inclusive political settlements that lead to good governance practices. DFID is *not* an institution for the propagation of tyranny, corruption or illiberal politics. Engaging with informal security and justice actors can mean dealing with some highly unsavoury characters involved in highly unsavoury activities (such as female circumcision or the recruitment of child soldiers). As one consultant explained, SJSR involves working with 'the sort of guys who finish up in charge of armies, police forces [and] intelligence services ... You are not always talking about pleasant individuals' (Biesheuvel 2008). This is not always comfortable territory for a liberal organization. As Charles Call and Susan Cook explain, 'local or traditional forms of governance require difficult choices and perhaps the sacrifice of values liberals hold dear. Traditional, legitimate forms of authority are often repressive of women's rights, individual rights, property rights, minority rights, and other rights' (Call and Cook 2003: 243). Engaging with oppressive security or justice practices is inimical to DFID's core business and the institutional ethos that staff share. The difficulty DFID staff have, for instance, in accepting the need to fund Sierra Leone Police training in non-lethal force demonstrates the lack of enthusiasm within the organization for supporting practices perceived to be in any way coercive. It is questionable then to what extent DFID could engage with the kinds of informal actors this book has been dealing with, without appearing illiberal, or being accused of violating the core principles and values it is supposed to uphold, thereby jeopardizing legitimacy both domestically and within the organization itself.

Finally, as a department of the British Government, and a development agency that rejects aid conditionality, DFID programmes must conform to the wishes of the sovereign government of the countries in which they work. It is thus not only up to DFID (and the British government and public from which it derives its support) as to whether or not it engages with informal security and justice actors, it is also dependent on the will of the Government of Sierra Leone. More research is needed on the Government of Sierra Leone's perceptions of the chieftaincy system and secret societies in order to know how much room for manoeuvre exists in this regard. While chiefs, secret societies and state politicians certainly derive support from each other, particularly around election time, there is also an historic divide between the 'progressive' Freetown peninsula and the interior provinces, which some Freetonians perceive to be backward and traditional. While the organizational politics of development agencies, as set out here, are critically important in defining the scope of the possible in SJSR interventions, so too are the political dynamics of the host government.

Bureaucratic and political natures limit 'thick' understandings

The impact of the bureaucratic and political nature of donors (not just DFID) is two-fold. First, bureaucratic and political pressures make it difficult for donors and non-governmental organizations (NGOs) to be upfront about the complexity of the issues they face. This makes achieving a 'thick' understanding of context and problems – argued throughout this book as critical to a full understanding of the causes of war – difficult. As Sue Unsworth explains:

> [Development agencies] want to eliminate poverty, curtail corruption, protect human rights and nurture democracy. Politicians who head bilateral agencies want to achieve these desirable goals within short time horizons. They have strong incentives to demonstrate progress – for example in achieving the Millennium Development Goals – and to tell an optimistic story to their own taxpayers ... Agencies have to reckon with their own domestic lobby groups and legislatures ... So it is difficult for agencies and their political leaders to acknowledge the depth and intractability of the challenges involved in tackling issues such as corruption and human rights.
>
> (Unsworth 2009: 890)

Thus, the bureaucratic and political nature of donors makes it difficult for them to develop, let alone act on, 'thick' understandings of the problems they encounter in their work. This means that donors are not set up to achieve the very understandings needed on which to base sustainable solutions to development problems. This is not to suggest that donors can never achieve 'thick' understandings of problems, but this largely happens due to the competence and innovations of particular staff, and is not facilitated (in fact, it is inhibited) by the nature of donor organizations.

Bureaucratic and political natures lead to state-centred SJSR

Second, donors' bureaucratic and political natures make them biased towards a statist worldview. DFID's bureaucratic nature predisposes the organization to engage with legal-rational actors. As Barnett and Finnemore explain:

> The course of action likely to be preferred by rational-legal authorities are, not surprisingly, rational-legal ones. Left to their own devices, bureaucracies are likely to craft policies that promote rational (in the Weberian sense), impersonal, rule-governed, and technocratic approaches to social tasks.
>
> (Barnett and Finnemore 2004: 43)

In addition, DFID's political nature means that the organization must answer to the government and the home public in a way that deters engagement with 'risky' actors, such as informal security and justice actors and the articulation of 'thick' understandings of development problems that are more complicated than the simplistic aid messages relied on for domestic consumption. The effect of these bureaucratic and political natures is that donors fall back on statist approaches to development. The state is the obvious contender demonstrating legal-rationalism and liberal democratic qualities (or, at least, having the greatest potential to demonstrate them). It is this combination of bureaucratic legal-rationality, alongside a political commitment to liberal democracy on the part of DFID and the lack of both of these attributes on the part of informal security and justice providers, that renders the partnership between the two problematic. DFID's inability to engage with informal security and justice actors, then, is not explained by ignorance or complacency. Rather, it is explained through an examination of DFID's political and bureaucratic nature itself, which acts to limit its potential engagements.

The situation renders Weber's fears about bureaucracy somewhat prophetic. Edward Page and Bill Jenkins (2005: 182) explain that Weber's 'conclusions about bureaucracy were about its potential to create an "iron cage of bondage" … a system in which a series of powerful constraints limited what is perceived to be possible or desirable.' The metaphor should not be pushed too far. DFID staff are not so embedded in their liberal, bureaucratic worldview that they cannot see the wood from the trees. In fact it is precisely this awareness on the part of DFID staff that makes the organization's lack of engagement with the informal so surprising and interesting. Rather, DFID's liberal and bureaucratic natures combine to render certain goals and methods of achieving those goals more amenable than other courses of action.

DFID *could* choose to go against its bureaucratic and political nature by engaging with informal security and justice actors to sensitize them and improve their services, with the aim of providing improved levels of policing and justice to all Sierra Leoneans. Yet this course of action would require a move away from normal operating procedures and institutional thinking, becoming more difficult to implement than engagement with liberal, bureaucratic actors (or those with the potential to be). This involves substantial work and political (and professional) risk when there are actors with whom DFID can engage in a more straightforward manner, who possess the very attribute that DFID seeks to promote – the state.

Normative bias of SJSR

This statist approach fits with wider Western donor discourse, in which the state is viewed as the vehicle for good governance (or, as it is increasingly termed, 'good enough governance') and liberal democracy (for discussion see Grindle 2007: 533–74). It is the most internationally accepted building block of the very attributes of liberalism and legal-rationalism that DFID exhibits and seeks to promote. As DFID's policy on governance, development and democratic politics suggests:

> An effective state is the single most important factor in determining whether progress takes place ... Whether states are effective or not – whether they are capable of preventing violent conflict, fulfilling human rights obligations, helping business grow, and delivering essential public services to their citizens – is the single most important factor that determines whether or not successful development takes place.
>
> (2007a: 1–2)

Thus, in attempting to build peace in post-conflict Sierra Leone, DFID has adopted a state building framework. This is not uncommon in peacebuilding efforts, which have become increasingly coterminous with state building (Stepputat *et al.* 2007: 3–4; Chappuis and Hänggi 2009: 31; Paris 2004). DFID, itself a state actor, seeks to create order through a state-logic by reforming primarily state security and justice forces within its SJSR programme. This state building approach, while often represented as a natural and technocratic response to governance breakdown from a Western viewpoint, is, of course, not devoid of a normative character (Peake *et al.* 2008: 166). As Fairlie Chappuis and Heiner Hänggi note:

> In so far as the nature of the legitimacy of the state remains tied to its representation function, it is firmly embedded in an international discourse of liberal democratic governance. This brings a distinctly normative angle to the SSR agenda which further distinguishes SSR from technical military or security focussed assistance.
>
> (Chappuis and Hänggi 2009: 39)

Thus while DFID operates with its own political and bureaucratic culture that limits its field of activities, the concept of SJSR is also not without related normative baggage of its own. SJSR is not simply the technical reform – of any kind – of a security or justice sector. The nature of the reforms that have built up to inform our understanding of the concept of SJSR is in fact highly specific, related to Weberian ideas about the state monopoly of violence, 'good governance' safeguards for the security sector (such as democratic civilian control and accountability) and the importance of the rule of law (Egnell and Halden 2009: 27–54; Stepputat *et al.* 2007: 4–5; Chanaa 2002). These are undoubtedly desirable goals. However, they are derived from particular historical experiences that have shaped the normative slant of SJSR, as we think of it now. The normative commitment to the Weberian state (and liberal, legal-rational rules of good governance) within SJSR was originally formulated to reform security sectors that were *too* strong and *too* effective

(Krogstad 2012: 263). This is not the experience in many of the contexts, such as Sierra Leone, where SJSR is now being deployed.

Because the concepts that have come to be associated with SJSR – civilian democratic control and accountability – are understood through a state-centric framework: controlled *by* a democratic state; accountable *to* higher political authorities (in turn, at least in principle, accountable to the people), this predisposes SJSR to successful results with state security and justice actors. It is state actors, already embedded in a framework that can, with reform, ensure the kinds of security governance and rule of law, that SJSR aims for. On the other hand, successful reform is not so straightforward when dealing with security and justice actors that fall outside of the state structures vested with ensuring democratic control, accountability and discipline. Justice, security, democracy and human rights are all seen to be most effectively ensured by a centralized state authority, properly structured and rule-bound by legal-rationalism. Informal actors, conversely, represent unaccountability and a lack of oversight, rendering them unmanageable forces. The goalposts for successful SJSR therefore depend upon a state framework and if this is lacking, then what success looks like is not clear. A policing and justice consultant interviewed notes the challenges posed by the lack of bureaucratic state structure amongst informal actors:

> When you work with non-state you don't have that institutional structure to work with [like you have with the state]. You know, there isn't a big door and a big man sitting behind a desk you can talk to like a Chief Justice or an IGP. You are working with different structures and the very thing that makes them so successful is the fact that they are traditional [and not the state].
>
> (Biesheuvel 2008)

If SJSR is predicated on the very institutional structure that informal security and justice actors lack, then the ability of SJSR to achieve its intended outcomes through engagement with informal actors might not be realistic. If the concepts of accountability, democratic control and discipline at the heart of SJSR could be recalibrated to apply outside of the bureaucratic state – for instance, by linking accountability to community groups or civil society, rather than to government – then the normative agenda of SJSR might not exclude successful reform of the informal.

Conclusion

This chapter has addressed three outstanding questions raised throughout this book: why won't state-centred security and justice reforms lead to the decline of informal actors?; why has there been more engagement with informal actors in justice reforms than in security reforms?; and why do donors seemingly find it so hard to engage with informal security and justice actors? In answering these questions, the longevity and malleability of informal practices; the importantly different relationships between security and the state and justice and the state; and the bureaucratic and political nature of donor organizations themselves have been seen to be determining factors. Ultimately, the answers suggest that informal security and justice practices are here to stay, although not necessarily in their 'traditional' form, and thus must be included in reforms if security and justice reforms are to be comprehensive and engage with the manner in which people actually access security and justice. In making such engagements, it is important to consider the functions of security and justice as interrelated, but distinct, goods, which will lend themselves to engagement with informal actors in different ways. In the end, however, the political and bureaucratic nature of donors may disallow these organizations from making the kinds of engagements necessary to fundamentally alter security and justice practices.

DFID needs to consider what role it can play in security and justice sectors in future operations. The policing and justice programmes in Sierra Leone have undoubtedly made positive contributions to post-conflict life. Both the police and judiciary are more trusted and utilized institutions than they were previously – albeit by only some segments of society. But it would be a stretch to say that these improved services have fundamentally altered the manner in which the majority of Sierra Leoneans access security and justice. This still occurs largely through informal and often illiberal actors, dissatisfaction with whom was a contributing cause of the civil war. Does this mean that DFID should not do SJSR in future? Or does it simply mean that it needs to be more cognisant of its limitations and the hubris involved in social engineering attempts and accept that SJSR (as it has been practiced by DFID in Sierra Leone) will never fundamentally alter practices of security and justice or address the full spectrum of conflict causes? Scheye and Andersen characterize the dilemma DFID faces:

> if donors want to support SSR in fragile states, while maintaining good development practices, they may need to recognise and accept the risks of working with nonstate actors who may not respect, adhere to, or believe in international human rights standards. Donors, of course, can choose not to engage in SSR under such circumstances, but, if they do wish to engage, the pertinent question may not be whether a nonstate justice and security provider accepts Western standards or not, but rather how donor assistance can improve the lives of citizens subjected to such service providers.
>
> (Scheye and Andersen 2007: 240)

DFID must decide whether there is space within its political, bureaucratic and statist nature to accommodate the kinds of actors that engaging with security and justice tasks puts the organization in contact with, or whether its role in security and justice programming needs to be limited to practices that fit more comfortably with the donors' goals and culture. This dilemma has not been arrived at due to wrong turns or bad decisions. To paraphrase Barnett and Finnemore, as DFID has recognized that its worldview was incomplete and that achieving its goal of poverty reduction required it to take into account other variables, such as security and justice, it expanded its work into new fields (2004: 44). The challenge, however, is to determine whether the organization, as it stands, is politically and bureaucratically capable of making the engagements that success in this new field requires. That is, engaging with the informal actors who are the predominant security and justice providers and whose failures were a contributing cause of the civil war in Sierra Leone. As Scheye and Andersen (2007: 240) rightly warn, 'the challenge is a forbidding one.'

Note

1 'An ideal type (not to be confused with an ideal) is a theoretical construct, combining several features of a phenomenon in their purest and most extreme form. An ideal type as such is never found in actual reality; it is a conceptual tool which simplifies and exaggerates reality for the sake of conceptual clarity' (Etzioni-Halvey 1983: 29).

Conclusion

Living with or overcoming political and bureaucratic confines

> A village, city, or language is the jointly created, partly unintended product of many, many hands. To the degree that the authorities insist on replacing this ineffably complex web of activity with formal rules and regulations, they are certain to disrupt the web in ways that they cannot possibly foresee ... Cities with a long history may be called 'deep' or 'thick' cities in the sense that they are the historical product of a vast number of people from all stations (including officialdom) who are long gone. It is possible, of course, to build a new city or a new village, but it will be a 'thin' or 'shallow' city, and its residents will have to begin ... to make it work in spite of the rules.
>
> (Scott 1998: 256)

Donor-supported reforms of the security and justice sectors in Sierra Leone have certainly been successful in forging an improved state police service and formal judiciary. Some level of policing is now being provided to women in urban areas and the formal justice system is more accessible to parts of the population. These are undoubtedly big achievements when considering the low base from which Sierra Leone's security and justice sectors began reforms. Yet both case studies revealed that an overwhelming focus on the state security and justice sectors meant that informal actors, who are central to security and justice provision, and indeed are often the dominant providers in Sierra Leone, were not included within reforms. Improvements in these sectors are thus 'thin' in their current form, and are yet to grow roots or become 'thick' practices. By not engaging with the thick practices of informal security and justice that exist in Sierra Leone, reforms have created a 'thin' construct over top of a web of complex and 'thick' practices that continue to operate beneath the surface.

This book has argued that the UK Department for International Development (DFID) internalized an understanding of the causes of war in Sierra Leone that focused primarily on state failure. As set out in Chapter 1, this, combined with a belief in the interconnections between security and development, led to over 15 years of security and justice reform programmes that have overwhelmingly focused on the state security and justice apparatus. This approach fails to recognize that the war in Sierra Leone was also critically about failures of the informal governance of the chieftaincy system, seen to hold in place a corrupt and inequitable social order, maintained through chiefs' security, justice and governance functions that were elaborated in the second chapter. The case studies in Chapters 3 and 4 demonstrated that this state-centric understanding of the causes of conflict infiltrated DFID's reform programmes and left key aspects of security and justice that have the greatest impact on the day to day lives of the majority of Sierra Leoneans unreformed. Not engaging with informal security and justice has therefore limited the overall results of DFID's security and justice reforms. Yet this failure to engage with the informal is not simply due, as one might expect, to DFID's lack of knowledge or awareness. Rather, it is due to the political and bureaucratic confines that, as a donor, DFID operates within. As a result, the space in which to implement the kinds of engagements that are needed to sustainably improve security and justice in places like Sierra Leone may be limited. This conclusion sketches out the implications of these findings for donors and points to some ideas as to what they might be able to do about them.

Living with the confines: The security-development nexus

DFID's political and organizational limitations set out in Chapter 5 go further than just stymieing engagement with informal security and justice actors. They also raise questions about DFID's involvement in security and justice work more broadly. In its increasing engagements with security tasks DFID is partnering with the Ministry of Defence (MoD) and the Foreign and Commonwealth Office (FCO), often through the Stabilisation Unit. While it is clearly important for the various actors sharing the development space to coordinate, questions remain about the viability of these cross-departmental partnerships in practice. If development organizations, like DFID, work with particular logics (based on a commitment to ethical politics that provides them with authority) that are insulated from logics of security (which rest upon alternative sources of authority and internalize different normative commitments), when such organizations end up involved in security practices, their guiding commitments are incongruous and have the potential to clash or work at cross purposes (Meharg 2007: 135).

There are reasons why security organizations and development organizations are historically different. Development agencies have fostered internal cultures that are oriented towards traditional development practices – education, healthcare and human rights promotion, for example – that are often deeply internalized by development practitioners and serve agency interests. Security tasks, on the other hand, often involve dealing with (and engaging in) direct violence and highly unsavoury actors in increasingly non-state contexts through a strict chain-of-command. These are situations conventionally deemed so exceptional that usual politics is suspended in favour of a securitized response (Weaver 1995: 46–86). DFID's ability to work with such actors and in such environments, while also maintaining its organizational culture, might only be possible to a limited degree. This is not to suggest that security professionals pay no attention to human rights or ethical concerns, for example, but the weight of such considerations in their decision-making is balanced with other concerns that are borne out of their own organizational and professional cultures, different to those cultivated by development organizations. One cannot simply bolt on security logics to development logics and assume the two will not contradict. Even if working towards a shared goal – such as improved policing and justice, security and development actors are likely to pursue it through different, and potentially conflicting, means. This became apparent in Sierra Leone in relation to tensions between DFID staff and their policing consultants regarding the use of lethal weapons by the police, as Erlend Krogstad captures:

> The rift that had appeared between DFID and its consultants on the issue of weapons was not rooted in a disagreement about the right policing model, but in deeper differences about what the target of reform was, and what counted as relevant knowledge in order to achieve it. On the one hand, DFID continued to view police reform in terms of a development effort targeting communities. To this end, the liberal-managerial assumptions accompanying the initial goal of Local Needs Policing seemed appropriate. On the other hand, its consultants had come to perceive the goal as equipping the police to neutralise the state's armed contenders. This, they thought, required a different form of expertise from the one DFID had on offer.
>
> (Krogstad 2012: 275)

Security and development fields are institutionally distinct (in policy worlds, as in academia), with often opposing worldviews that can result in antagonistic relationships in increasingly shared humanitarian and development spaces (Meharg 2007: 117; Stern and Öjendal 2010: 7). This was apparent in its most basic form in social settings in Freetown where, during post-conflict reconstruction efforts, the two worlds met and security personnel referred to development workers as 'tree huggers', while development practitioners talked about security forces as lacking cultural understanding, intelligence and being heavy handed. Rachel Kleinfeld notes the different professional logics even within the field of security and justice sector reform (SJSR), between security and justice practitioners: 'Lawyers, who make up the bulk of rule-of-law practitioners, tend to be different types of people and move in different circles from the security officials who focus on reforms more directly related to law and order' (2005: 11).

These opposing commitments and worldviews cannot easily be melded together without compromise. Indeed, civil-military relations theory was developed precisely to assist in navigating this unusual relationship between two culturally (in the organizational sense) divergent actors (Mychajlyszyn 2007: 176–7). Civil-military relations literature maintains that differences in organizational culture can hamper integration of security and development activities (Mychajlyszyn 2007: 182). The problems of coherence between development and security practitioners thus might be more than just procedural failures that can be amended with increased communication and coordination (Biesheuvel 2008). They might, rather, be indicative of distinct organizational cultures and goals that, while seemingly integrated at the policy level, are more intractable in practice (de Coning 2008: 55; 56). The boundary between the concepts of security and development, whilst penetrable at a conceptual level requires far more difficult transformations of mind-sets and practices on the ground. DFID's political and bureaucratic nature may constrain it in making such transformations, and thus limit its ability to effectively engage in security tasks.

As a result, it is important to consider that donors simply might not be able to do everything that sustainably and comprehensively transforming security and justice provision might entail. Michael Barnett and Martha Finnemore note that bureaucracies tend to expand their mandates and expertise when new fields of work are revealed as relevant for their broader mission and, in doing so, define problems and solutions in ways that legitimize and even require more bureaucratic involvement (2004: 2; 9). Thus, as security was increasingly perceived to influence development, DFID's work in this area duly expanded. Yet what happens when the area of work that the bureaucracy moves into requires fundamentally different political and organizational cultures than the bureaucracy has built up and which facilitate its other areas of work? If donors are not able to alter the ways they work, then they may have to consider the possibility that they are not politically or organizationally equipped to carry out the kinds of security and justice reforms needed to comprehensively and sustainably transform security and justice provision. This would clearly have significant implications for programming, given the substantial investments donors have made in the areas of security and justice, particularly with the strong emphasis currently placed on working in fragile and conflict-affected contexts.

Overcoming the confines: What donors can do differently

Informal security and justice actors, despite their flaws, present an opportunity for donors to tap into alternative forms of knowledge that provide more specific understandings of context than the formal state is capable of and can help to build grass roots legitimacy and local relevance of donor programming (Scott 1998; Sklar 2003). Informal security and justice actors operate with different forms of knowledge to those of the state. This knowledge has generally not been deemed as relevant or useful in SJSR. While the formal state operates according to legal-rationalism, seen to be necessary for working with donors in Chapter 5, informal security and justice actors, like chiefs in Sierra Leone, lack this bureaucratic knowledge but are capable instead of more intimate and less abstract forms of knowledge. Unlike the state, chiefs do not need to develop an abstract idea of citizens – they personally know their subjects and can therefore account for their position, interests and needs in a more personalized manner than the state could ever be capable of. Of course, this knowledge has not always been deployed by chiefs for benevolent purposes and indeed, intimate knowledge of subjects or citizens has the potential for tailored and personalized oppression as much as enlightened governance, as Chapter 2 demonstrated. Yet the very possession of this kind of knowledge should be noted by development partners as a potential counterweight to the relatively blunt instruments of comprehending citizens that states develop through abstractions and the invention of a standardized 'common man' whose needs and interests they then try to meet. James Scott explains these different forms of knowledge by drawing a parallel between the state's need to abstract and simplify complexity and the character of maps:

> [S]tate simplifications … have the character of maps. That is, they are designed to summarise precisely those aspects of a complex world that are of immediate interest to the mapmaker and ignore the rest. To complain that a map lacks nuance and detail makes no sense unless it omits information necessary to its function. A city map that aspired to represent every traffic light, every pothole, every building, and every bush and tree in every park would threaten to become as large and as complex as the city that it depicted. And it would certainly defeat the purpose of mapping, which is to abstract and summarise.
>
> (Scott 1998: 87)

Informal actors possess knowledge of the local complexity that the state cannot possibly know, because it can see only in abstract and simplifying terms, in part, at least, due to its bureaucratic character which aims to compartmentalize common problems in order to develop common solutions. Yet in the case of Sierra Leone, there is an opportunity to combine the abstract knowledge of state security and justice sectors, attuned to large-scale delivery of relatively standardized security and justice services, with the locally specific knowledge of informal actors in a manner that at least has the potential to allow for more context-specific approaches to security and justice. This can help to build local ownership beyond just government buy-in. As Richard Sklar notes:

> Increasingly … [the moral authority of traditional leaders] is reckoned in Africa to be a political resource of potentially great value. Wisely used, it

> can help to maintain civic morale and social order during the current era of extremely difficult transitions ... A separate source of authority, embedded in tradition, could be used to reinforce social stability without the abandonment of democratic reforms. Traditional governments would then prove themselves to be superior shock absorbers for the African ships of state during the stormy passages of these turbulent times.
>
> (Sklar 2003: 17)

Informal security and justice actors may thus have the potential to provide the 'localness' that donors require and alternative forms of knowledge to achieve country ownership, sustainability and locally tailored reforms.

The irony, of course, is that donors also 'see like states' (to use Scott's phrase) and therefore overlook the potentially valuable forms of knowledge that informal security and justice actors possess. This book has argued that this happens because of the bureaucratic and political nature of donors, which limits their worldview to a statist representation of a complex reality that can only be perceived through 'thick' understandings. DFID's bureaucratic and political nature renders engagement with formal state structures significantly more straightforward than engagement with informal actors that operate according to different logics. Specifically, DFID's bureaucratic nature and political commitments lead it to a view of the causes of conflict and nature of security and justice provision that privileges the state. This understanding filters through DFID's post-conflict recovery response, resulting in an overwhelmingly state-centric SJSR programme that leaves informal security and justice actors unreformed. This restricts the ability of its SJSR efforts to comprehensively address the thickly understood causes of conflict and sustainably transform security and justice provision in Sierra Leone. These limitations bring into question DFID's increasing involvement in security tasks as development processes more broadly, given the 'iron cage of bondage' that they find themselves in.

If donors *are* determined to better equip themselves in order that they can work more effectively in the security and justice fields, then they will need to make changes to their current modes of operation. Some recommendations on where to start are set out below. These can be broken into four key areas where change is needed: creating political space; investing in 'thick' analysis; recruiting and promoting different skill sets; and breaking away from standard programming approaches. These are undoubtedly not the only changes to be made, but they have emerged from this research as the most pressing issues that prevent donors from engaging in SJSR comprehensively and with the full gamut of security and justice providers.

Creating political space

Given that donors gain a mandate to carry out their work by building legitimacy through support from their domestic public and government, as set out in Chapter 5, there is a need to prise open a larger space in which donors can manoeuvre. To create this space, donors need to repackage the way in which aid is 'sold' domestically. For too long aid has been understood as charity, usually given through project aid to 'worthy' recipients, such as malnourished children, women lacking educational opportunities and the sick and vulnerable – categories of people that are seen to constitute 'the deserving poor' (Wood 2008). This has done little to build an understanding of the complexity of the underlying causes of the problems that aid is meant to address. The over-simplification of the way that aid is communicated is noted by Chris Brown in his critique of aid concerts such as Live Aid:

> The remedy for African starvation that Geldof incessantly plugged – in essence and in his words, 'give me your fucking money' – was simplistic in the extreme, made no attempt to approach the causes of famines, and left a generation of young people with the quite false belief that transferring wealth to the poor is both easy to do and a solution to something.
> (Brown 2010: 423)

He goes on to note the limitations of the wristbands of Make Poverty History and similar celebrity aid public relations (Brown 2010: 243). But beyond these public aid campaigns, the modalities of aid have changed, with shifts towards putting aid recipient governments in the driving seat, for instance through budget support, where donor money is transferred directly to recipient governments to supplement their national budgets and spend according to their own priorities.

As aid modalities have changed to recognize that, in fact, aid might be more effective if it works 'with the grain' of entrenched political realities that are often illiberal, patrimonial and patriarchal, the public relations of aid has not kept pace (Kelsall 2008; Golooba-Mutebi 2011; Unsworth 2010). While this new message might not seem palatable to public audiences, demonstrating why, for example, engaging with chiefs will improve development, is important in creating the space aid agencies need to implement the programmes they believe will most effectively reduce poverty. Donors are painfully aware of the limited public support for aid, particularly in times of fiscal austerity. Perhaps an important step towards addressing the obstacles donors face in engaging with informal security and justice actors is to think more carefully about how aid spending is represented to the public and to start to communicate the more complicated (but also more realistic) messages about development. Initial research on public perceptions of aid, conducted through focus groups across the UK, suggests that an appetite exists for this more complex and honest approach (Glennie *et al.* 2012: 2). Ultimately, if the development community are satisfied that engaging with actors such as chiefs is likely to improve the quality of security and justice services, then they need to be able to make the case convincingly to domestic audiences.

Doing so may seem risky given the potentially negative response, yet continuing to pretend that aid is soft and furry only limits the ability of donors to engage in the gritty work that we know to be necessary for effective development outcomes, especially in the security and justice sectors in fragile and conflict-affected contexts.

The need for 'thick' understandings

While much development work exhibits a lack of context awareness, this is acute in the justice and security sectors, where blueprint approaches that seek to transplant a model developed for one context to another are particularly resilient. Understanding context, however, needs to go beyond country-level analysis that is frequently relied upon in 'drivers of change' and 'political-economy analysis' approaches to become 'thick'. If donors do not invest in understanding the complexity of the situations they are working within, their chances of making sustainable changes to that environment are slim.

The constellation of security, safety, justice and rule of law that governs a community relates directly to the unique political settlements at play and, as such, varies in important ways even within a country. Donors need to be savvy about the interconnections between justice, security, interests and power and understand that altering who is responsible for justice and security will consolidate and reallocate power in crucial ways. A failure to understand the political-economy of informal actors was apparent in DFID's Chiefdom Governance Reform Programme, examined in Chapter 1, where insufficient understanding on the part of DFID about how chiefs and their patronage networks and justice systems were connected to the very grievances that instigated conflict meant that the programme failed and was ultimately dismantled in 2002. The lesson to be learnt from this experience is not that informal actors should become peripheral to reforms, but rather that effective engagement demands a deeper understanding of the many ways in which informal actors provide services and exercise power within communities. Engagement needs to be built on an acute understanding of the micro-level context in which programmes work. By developing a thicker understanding of local authority structures, allegiances and service providers, donors can build programmes that engage with practices that have deep roots in society and that will weather the political and social storms of the future better than thinly planted reforms.

Importantly, however, as was seen in Chapter 5, the ability of donors to develop 'thick' understandings of their environment and the problems they face is constrained by the very bureaucratic and political features of donor organizations themselves. As Will Hout notes, the reason 'why development agencies are apparently unable to apply the outcomes of political-economy analysis requires a theoretical interpretation of the very political economy of the aid agencies themselves' (2012: 406). He goes on to explain that '[t]he lofty goals of understanding realities better may ... "not be well aligned with donor incentives to demonstrate short term impact, respond to their own tax-payers and lobby groups, and to spend the allocated aid resources"' (Hout quoting Dahl-Østergaard, 2012: 410). That is, it may be the down-stream operational aspects of donors that undermine their ability to cultivate the kind of thick analysis needed for working effectively with security and justice actors. To develop thick understandings of contexts and problems, donors also need to make operational changes to recruitment, career advancement and programming approaches, so that incentives are aligned with valuing thick analysis.

Recruiting and promoting different skill sets

In order to develop the 'thick' understandings of context needed to engage effectively with informal security and justice actors, donors need to recruit and promote people with different skill sets that focus less on generic or technical knowledge, and more on country or regional expertise (Unsworth 2009: 890). Currently, most donor recruitment calls for broad knowledge of governance-related themes (such as service delivery, corruption and statebuilding) or technical capacities (in relation to the security and justice sectors, this often includes a background as a police officer or lawyer). Of course, these skill sets can be useful to security and justice programming, but they also prioritize certain forms of knowledge which have an impact on how programmes look as a result. These skill sets reinforce, perhaps unintentionally, a blueprint approach, drawing on expertise in how security and justice operate within donor countries and often highly normative 'good governance' approaches to how states *should* function. While this might not be the intention of donors, the kinds of knowledge that human resourcing prioritizes can be seen to infer that developing country deficits are best dealt with through transferring skills attuned to the functioning of Western political systems. This raises questions about how far we have broken away from a modernization theory approach, whereby the political configurations of Western countries are seen as the ideal that developing countries are working towards, and thus the skills and expertise perceived as necessary to the function of political configurations in the West are deemed the most relevant for developing countries. This is at odds with the wide academic literature that highlights the unclear trajectory of development and state reforms in developing countries, and rejects such a teleological approach (Stepputat *et al.* 2007: 6; Migdal 1988: 25; Chazan, 1988: 121–3; Herbst 2000: 270). Mark Beissinger and Crawford Young speak to this uncertain future:

> There no longer appears to be a clearly defined end point in the processes of adaptation in course. Although the tug of liberal democracy and market economy is strong, as a referential emblem of 'normality' and as a global cachet of respectability, given the enormous problems of stateness that

> affect these regions there is no longer a certainty that these represent the eventual destinations.
>
> (Quoted in Young 2004: 48)

Indeed, as Stephen Ellis posits, '[h]ealthier states will need to reflect the actual politics of their societies, including some unconventional arrangements' (2007: 160). In recruiting the kind of technical experts that are constitutive of security and justice sectors as they operate in the West, donors overlook the importance of the local knowledge that more anthropological or area studies experts provide. These under-utilized experts are more likely to speak local languages (in which most informal security and justice systems operate) and understand socio-political and economic dynamics from a bottom-up and local perspective, rather than from the perspective of international development debates. Incorporating these skill sets – to say nothing of hiring more local staff – alongside more generic and technical experts would help to provide donors with 'thicker' understandings of context.

In addition to recruiting people with such skill sets, donors must also learn to promote them within their organizations as valuable commodities. Currently career advancement within donor organizations is largely based on accruing experience in a number of country contexts and demonstrating an ability to 'move money' and submit reports showing programme success on time and on budget (Hout 2012: 408; Unsworth 2009: 890; Natsios 2010: 44–5). This overlooks the importance of developing deep knowledge of a single country or region, focusing on long-term development results rather than short-term programming cycles, and piloting risky strategies that will not always work. This is clearly related to the political and bureaucratic constraints that donors work within, as set out in Chapter 5. It is important that donors recognize that these characteristics may actually make them less effective at their job of supporting transformations in security and justice, and fighting poverty more broadly.

Breaking away from standard programming approaches

Donors' standard operating procedures mean that they are poorly equipped to develop the thick knowledge necessary to engage in the complex task of security and justice reform. In country offices, donors are invariably based in capital cities, at a remove from the places where informal security and justice thrive. Staff are routinely rotated in and out of country on two to three year cycles. In Sierra Leone, DFID staff have often moved on at the same time as the large multi-year security and justice programmes have changed hands, meaning that the new programme cycle has the impression of beginning with a 'clean slate', inhibiting efforts to build on accrued knowledge or past approaches and relationships. Indeed, with donors increasingly utilizing large consulting companies to implement their projects, it is these consultancies, as much as donors themselves, who need to take on board these findings.

The financing models preferred by donors are also not suited to engaging with informal security and justice actors. First of all, the business models of many development agencies are based on spending large amounts of money with a small number of fulltime staff. This is particularly true of DFID. In reality, this means that DFID staff themselves do not have the time to be heavily involved in programming – which is rather outsourced to consultants. The cumbersome procurement processes involved in contracting these consultants almost certainly rule out bids from local organizations, especially now that pre-selection often occurs through what are known as 'framework agreements' so that donors can limit the pool of potential applicants to those that have already passed required benchmarks in relation to accounting, reporting, value for money, and so on. Once one of a handful of large consulting outfits has (invariably) won the bid, pressure is on them to 'move the money' as quickly as possible to meet donor deadlines. Of course, this is not to suggest that implementers do not care about the quality of programming, but that the incentives at play mean priorities can easily become skewed to fulfilling bureaucratic requirements, rather than engaging in the most effective forms of programming (Natsios 2010).

Engagement with informal security and justice actors does not lend itself to big budget programmes. While some interventions may focus on complex and long-term issues, such as the relationships between formal and customary law, it is increasingly recognized that most are likely to be targeted, small scale projects that provide training and buy small items like whistles, bicycles and notepads, rather than large social engineering efforts (Scheye 2009b: 43). Given the emphasis on 'moving money', or 'the burn rate', as it is sometimes called, this kind of engagement is often not prioritized. What is more, projects that work with informal security and justice actors in one locale, even when successful, are often not suited to a nationwide roll-out. Replicating initiatives that work in one community in other parts of the country might be an attractive strategy for donors trying to achieve large scale results and spend money quickly, but while rolling out effective practices might seem beneficial, results from engaging with informal security and justice providers are more likely to be limited to specific communities, differentiated within a country and not large scale and replicable. There may well be local level security and justice practices that can benefit from donor assistance – but these are most likely to be limited to specific communities and donors need to accept that the solution to societal problems is unlikely to lie in one community, able to be scaled-up countrywide.

Alternative financing models are therefore necessary to work with informal security and justice actors. Smaller amounts of funding need to be available to support pilot projects. Experimentation will be necessary to test out innovative approaches that might or might not work – and accepting this risk is imperative. Community-based or non-government organizations might also be potential partners to assist donors in navigating how to work with informal security and justice actors, and they may help to alleviate the difficulty of ticking the accounting and reporting boxes. Such organizations would need to be locally credible and donors should be aware of potentially competing agendas.

Perhaps bureaucracy is not the iron cage that Weber feared and donors can make the changes necessary to work effectively with informal security and justice actors. To do so, donors must be able to develop 'thick' understandings of contexts and problems. Such understandings go beyond 'context awareness' to engaging with local modes of knowledge that informal security and justice practices are steeped in. Achieving 'thick' understandings, and being able to act on them, also requires other changes in the ways that donors work. There is a need to create more political space for manoeuvre so that donors have greater freedom to pursue unconventional development strategies that they believe are most likely to work. This space will only be carved out, however, by embarking on a more honest dialogue with home publics about the realities of development. In addition, donors must adapt their operational practices, in terms of recruitment, career advancement, procurement and funding mechanisms to incentivize 'thick' analysis and best equip donors for success in working with informal security and justice actors.

Beyond the iron cage of bondage?

This book has demonstrated how DFID's ability to engage with informal security and justice actors is limited by its bureaucratic and political nature. Can this be transcended to ensure better SJSR in future, or are these features intrinsic to development agencies themselves? As suggested here, if donors can carve out a more flexible political space, develop thick understandings of contexts and problems, recruit and retain different skill sets, and change their standard operating procedures, then the confines of their political and bureaucratic commitments might become less restrictive. But if these changes cannot be made, donors may need to accept that their ability to engage in comprehensive and sustainable transformation of the security and justice sectors in many countries will, inevitably, be limited.

Given the central role that donors play in implementing SJSR, it is surprising that so little research has been dedicated to examining the workings and politics of donors themselves and the influence this has on programming. This book has made some initial inroads to this research but more could be done to understand the political-economy of donors themselves, as well as of the implementing agencies who often deliver security and justice programmes on the ground. Rather than focusing solely on the difficult questions of operationalization of peacebuilding strategies in specific country settings, research also needs to undertake a more rigorous examination of how the nature of donors themselves influence programme outcomes. Even if research findings suggest that no space exists within donor organizations to forge new ways of working, this would assist in providing a better understanding of their capabilities and limitations and thus defining the scope of their operations in the field.

While the story told here is of a specific organization doing SJSR in the context of Sierra Leone, the findings should be insightful for other development agencies engaged in SJSR in complex security environments. The challenges of informal security and justice actors for SJSR programmes have been noted in places as diverse as Timor-Leste (Peake *et al.* 2007), Afghanistan (Sedra 2007), Iraq (Ucko 2008: 341–73) and Somalia (Menkhaus 2007) – to name but a few. The prevalence of this problem across diverse contexts suggests that unpacking how these actors can be engaged or why they cannot, will be of crucial importance in honing post-conflict peacebuilding strategies. This is particularly relevant as development agencies increasingly become involved in security and justice programming. While it is comforting to believe that development organizations are uniquely placed to focus reforms on enabling the security and justice sectors to contribute to broader developmental goals, the practicability of such tasks needs serious consideration. As the case of DFID in Sierra Leone attests, development organizations might be limited by their political mandate and bureaucratic nature in engaging with the kinds of actors that often provide security and justice functions in fragile contexts. Reforming the actors who have been powerful or coercive enough to maintain control over people throughout appallingly brutal political transformations was never going to be an easy task. This is not in any way to suggest that SJSR should be conducted solely by defence departments and security forces, but that the practicable role of development organizations should be considered in light of what they are capable of and to what extent this will help to provide the best possible security and justice for the majority of people in any given country.

If development agencies are not able to engage with the thorny and morally dubious actors that are involved in informal security and justice provision, or even those actors who merely operate according to non-bureaucratic processes, then the nature of their contribution to SJSR needs to be reappraised. It is all well and good to hope that, over time, fealty towards informal security and justice providers will weaken, as the state apparatus improves. Yet there is little precedent in Sierra Leone, or Africa more broadly, to suggest that this shift will occur in the near future, as evidenced by the growing literature on the continuing role of informal institutions in African governance (Kyed and Buur 2007; Vaughan 2005; Andersen, Møller and Stepputat 2007; Baker 2006b: 31–46; Blundo and Olivier de Sardan 2006). Practitioners may well need to put their hopes for a legal-rational, Weberian state on the backburner and focus in the meantime on improving the kinds of states that *actually exist* in Africa. Helene Kyed and Lars Buur describe the challenge:

> The fear of the sceptics is that the gains promised by democracy with regard to equity, human rights, and gender equality will be lost if the rudder of development and governance is handed over to an indeterminate huddle of unelected patriarchal leaders in the name of efficient, localised governance, cultural diversity, and the inclusion of local communities.
> (Kyed and Buur 2007: 11)

To engage with informal security and justice actors, however, is merely to recognize already lived realities. In Sierra Leone, this reality is a weak but resilient state that exists alongside many equally resilient informal actors that exercise authority over the day to day affairs of people's lives, including their security and justice. Not only are both of these responsible for dispensing security and justice, but it was also the failure of both that precipitated the civil war. Addressing the causes of conflict and improving security and justice for Sierra Leoneans therefore means engaging with both; and importantly, finding the appropriate development partners willing and able to do so.

Bibliography

Abdullah, I. (1998) 'Bush Path to Destruction: the origin and character of the Revolutionary United Front', *Journal of Modern African Studies*, 36(2): 203–35.

—. (ed.) (2004) *Between Democracy and Terror: The Sierra Leone War*, Dakar: CODESRIA.

Abraham, A. (1978) *Mende Government and Politics under Colonial Rule*, Freetown: Sierra Leone University Press.

Abrahamsen, R. (2000) *Disciplining Democracy: Development discourse and good governance in Africa*, London: Zed Books.

—. (2004) 'A Breeding Ground for Terrorists', *Review of African Political Economy*, 31(102): 677–84.

Abrahamsen, R. and P. Williams (2001) 'Ethics and Foreign Policy: the antinomies of New Labour's 'third way' in sub-Saharan Africa', *Political Studies*, 49(2): 249–64.

Acemoglu, D., Reed, T. and Robinson, J.A. (2013) 'Chiefs: Elite Control of Civil Society and Economic Development in Sierra Leone', National Bureau of Economic Research Working Paper No. 18691. Online, available at: http://www.nber.org/papers/w18691 (accessed 7 June 2013).

AFP (2008) 'Sierra Leone Government to Ban Female Circumcision: minister'. Online, available at: http://www.forwarduk.org.uk/news/news/172 (accessed 17 August 2009).

African Human Security Initiative (2009) 'Sierra Leone: A country review of crime and criminal justice', *Institute for Security Studies Monograph* 160. Online, available at: http://dspace.cigilibrary.org/jspui/bitstream/123456789/30961/1/M160FULL.pdf?1 (accessed 7 June 2013).

Albrecht, P. (2010) 'Betwixt and between: chiefs and reform of Sierra Leone's justice sector', DIIS Working Paper 33. Online, available at: http://www.diis.dk/graphics/Publications/WP2010/WP2010-33-Albrecht-Betwixt-and-between_web.pdf (accessed 7 June 2013).

Albrecht, P. and Jackson, P. (2009) *Security System Transformation in Sierra Leone, 1997–2007*, Birmingham: Global Facilitation Network for Security Sector Reform.

Albrecht, P. and Kyed, H.M. (2011) 'Introduction: non-state and customary actors in development programs', in P. Albrecht, H.M. Kyed, D. Isser and E. Harper (eds) *Perspectives on Involving Non-state and Customary Actors in Justice and Security Reform*, Rome: DIIS and IDLO.

Alie, J.A.D. (2005) 'The Kamajor Militia in Sierra Leone: liberators or nihilists?', in D.J. Francis (ed.) *Civil Militia: Africa's intractable security menace*, Aldershot: Ashgate.

—. (2008) 'Reconciliation and Traditional Justice: tradition-based practices of the Kpaa Mende in Sierra Leone', in L. Huyse and M. Salter (eds) *Traditional Justice and Reconciliation after Violent Conflict: learning from African experiences*, Stockholm: International Institute for Democracy and Electoral Assistance.

Alldridge, T.J. (1970 [1910]) 'A Transformed Colony, Sierra Leone as it was, and as it is: its progress, peoples, native customs and undeveloped wealth', Westport, CT: Negro Universities Press.

Alterman, O. Binienda, A., Rodella, S. and Varzi, K. (2003) 'The Law People See: the status of dispute resolution in the provinces of Sierra Leone in 2002', Freetown: National Forum for Human Rights.

Andersen, L. (2007) 'What to do? The dilemmas of international engagement in fragile states', in L. Andersen, B. Møller and F. Stepputat (eds) *Fragile States and Insecure People? Violence, security and statehood in the twenty-first century*, New York, NY: Palgrave Macmillan.

Andersen, L., Møller, B. and Stepputat, F. (eds) (2007) *Fragile States and Insecure People? Violence, security and statehood in the twenty-first century*, New York, NY: Palgrave Macmillan.

Anderson, L. (2004) 'Antiquated before they can ossify: States that fail before they form', *Journal of International Affairs*, 58(1): 1–16.

Archibald, S. and Richards, P. (2002) 'Converts to Human Rights? Popular debate about war and justice in rural central Sierra Leone', *Africa*, 72(3): 339–67.

Aryeetey, E. (1996) 'Formal and Informal Economic Activities', in S. Ellis (ed.) *Africa Now: people, policies, institutions*, Oxford: James Currey.

Awoko News (2010) 'JSDP trains 88 chiefdom police in Moyamba'. Online, available at: http://awoko.org/2010/05/26/jsdp-trains-88-chiefdom-police-in-moyamba/ (accessed 7 June 2013).

Ayittey, G.B.N. (1999) *Africa in Chaos*, New York, NY: St Martin's Press.

Bagayoko, N. (2012) 'Introduction: Hybrid Security Governance in Africa', *IDS Bulletin*, 43(4): 1–13.

Baker, B. (2005) 'Who Do People Turn to for Policing in Sierra Leone?', *Journal of Contemporary African Studies*, 23(3): 371–90.

—. (2006a) 'Beyond the State Police in Urban Uganda and Sierra Leone', *Afrika Spectrum*, 41(1): 55–76.

—. (2006b) 'The African post-conflict policing agenda in Sierra Leone', *Conflict, Security and Development*, 6(1): 25–41.

—. (2006c) 'Post-Settlement Governance Programmes: what is being built in Africa?', in O. Furley and R. May (eds) *Ending Africa's Wars*, Aldershot: Ashgate.

—. (2007) 'Nonstate Providers of Everyday Security in Fragile African States', in L. Andersen, B. Møller and F. Stepputat (eds) *Fragile States and Insecure People? Violence, security and statehood in the twenty-first century*, New York, NY: Palgrave Macmillan.

—. (2008) Personal interview, 12 September.

Baker, B. and Scheye, E. (2007) 'Multilayered Justice and Security Delivery in Post-Conflict and Fragile States', *Conflict, Security and Development*, 7(4): 503–28.

Ball, N., Biesheuvel, P., Hamilton-Baillie, T. and Olonisakin, F. (2007) 'Security and Justice Sector Reform Programming in Africa', Evaluation Working Paper 23, London: Department for International Development.

Barnes, K. with Albrecht, P. And Olson, M. (2007) 'Addressing Gender-Based Violence in Sierra Leone: mapping challenges, responses and future entry points', London: International Alert.

Barnett, M. and Finnemore, M. (1999) 'The Politics, Power, and Pathologies of International Organizations', *International Organization*, 53: 699–732.

Barnett, M. and Finnemore, M. (2004) *Rules for the World*, Ithaca, NY: Cornell University Press.

Barrows, W. (1976) *Grassroots politics in an African State: integration and development in Sierra Leone*, London: Africana Publishing Company.

Bash-Taqi, R., Country Director, Health Poverty Action Sierra Leone (2012) Personal interview, 16 October.

Bassie, L., Chief of Staff, Keili, F., Assistant to the Chief of Staff and Sannoh, A., Director of Cabinet and Parliamentary Affairs, Office of National Security (2009) Personal interview, 7 April.

Bastian, S. and Luckham, R. (2003) *Can Democracy de Designed?*, London: Zed Books.

BBC News (2001) 'Blair Promises to Stand By Africa'. Online, available at: http://news.bbc.co.uk/1/hi/world/africa/1575428.stm (accessed 11 November 2008).

—. (2006) 'Sierra Leone Anger at FGM Asylum in UK'. Online, available at: http://news.bbc.co.uk/go/pr/fr/-/1/hi/world/Africa/6065682.stm (accessed 17 August 2009).

—. (2009) 'UK to spend £1bn on 'war' nations'. Online, available at: http://news.bbc.co.uk/go/pr/fr/-/1/hi/uk-politics/8135413.stm (accessed 6 July 2009).

Berdal, M. (2009) *Building Peace after War*, Abingdon: Routledge.

Berg, E. (2000) 'Why Aren't Aid Organisations Better Learners?' Expert Group on Development Issues Seminar. Online, available at: http://www.observatoritercer-sector.org/pdf/centre_recursos/2_14_why_00406.pdf (accessed 7 June 2013).

Biddle, K., former-Inspector General of the Sierra Leone Police and Head of Commonwealth Community Safety and Security Project (2008), Personal interview, 13 September.

—. (2013) 'Re: Permission to use quotes in book on Sierra Leone SJSR'. Email sent to author (20 May 2013).

Biddle, K., Clegg, I. and Whetton, J. (1998) 'Evaluation of ODA/DFID support to the police in developing countries: synthesis study', Evaluation Report 648, Swansea: University of Wales and the Department for International Development.

Biesheuvel, P., Libra Advisory Group (2008) Personal interview, 17 October.

Biesheuvel, P., Hamilton-Baillie, T. and Wilson, T. (2007) 'Sierra Leone Security Sector Reform Programme: output to purpose review'. Online, available at: http://s4rsa.wikispaces.com/file/view/SILSEP_07.doc. (accessed 6 August 2009).

Binyon, M. (2000) 'Labour's expensive African albatross', *The Times*, 8 May.

Blair, T. (2001) 'Speech to the Labour Party Conference'. Online, available at: http://www.guardian.co.uk/politics/2001/oct/02/labourconference.labour6 (accessed 30 April 2010).

Bledsoe, C. (1984) 'The Political Use of Sande Ideology and Symbolism', *American Ethnologist*, 11(3): 455–72.

—. (1990) '"No Success without Struggle": social mobility and hardship for foster children in Sierra Leone', *Man*, 25(1): 70–88.

Blundo, G. and Olivier de Sardan, J-P. (2006) 'Everyday Corruption in West Africa', in G. Blundo and J-P Olivier de Sardan (eds) *Everyday Corruption and the State*, London: Zed Books.

Blundo, G. and Le Meur, P-Y. (2009) 'An Anthropology of Everyday Governance: collective service delivery and subject-making', in G. Blundo and P-Y. Le Meur (eds) *The Governance of Daily Life in Africa*, Leiden: Brill.

Bo Bike Riders Association (2009) Personal interview, 18 March.

Bo Family Support Unit staff, Sierra Leone Police (2009) Personal interview, 19 March.

Bøås, M. (2001) 'Liberia and Sierra Leone – Dead Ringers? The logic of neopatrimonial rule', *Third World Quarterly*, 22(5): 697–723.

Bob-Kandeh, M., President, Market Women's Association (2009) Personal interview, 4 March.

Boege, V., Brown, A., Clements, K. and Nolan, A. (2009) 'On Hybrid Political Orders and Emerging States: what is failing – states in the Global South or research and politics in the West?', Berlin: Berghof Research Centre for Constructive Conflict Management.

Boersch-Supan, J. (2010) 'Intergenerational Conflict in Post-Conflict Sierra Leone', Paper presented at the African Studies Association United Kingdom Conference, Oxford, United Kingdom, 16–19 September 2010.

Borger, J. (2007) 'I would not be speaking to you if it weren't for the risks Blair took', *The Guardian*. Online, available at: http://www.guardian.co.uk/world/2007/may/26/tonyblair.foreignpolicy (accessed 11 November 2008).

Bowcott, O. and Mark, M. (2012) 'Charles Taylor found guilty of abetting Sierra Leone war crimes', *The Guardian*. Online, available at: http://wwvw.guardian.co.uk/world/2012/apr/26/charles-taylor-guilty-war-crimes (accessed 7 June 2013).

Bowers, E. (2007) 'FGM Practitioners sway elections in Sierra Leone', *Women's E-News*. Online, available at: http://www.womensenews.org/article.cfm/dyn/aid/3305 (accessed 17 August 2009).

Broadbent, E. (2012) 'Research-based evidence in African policy debates: chieftaincy reform in Sierra Leone', Case Study 4, Evidence-based Policy in Development Network and Mwananchi. Online, available at: http://www.mwananchi-africa.org/storage/126565_ebpdn_SL.pdf (accessed 24 April 2013).

Brown, C. (2010) 'Bob Dylan, Live Aid, and the Politics of Popular Cosmopolitanism', in C. Brown (ed.) *Practical Judgement in International Political Theory*, Abingdon: Routledge.

Bryden, A., N'Diaye, B. and Olonisakin, F. (2008) 'Understanding the Security Challenges of Security Sector Governance in West Africa', in A. Bryden, B. N'Diaye and F. Olonisakin (eds) *Understanding the Security Challenges of Security Sector Governance in West Africa*, Berlin: Lit Verlag.

Call, C.T. and Cook, S.E. (2003) 'On Democratisation and Peacebuilding', *Global Governance*, 9(2): 233–46.

Call, C. with Wyeth, V. (eds) (2008) *Building States to Build Peace*, Boulder, CO: Lynne Rienner Publishers.

Carlson, K. (2009) 'Sierra Leone Calling: CSU professor, ex-pupil help with Childbirth', *The Modesto Bee*. Online, available at: http://www.modbee.com/loca/story/647024.html (accessed 26 August 2009).

Carothers, T. (1998) 'The Rule of Law Revival', *Foreign Affairs*, 77(2): 95–106.

Castillejo, C. (2009) 'Building Accountable Justice in Sierra Leone', Working Paper 76, Madrid: FRIDE.

Centre for Development Research University of Bonn (undated) 'Institutional Mapping and Bibliography on State Failure and Good Governance'. Online, available at: http://www.state-failure.de/directory/4.htm#4.2.1 (accessed 14 November 2008).

Chabal, P. and Daloz, J-P. (1999) *Africa Works: Disorder as Political Instrument*, Oxford: James Currey.

Chanaa, J. (2002) *Security sector reform: Issues, challenges and prospects*, London: International Institute for Strategic Studies.

Chappuis, F. and Hänggi, H. (2009) 'The Interplay between Security and Legitimacy: security sector reform and statebuilding', in J. Raue and P. Sutter (eds) *Facets and Practices of Statebuilding*, Leiden: Martinus Nijhoff Publishers.

Chazan, N. (1988) 'Patterns of State-Society Incorporation and Disengagement in Africa', in D. Rothchild and N. Chazan (eds) *The Precarious Balance: state and society in Africa*, Boulder, CO: Westview.

Chirayath, L., Sage, C. and Woolcock, M. (2005) 'Customary Law and Policy Reform: engaging with the plurality of justice systems', Background paper, World Development Report 2006. Online, available at: http://siteresources.worldbank.org/INTWDR2006/Resources/477383-1118673432908/Customary_Law_and_Policy_Reform.pdf (accessed 4 May 2010).

Chopra, T. and Isser, D. (2011) 'Women's access to justice, legal pluralism and fragile states', in P. Albrecht, H.M. Kyed, D. Isser and E. Harper (eds) *Perspectives on Involving Non-state and Customary Actors in Justice and Security Reform*, Rome: DIIS and IDLO.

Clarke, J.I. (1969) *Sierra Leone in Maps*, London: University of London Press.

Collier, G. (1970) *Sierra Leone: experiment in democracy in an African nation*, London: University of London Press.

Collier, P. (2001) 'Economic Causes of Civil Conflict and Their Implications for Policy', in C.A. Crocker, F. Osler Hampson and P. Aall (eds) *Turbulent Peace: the challenge of managing international conflict*, Washington, DC: United States Institute of Peace.

Commission for Africa (undated) 'Story of the Commission for Africa'. Online, available at: http://www.commissionforafrica.org/english/about/story.html (accessed 11 November 2008).

Commission for Africa (2005) 'Our Common Interest: Report of the Commission for Africa'. Online, available at: http://webarchive.nationalarchives.gov.uk/20050606200944/http://www.commissionforafrica.org/english/report/thereport/english/11-03-05_cr_report.pdf (accessed 7 June 2013).

Conteh-Morgan, E. and Dixon-Fyle, M. (1999) *Sierra Leone at the End of the Twentieth Century*, New York, NY: Peter Lang.

Cook, R. (1997) 'Robin Cook's speech on the government's ethical foreign policy'. Online, available at: http://www.guardian.co.uk/world/1997/may/12/indonesia.ethicalforeignpolicy (accessed 7 June 2013).

Crawford-Garrett, B. (2012) 'Sierra Leone: a case the international community finally got somewhat right', in D.J. Francis (ed.) *When War Ends: building peace in divided communities*, Farnham: Ashgate.

Dalby, S. (1997) 'Contesting an essential concept: reading the dilemmas in contemporary security discourse', in K. Krause and M.C. Williams (eds) *Critical Security Studies: cases and concepts*, London: UCL Press.

Dale, P. (2008) 'Access to Justice in Sierra Leone: A Review of the Literature', World Bank Justice for the Poor Programme. Online, available at: http://www.daco-sl.org/encyclopedia/1_gov/1_4/JSDP/jsdp_access_justiceSL_Litreview.pdf (accessed 21 September 2009).

Decker, K., Sage, C. and Stefanova, M. (2005) 'Law or Justice: building equitable legal institutions', World Bank. Online. available at: http://siteresources.worldbank.org/INTWDR2006/Resources/477383-1118673432908/Law_or_Justice_Building_Equitable_Legal_Institutions.pdf (accessed 26 October 2009).

de Coning, C. (2008) 'Civil-military coordination and complex peace building systems', in C. Andersen (ed.) *Civil-Military Cooperation in Post-Conflict Operations*, London: Routledge.

de Haan, A. and Everest-Phillips, M. (2007) 'Can new aid modalities handle politics?' UNU-WIDER Research Paper No. 2007/63. Online, available at: http://www.wider.unu.edu/publications/working-papers/research-papers/2007/en_GB/rp2007-63/ (accessed 7 June 2013).

Denney, L. and Ibrahim, A.F. (2012) 'Violence Against Women in Sierra Leone: how women seek redress', ODI Country Evidence. Online, available at: http://www.odi.org.uk/sites/odi.org.uk/files/odi-assets/publications-opinion-files/8175.pdf (accessed 7 June 2013).

Denzer, L. (1971) 'Sierra Leone – Bai Bureh', in M. Crowder (ed.) *West African Resistance*, London: Hutchinson and Company.

Department for International Development (1997) 'Eliminating World Poverty: a challenge for the 21st century', White Paper on International Development, London: Department for International Development.

—. (1998) 'Poverty and the Security Sector', London: Department for International Development.

—. (2000a) 'Justice and Poverty Reduction', London: Department for International Development.

—. (2000b) 'Eliminating World Poverty: making globalisation work for the poor', White Paper on International Development. Online, available at: http://www.dfid.gov.uk/Documents/publications/whitepaper2000.pdf (accessed 11 May 2010).

—. (2000c) 'Security Sector Reform and the Management of Military Expenditure: high risks for donors, high returns for development', London: Department for International Development.

—. (2001) 'The Causes of Conflict in sub-Saharan Africa', London: Department for International Development, Foreign and Commonwealth Office and Ministry of Defence.

—. (2002a) 'Understanding and Supporting Security Sector Reform', London: Department for International Development.

—. (2002b) 'Safety, Security and Accessible Justice: putting policy into practice', London: Department for International Development.

—. (2002c) 'International Development Act 2002: an overview', London: Department for International Development. Online, available at: http://www.dfid.gov.uk/aboutDFID/devact2002overview.asp (accessed 10 November 2008).

—. (2003) 'Sierra Leone: a long-term partnership for development'. Online, available at: http://www.dfid.gov.uk/Documents/publications/sl-long-term-partnership.pdf (accessed 8 December 2009).

—. (2004a) 'Non-state Justice and Security Systems', London: Department for International Development.

—. (2004b) 'Poverty Reduction Framework Agreement between the UK and Sierra Leone'. Online, available at: http://www.dfid.gov.uk/Documents/publications/sierraleone-prf-arrangement.pdf (accessed 7 December 2009).

—. (2004c) 'Public Information Note: drivers of change'. Online, available at: http://139.184.194.47/docs/open/DOC59.pdf (accessed 7 June 2013).

—. (2005a) 'Why we need to work more effectively in fragile states', London: Department for International Development.

—. (2005b) 'Conflict Reduction and Humanitarian Assistance'. Online, available at: http://www. 62.189.42.51/DFIDstage/AboutDFID/files/conflict_main.htm#The%20humanitarian%20response (accessed 26 November 2008).

—. (2007a) 'Governance, Development and Democratic Politics: DFID's work in building more effective states', London: Department for International Development.

—. (2007b) 'DFID Annual Report 2007: development on the record', London: Department for International Development.

—. (2007c) 'Explanatory Note on Security and Access to Justice for the Poor'. Online, available at: http://www.dfid.gov.uk/Documents/publications/security-access-justice.pdf (accessed 9 December 2009).

—. (2008) 'Evaluation of DFID Country Programmes: Sierra Leone', London: Department for International Development.

—. (2009a) 'Security and Justice'. Online, available at: http://www.dfid.gov.uk/Global-Issues/How-we-fight-Poverty/Conflict-and-Security/new-sub-theme-page/ (accessed 4 November 2009).

—. (2009b) 'History'. Online, available at: http://www.dfid.gov.uk/About-DFID/History1/ (accessed 3 May 2010).

—. (2010) 'The Politics of Poverty: Elites, Citizens and States: findings from ten years of DFID-funded research on governance and fragile states 2001–2010'. Online, available at: http://r4d.dfid.gov.uk/PDF/Outputs/FutureState/dfid_Politics_BOOKMARK_SINGLESNEW.pdf (accessed 7 June 2013).

Department for International Development, Ministry of Defence and the Foreign and Commonwealth Office (2003) 'Security Sector Reform Policy Brief', London: Department for International Development, Ministry of Defence and the Foreign and Commonwealth Office.

—. (2004) 'The Africa Conflict Prevention Pool: an information document', London: Department for International Development, Ministry of Defence and the Foreign and Commonwealth Office.

Dolan, C. (1998) 'Conference Report: principled aid in an unprincipled world', *Development in Practice*, 8(3): 372–373.

Donais, T. (2009) 'Inclusion or Exclusion? Local ownership and security sector reform', *Studies in Social Justice*, 3(1): 3–26.

Dorman, A.M. (2009) *Blair's Successful War: British military intervention in Sierra Leone*, Farnham: Ashgate.

Douglas, M. (1986) *How Institutions Think*, New York, NY: Syracuse University Press.

Duffield, M. (2001) *Global Governance and the New Wars*, London: Zed Books.

—. (2007) *Development, Security and Unending War*, Cambridge: Polity Press.

Easterly, W. (2002) 'The cartel of good intentions: the problem of bureaucracy in foreign aid', Center for Global Development, Working Paper 4. Online, available at: http://dx.doi.org/10.2139/ssrn.999981 (accessed 7 June 2013).

Economic Commission for Africa (2007), 'Relevance of African Traditional Institutions of Governance', Addis Ababa: Economic Commission for Africa.

Egnell, R. and Halden, P. (2009) 'Laudable, Ahistorical and Overambitious: security sector reform meets state formation theory', *Conflict, Security and Development*, 9(1): 27–54.

Ellis, S. (1996) 'Conclusion: Africa's future and the world', in S. Ellis (ed.) *Africa Now: people, policies, institutions*, Oxford: James Currey.

—. (1999) *The Mask of Anarchy: the destruction of Liberia and the religious dimensions of an African civil war*, London: Hurst & Company.

—. (2007) 'How to Rebuild Africa', in P.N. Lyman and P. Dorff (eds) *Beyond Humanitarianism*, New York, NY: Council on Foreign Relations.

Ellis, S. and Ter Haar, G. (2004) *Worlds of Power: religious thought and political practices in Africa*, London: Hurst & Company.

Englebert, P. (2000) 'Pre-Colonial Institutions, Post-Colonial States, and Economic Development in Tropical Africa', *Political Research Quarterly*, 53(1): 1–30.

—. (2005) 'Back to the Future? Resurgent indigenous structures and the reconfiguration of power in Africa,' in O. Vaughan (ed.) *Tradition and Politics: indigenous political structures in Africa*, Trenton, NJ: African World Press.

—. (2009) *Africa: unity, sovereignty and sorrow*, Boulder, CO: Lynne Rienner.

Ero, C. (2001) 'A critical assessment of Britain's Africa policy', *Conflict Security and Development*, 1(2): 51–71.

Etzioni-Halvey, E. (1983) *Bureaucracy and Democracy: a political dilemma*, London: Routledge and Kegan Paul.

Evans, R. (undated) 'Security Sector Transformation from a Development Donor Perspective'. Online, available at: http://www.dcaf.ch/Chapter-Section/Security-Sector-Transformation-from-a-Development-Donor-Perspective (accessed 7 October 2008).

Eyben, R. (2005) 'Donors' Learning Difficulties: Results, Relationships and Responsibilities', *IDS Bulletin*, 36(3): 98–107.

Fakondo, K. (2008) 'Reforming and Building Capacity of the Sierra Leone Police, 1997–2007', Working Paper 8, Security System Transformation in Sierra Leone, 1997–2007, Birmingham: Global Facilitation Network for Security Sector Reform. Online, available at: http://www.ssrnetwork.net/documents/Publications/SierraLeoneWPs/working%20paper%208.pdf (accessed 7 June 2013).

Fakondo, K., Assistant Inspector General, Sierra Leone Police (2009) Personal interview, 25 February.

Fanthorpe, R. (1998) 'Locating the Politics of a Sierra Leonean Chiefdom', *Africa*, 68(4): 558–83.

—. (2001) 'Neither Citizen nor Subject? "Lumpen" agency and the legacy of native administration in Sierra Leone', *African Affairs*, 100(400): 363–86.

—. (2003) 'Humanitarian aid in post-war Sierra Leone: the politics of moral economy', in S. Collinson (ed.) *Power, livelihoods and conflict: case studies in political economy analysis for humanitarian action*, Humanitarian Policy Group Report. Online, available at: http://www.odi.org.uk/sites/odi.org.uk/files/odi-assets/publications-opinion-files/289.pdf (accessed 7 June 2013).

—. (2004) 'Post-war reconstruction in rural Sierra Leone: what political structures may prove viable?', Final Report for the Department for International Development Security Sector Reform Project. Online, available at: http://r4d.dfid.gov.uk/PDF/Outputs/Mis_SPC/R8095FinalReport.pdf (accessed 7 June 2013).

—. (2005) 'On the limits of liberal peace: chiefs and democratic decentralisation in post-war Sierra Leone', *African Affairs*, 105(418): 27–49.

—. (2007) 'Sierra Leone: the influence of the secret societies, with special reference to female genital mutilation', United Nations High Commission for Refugees. Online, available at: http://www.unhcr.org/refworld/pdfid/46cee3152.pdf (accessed 27 July 2010).

Fanthorpe, R., Lavali, A. and Gibril Sesay, M. (2011) 'Decentralisation in Sierra Leone: impacts, constraints and prospects, Study commissioned by DFID. Online, available at: http://www.dfid.gov.uk/R4D/PDF/Outputs/Mis_SPC/Decentralization ResearchReportFINAL.pdf (accessed 7 June 2013).

Feika, H., Coordinator, Bo Peace and Reconciliation Movement (2011) Personal interview, 17 March.

Fenrich, J., Galizzi, P. and Higgins, T.E. (eds) (2011) *The Future of African Customary Law*, Cambridge: Cambridge University Press.

Ferguson, J. (1994) *The Anti-Politics Machine*, Minneapolis, MN: University of Minnesota Press.

—. (2006) *Global Shadows: Africa in the neoliberal world order*, Durham, NC: Duke University Press.

Ferme, M.C. (2001) *The Underneath of Things: violence, history and the everyday in Sierra Leone,* Berkley, CA: University of California Press.

Finnegan, R. and Murray, D.J. (1970) 'Limba Chiefs', in M. Crowder and O. Ikime (eds) *West African Chiefs: their changing status under colonial rule and independence*, New York, NY: Africana Publishing Corporation.

Fithen, C. and Richards, P. (2005) 'Making War, Crafting Peace', in P. Richards (ed.) *No War No Peace*, Oxford: James Currey.

Fofanah, A., Justice of the High Court of Sierra Leone (2009) Personal interview, 10 March.

Forrest, J.B. (1998) 'State Inversion and Nonstate Politics', in L.A. Villalon and P.A. Huxtable (eds) *The African State at a Critical Juncture: between disintegration and reconfiguration,* Boulder, CO: Lynne Rienner Publishers.

Friedman, J. (2011) 'Building Strategic Capacity in the Police: Sierra Leone 1998–2008', Innovations for Successful Societies, Princeton University. Online, available at: https://www.princeton.edu/successfulsocieties/content/data/policy_note/PN_id181/Policy_Note_ID181.pdf (accessed 4 February 2013).

Fukuyama, F. (2004) *State-Building: governance and world order in the 21st century*, Ithaca, NY: Cornell University Press.

Fullerton Joireman, S. (2001) 'Inherited Legal Systems and Effective Rule of Law: Africa and the colonial legacy', *Journal of Modern African Studies*, 39(4): 571–596.

Fyfe, C. (1962) *A History of Sierra Leone*, Oxford: Oxford University Press.

Fyle, C.M. (1981) *The History of Sierra Leone*, London: Evans Brothers.

Gabelle, C., Governance Advisor, DFID (2009) Personal interview, 27 February.

Gaima, E., Coordinator, Decentralisation Secretariat (2009) Personal interview, 6 March.

Gallagher, J. (2009) 'Healing the scar? Idealising Britain in Africa, 1997–2007', *African Affairs*, 180(432): 435–51.

Gberie, L. (2005) *A Dirty War in West Africa: the RUF and the destruction of Sierra Leone*, London: C. Hurst & Company.

—. (2009) 'Rescuing a Fragile State: the case of Sierra Leone', in L. Gberie (ed.) *Rescuing a Fragile State: Sierra Leone 2002–2008*, Waterloo, ON: Wilfred Laurier University Press.

Gbla, O. (2008) 'Security Sector Reform under International Tutelage in Sierra Leone', *International Peacekeeping*, 13(1): 78–93.

—. Dean of Faculty of Social Science and Law, University of Sierra Leone (2009) Personal interview, 3 March.

Geertz, C. (1975) *The Interpretation of Cultures*, London: Hutchinson.

Ghai, Y. (1987) 'Law, Development and African Scholarship', *The Modern Law Review*, 50(6): 750–76.

Gibrill, H. (2007) 'The Disintegration and Restoration of State Authority in Sierra Leone', in G. Klay Kieh Junior (ed.) *Beyond State Failure and Collapse: making the state relevant in Africa*, Plymouth: Lexington Books.

Giddens, A. (1979) *Central Problems in Social Theory: Action, structure and contradiction in social analysis,* Berkley, CA: University of California Press.

Glennie, A., Straw, W. and Wild, L. (2012) 'Understanding public attitudes to aid and development', Institute for Public Policy Research and the Overseas Development Institute. Online, available at: http://www.odi.org.uk/sites/odi.org.uk/files/odi-assets/publications-opinion-files/7708.pdf (accessed 7 June 2013).

Glentworth, G., Senior Governance Advisor, DFID (2008) Personal interview, 17 October.

Golooba-Mutebi, F. (2011) 'Rooting Governance in African Realities: are customary institutions an answer?', in International Idea (ed.) *Customary Governance and Democracy Building: Exploring the Linkages*, Stockholm: International IDEA.

Golub, S. (2003) 'Beyond Rule of Law Orthodoxy: the legal empowerment alternative', Working Paper 41, Carnegie Endowment for International Peace. Online, available at: http://www.carnegieendowment.org/files/wp41.pdf (accessed 27 October 2009).

—. (2006) 'A House without a Foundation', in T. Carothers (ed.) *Promoting the Rule of Law Abroad: in search of knowledge*, Washington, DC: Carnegie Endowment for International Peace.

Government of Sierra Leone (2006) 'Project Concept Note: enhancement of security and transitional justice', Freetown: Government of Sierra Leone. Online, available at: http://www.betterpeace.org/node/776 (accessed 7 June 2013).

—. (2007) 'Justice Reform Strategy and Investment Plan, 2008–2010'. Online, available at: http://www.daco-sl.org/encyclopedia/4_strat/4_1/justice_sector_reform08-10.pdf (accessed 23 December 2009).

Grindle, M.S. (2004) 'Good Enough Governance: poverty reduction and reform in developing countries', *Governance*, 17(4): 525–48.

Grindle, M.S. (2007) 'Good Enough Governance Revisited', *Development Policy Review*, 25(5): 533–574.

Hänggi, H. (2004) 'Conceptualising Security Sector Reform and Reconstruction', in A. Bryden and H. Hänggi (eds) *Reform and Reconstruction of the Security Sector*, Munster: Lit Verlag and The Centre for the Democratic Control of Armed Forces.

Hardin, K. (1993) *The Aesthetics of Action: continuity and change in a West African town*, Washington, DC: Smithsonian Institute Press.

Harrison, D. (1988) *Sociology of Modernisation and Development*, London: Routledge.

Held, D. (2006) *Models of Democracy*, 3rd edn, Cambridge: Polity.

Herbst, J. (2000) *States and Power in Africa*, Princeton, NJ: Princeton University Press.

Hobsbawm, E. (1983) 'Introduction: inventing traditions', in E. Hobsbawm and T. Ranger (eds) *The Invention of Tradition*, Cambridge: Cambridge University Press.

Hobsbawm, E. and Ranger, T. (eds) (1983) *The Invention of Tradition*, Cambridge: CUP.

Hoffman, D. (2011) *The War Machines: young men and violence in Sierra Leone and Liberia*, Durham, NC: Duke University Press.

Hoffman, E. (2008) 'Reconciliation in Sierra Leone: local processes yield global lessons', *The Fletcher Forum of World Affairs*, 32(2): 129–41.

Holt-Rusmore, E.T. (2009) 'The Social Reintegration of Women: reconstructing womanhood and moving past post-conflict in Sierra Leone', *The Berkley Undergraduate Journal*, 22(1): 1–34.

Horlacher, G., Security Sector Reform Coordinator, DFID (2009) Personal interview, 12 February.

Horn, A. (2001) 'The Development of a Local Needs Policing Model', private document, October.

Horn, A. Project Manager, Commonwealth Safety and Security Project (2008) Personal interview, 10 October.

Horn, A. and Olonisakin, F. with Peake, G. (2006) 'United Kingdom-led Security Sector Reform in Sierra Leone', *Civil Wars*, 8(2): 109–23.

Hout, W. (2012) 'The Anti-Politics of Development: donor agencies and the political economy of governance', *Third World Quarterly*, 33(3) 405–22.

Howlett-Bolton, A.C. (2008) 'Aiming for Holistic Approaches to Justice Sector Development', Working Paper 7, Security System Transformation in Sierra Leone, 1997–2007, Birmingham: Global Facilitation Network for Security Sector Reform. Online, available at: http://www.ssrnetwork.net/documents/Publications/SierraLeoneWPs/working%20paper%207.pdf (accessed 7 June 2013).

Human Rights Watch (2009) 'World Report 2009 – Sierra Leone'. Online, available at: http://www.refworld.org/docid/49705f9246.html (accessed 7 June 2013).

Huntington, S. (1971) 'The Change to Change: Modernisation, Development and Politics', *Comparative Politics*, 3(3): 283–322.

Hurwitz, A. and Peake, G. (2004) 'Strengthening the Security-Development Nexus: assessing international policy and practice since the 1990s', Conference Report, New York, NY: International Peace Academy. Online, available at: http://www.un.org/esa/peacebuilding/Library/Strengthening_SecDev_Nexus_IPA.pdf (accessed 7 June 2013).

Huysmans, J. (2006) *The Politics of Insecurity: fear, migration and asylum in the EU*, London: Routledge.

IANSA, Oxfam and Saferworld (2007) 'Africa's Missing Billions: international arms flows and the cost of conflict', Oxfam Briefing Paper 107. Online, available at: http://www.oxfam.org/sites/www.oxfam.org/files/africas%20missing%20bils.pdf (accessed 7 June 2013).

Inglehart, R. and Baker, W.E. (2000) 'Modernisation, Cultural Change and the Persistence of Traditional Values', *American Sociological Review*, 65: 19–51.

IRIN News (2005) 'West Africa: rejecting FGM not an affront to tradition'. Online, available at: http://www.irinnews.org/Report.aspx?ReportId=57496 (accessed 17 August 2009).

—. (2007a) 'Female Genital Mutilation a vote-winner in Sierra Leone'. Online, available at: http://www.afrol.com/printable_article/15927 (accessed 17 August 2009).

—. (2007b) 'Sierra Leone: judiciary prepares for post-election disputes'. Online, available at: http://www.irinnews.org/Report.aspx?ReportId=73760 (accessed 2 October 2009).

—. (2009) 'Sierra Leone: chiefs ban genital cutting for girls under 18'. Online, available at: http://www.allafrica.com/stories/printable/200904160734.html (accessed 17 August 2009).

Isser, D. (ed.) (2011) *Customary Justice and the Rule of Law in War-Torn Societies*, Washington, DC: United States Institute of Peace.

Jackson, P. (2005) 'Chiefs, Money and Politicians: rebuilding local government in post-war Sierra Leone', *Public Administration & Development*, 25(1): 49–58.

—. (2006) 'Reshuffling an Old Deck of Cards? The politics of local government in Sierra Leone', *African Affairs*, 106(422): 95–111.

—. Director, Global Facilitation Network for Security Sector Reform (2008) Personal interview, 10 September.

—. (2011) 'Decentralised Power and Traditional Authorities: how power determines access to justice in Sierra Leone', *Journal of Legal Pluralism*, 63: 207–30.

Jacob, M. (2008) 'Engendering Security Sector Reform: Sierra Leone and Liberia compared', Workshop Report, Engendering Security Sector Reform. Online, available at: www.ssrnetwork.net/uploaded_files/4534.pdf#page=54 (accessed 22 July 2009).

Jearey, J.H. (1960) 'The Structure, Composition and Jurisdiction of Courts and Authorities Enforcing the Criminal Law in British African Territories', *International and Comparative Law Quarterly*, 9: 409–410.

Jensen, E.G. (2008) 'Justice and the Rule of Law', in C.T. Call and V. Wyeth (eds) *Building States to Build Peace,* Boulder, CO: Lynne Rienner Publishers.

Joko Smart, H.M. (1980) 'The Place of Islamic Law within the Framework of the Sierra Leone Legal System', *African Law Studies*, 18: 87–102.

Joko Smart, H.M. *Sierra Leone Customary Family Law*, Freetown: Fourah Bay College Press.

Jörgel, M. and Utas, M. (2007) 'The Mano River Basin Area: formal and informal security providers in Liberia, Guinea and Sierra Leone', Stockholm: Swedish Defence Research Agency.

Justice Sector Coordination Office (2008) 'Justice Sector Survey 2008', Freetown: Justice Sector Coordination Office and Government of Sierra Leone.

Kabbah, H. (2006) 'Sierra Leone Legal System and Legal Research'. Online, available at: http://www.nyulawglobal.org/globalex/Sierra_Leone.htm (accessed 20 September 2009).

Kamara, M., Provincial Security Committee Coordinator, Southern Province (2009) Personal interview, 18 March.

Kampfner, J. (2003) *Blair's Wars*, London: The Free Press.

Kandeh, J.D. (1999) 'Ransoming the State: elite origins of subaltern terror in Sierra Leone', *Review of African Political Economy*, 26(81): 349–66.

Kane, M., Oloka-Onyango, J. and Tejan-Cole, A. (2005) 'Reassessing Customary Law Systems as a Vehicle for Providing Equitable Access to Justice for the Poor', Paper presented at the New Frontiers of Social Policy Conference, Arusha.

Kaplan, R.D. (1994) 'The Coming Anarchy', *Atlantic Monthly*, February: 44–76.

Kargbo, A.S. (2009) 'Fiscal Decentralization: building the financial capacity of local governments', in Y. Zhou (ed.) *Decentralisation, Democracy and Development: recent experience in Sierra Leone*, Washington, DC: World Bank.

Kargbo, M.S. (2006) *British Foreign Policy and Conflict in Sierra Leone, 1991–2001*, Bern: Peter Lang.

Keen, D. (2003) 'Greedy Elites, Dwindling Resources, Alienated Youths: the anatomy of protracted violence in Sierra Leone', *International Politics and Society*, 2: 67–94.

—. (2005) *Conflict and Collusion in Sierra Leone*, Oxford: James Currey.

Kelsall, T. (2008) 'Going with the Grain in African Development?', *Development Policy Review*, 26(6): 627–55.

Kenema Family Support Unit staff, Sierra Leone Police (2009) Personal interview, 20 March.

Kent, A.D. (2007) 'Custody, Maintenance and Succession: the internalisation of women's and children's rights under customary law in Africa', *Michigan Journal of International Law*, 28: 507–38.

Kerr, R. (2008) 'International development and the New Public Management: projects and logframes as discursive technologies of governance,' in S. Dar and B. Cook (eds) *The New Development Management: Critiquing the Dual Modernization*, London: Zed Books.

Kleinfeld, R. (2005) 'Competing Definitions of the Rule of Law: implications for practitioners', Carnegie Endowment Paper No. 55. Online, available at: http://carnegieendowment.org/files/CP55.Belton.FINAL.pdf (accessed 7 June 2013).

Koroma, B. (2007) 'Local Courts Record Analysis Survey in Sierra Leone', Justice Sector Development Programme and the World Bank's Justice for the Poor Programme. Online, available at: http://web.worldbank.org/WBSITE/EXTERNAL/TOPICS/EXTLAWJUSTICE/EXTJUSFORPOOR/0,contentMDK:21172707~menuPK:3282963~pagePK:210058~piPK:210062~theSitePK:3282787,00.html#Sierra_Leone (accessed 4 October 2009).

Koroma, S., Director, TIMAP for Justice (2009) Personal interview, 12 March.

Krasner, S.D. (1983) *International Regimes*, Ithaca, NY: Cornell University Press.

Krause, K. and Jütersonke, O. (2005) 'Peace, security and development in post-conflict environments', *Security Dialogue*, 36(4): 447–62.

Krogstad, E.G. (2012) 'Security, development and force: revisiting police reform in Sierra Leone', *African Affairs*, 111(443): 261–80.

Kup, A.P. (1975) *Sierra Leone: a concise history*, London: David and Charles.

Kyed, H.M. and Buur, L. (2006) 'Recognition and Democratisation: "new roles" for traditional leaders in sub-Saharan Africa', DIIS Working Paper 11. Online, available at: http://www.diis.dk/graphics/Publications/WP2006/DIIS%20WP%202006-11.web.pdf (accessed 7 June 2013).

—. (2007) 'Introduction: traditional authority and democratisation in Africa', in L. Buur and H.M. Kyed (eds) *State Recognition and Democratisation in Sub-Saharan Africa*, Houndsmills: Palgrave Macmillan.

Labonte, M. (2008) 'Same Care, Different Driver? The impact of peacebuilding partnerships and the chiefdom system in Sierra Leone', *Journal of Peacebuilding and Development*, 4(1): 1–15.

Lawry-White, S. (2003) 'Review of the UK Government Approach to Peacebuilding', London: Department for International Development and the Performance Assessment Resource Centre.

Leftwich, A. (2006) 'From Drivers of Change to the Politics of Development: refining the analytical framework to understand the politics of the places where we work', Part 3: Final Report. Online, available at: http://www.gsdrc.org/docs/open/doc104.pdf (accessed 7 June 2013).

Lewis, R. (1954) *Sierra Leone: a modern portrait*, London: HMSO.

Littler, K. L. (1948) 'The Changing Position of Women in the Sierra Leone Protectorate', *Africa* 18(1): 1–17.

Little, K.L. (1967) 'The Mende Chiefdoms of Sierra Leone', in D. Forde and P.M. Kabbery (eds) *West African Kingdoms in the Nineteenth Century*, Oxford: Oxford University Press.

Lubkemann, S.C., Isser, D. and Banks, P.A.Z. III (2011) 'Unintended Consequences: constraint of customary justice in post-conflict Liberia', in D. Isser (ed.) *Customary Justice and the Rule of Law in War-Torn Societies*, Washington, DC: United States Institute of Peace.

Luckham, R. and Kirk, T. (2012) 'Security in Hybrid Political Contexts: an end-user approach', Justice and Security Research Programme Paper 2. Online, available at: http://www2.lse.ac.uk/internationalDevelopment/research/JSRP/downloads/JSRP2.LuckhamKirk.pdf (accessed 7 June 2013).

Lund, C. (2006) 'Twilight Institutions: public authority and local politics in Africa', *Development and Change*, 37(4): 685–705.

—. (2007) 'Twilight Institutions: an introduction', in C. Lund (ed.) *Twilight Institutions*, Oxford: Blackwell.

Macaulley, M., Campaign for Good Governance (2009) Personal interview, 1 April.

Magbity, J., Primary Justice Manager, Justice Sector Development Programme (2009) Personal interview, 8 April.

Maguire, S. (2012) 'Access to justice for women and girls in Sierra Leone: assessment and strategy', Access to Security and Justice Programme, private document.

Malan, M. (2003) 'The Challenge of Justice and Reconciliation', in M. Malan, S. Meek, T. Thusi, J. Ginifer and P. Coker (eds) *Sierra Leone – Building the Road to Recovery*, Monograph No. 80, Pretoria: Institute for Security Studies.

Mamdani, M. (1996) *Citizen and Subject: contemporary Africa and the legacy of late colonialism*, Princeton, NJ: Princeton University Press.

Mani, R. (2002) *Beyond Retribution: seeking justice in the shadows of war*, London: Polity Press.

Mann, K. and Roberts, R. (1991) 'Introduction: law in colonial Africa', in K. Mann and R. Roberts (eds) *Law in Colonial Africa*, London: James Currey.

Mannah, M. (2007) 'The Intestate Succession Bill: a discussion', Sierra Leone Court Monitoring Program. Online, available at: http://www.carl-sl.org/home/index.php?option=com_content&view=article&id=134:by-millicent-mannah&catid=4:articles&Itemid=23 (accessed 5 October 2009).

Manning, R.E. (2006) 'Crime and Conflict Statistics from Baseline GoBifo/ENCISS/Decentralisation Surveys', World Bank. Online, available at: http://www-wds.worldbank.org/external/default/WDSContentServer/WDSP/IB/2007/06/15/000020439_20070615142646/Rendered/PDF/400500Crime0Statistics01PUBLIC1.pdf (accessed 7 June 2013).

—. (2009) 'Landscape of Local Authority in Sierra Leone: how "traditional" and "modern" justice and governance systems interact', in Y. Zhou (ed.) *Decentralisation, Democracy and Development: recent experience in Sierra Leone*, Washington, DC: World Bank.

Manson, K. (2007) 'Traditional chiefs wield political influence in Sierra Leone', Voice of America. Online, available at: http://www.voanews.com/content/a-13-2007-08-10-voa52-66579857/555453.html (accessed 10 December 2012).

Marks, M. and Goldsmith, A. (2006) 'The state, the people and democratic policing: the case of South Africa', in J. Wood and B. Dupont (eds) *Democracy, Society and the Governance of Security*, Cambridge: Cambridge University Press.

Marriage, Z. (2006) *Challenging Aid in Africa: principles, implementation and impact*, New York, NY: Palgrave Macmillan.

Maru, V. (2005) 'The Challenges of African Legal Dualism: an experiment in Sierra Leone', *Justice Initiatives*, February: 18–22.

—. (2006) 'Between Law and Society: paralegals and the provision of primary justice services in Sierra Leone', Open Society Justice Initiative. Online, available at: http://www.soros.org/initiatives/justice/focus/legal_capacity/articles_publications/publications/between-law-and-society-20100310/between-law-and-society-20100310.pdf (accessed 4 March 2010).

Meharg, S.J. (2007) 'Clash of the Titans: navigating new identities in conflict geographies', in S.J. Meharg (ed.) *Helping Hands and Loaded Arms: navigating the military and humanitarian space*, Clementsport, NS: The Canadian Peacekeeping Press.

Mehler, A. (2009) 'Hybrid Regimes and Oligopolies of Violence in Africa: expectations on security provision "from below"', in M. Fischer and B. Schmelzle (eds) *Building Peace in the Absence of States: challenging the discourse on state failure*, Berlin: Berghof Research Centre for Constructive Conflict Management.

Meier, K.J. and O'Toole Junior, L.J. (2006) *Bureaucracy in a Democratic States: a governance perspective*, Baltimore, MD: Johns Hopkins University Press.

Members A, Promoters of Peace and Justice, Freetown (2009) Personal interview, 16 February.

Member B, Promoters of Peace and Justice, Freetown (2009) Personal interview, 3 March.

Member C, Promoters of Peace and Justice, Freetown (2009) Personal interview, 13 March.

Members D, Promoters of Peace and Justice, Bo (2009) Personal interview, 17 March.

Members E, Promoters of Peace and Justice, Kenema (2009) Personal interview, 20 March.

Menkhaus, K. (2007) 'Governance without Government in Somalia: spoilers, state building and the politics of coping', *International Security*, 31(3): 74–106.

Merry, S.E. (2006) *Human Rights and Gender Violence: translating international law into local justice*, Chicago, IL: University of Chicago Press.

Migdal, J.S. (1988) *Strong Societies and Weak States*, Princeton, NJ: Princeton University Press.

Ministry of Defence (no date) 'Factsheet: the Africa Conflict Prevention Pool'. Online, available at: http://www.operations.mod.uk/africa/acpp.htm (accessed 10 November 2008).

Mokuwa, E., Voors, M., Bulte, E. and Richards, P. (2011) 'Peasant Grievance and Insurgence in Sierra Leone: judicial serfdom as a driver of conflict', *African Affairs*, 110(440): 339–66.

Mosse, D. (2004) 'Is good policy unimplementable? Reflections on the ethnography of aid policy and practice', *Development and Change*, 35(4): 639–71.

Murray, C. (2009) *The Catholic Orangemen of Togo and other Conflicts I have Known*, London: Atholl.

Mustapha, A.R. and Larbi Jones, E. (2005) 'Change, Chieftaincy and Conflict in Three West African Communities', in O. Vaughan (ed.) *Tradition and Politics: indigenous political structures in Africa*, Trenton, NJ: African World Press.

Mychajlyszyn, N. (2007) 'Putting Policy into Practice: integrating post-conflict operations', in S.J. Meharg (ed.) *Helping Hands and Loaded Arms: navigating the military and humanitarian space*, Clementsport, NS: The Canadian Peacekeeping Press.

Natsios, A. (2010) 'The clash of the counter-bureaucracy and development', Washington, D.C.: Center for Global Development.

Newland, H.O. (1916) *Sierra Leone: its people, products and secret societies*, London: John Bale, Sons & Danielsson.

Ngombulango, L., Town Chief, Kenema (2009) Personal interview, 20 March.

North, D. (1981) *Structure and Change in Economic History*, New York, NY: W.W. Norton & Co.

OECD DAC (2005) 'Security System Reform and Governance', DAC Guidelines and Reference Series. Online, available at: http://www.oecd.org/development/incaf/31785288.pdf (accessed 7 June 2013).

OECD DAC (2007a) 'Principles for Good International Engagement in Fragile States and Situations'. Online, available at: http://www.oecd.org/dac/incaf/38368714.pdf (accessed 7 June 2013).

OECD DAC (2007b) 'OECD DAC Handbook on Security System Reform: supporting security and justice'. Online, available at: http://www.oecd.org/development/incaf/38406485.pdf (accessed 7 June 2013).

OECD DAC Network on Governance (2005) 'Lessons learned on the use of Power and Drivers of Change Analyses in development cooperation', Final Report. Online, available at: http://www.gsdrc.org/docs/open/DOC82.pdf (accessed 7 June 2013).

Officer in Charge, Lumley Family Support Unit, Sierra Leone Police (2009) Personal interview, 5 March.

Olonisakin, F. (2008) *Peacekeeping in Sierra Leone: the story of UNAMSIL*, Boulder, CO: Lynne Rienner Publishers.

O'Neill, D., Country Director, DFID (2009) Personal interview, 9 April.

Osteria, T.S. (2003) 'Achieving Gender Equality and Equity: ten years after the ICPD', Occasional Paper, The Yuchengco Center, De La Salle University, Manila. Online, available at: www.dlsu.edu.ph/research/centers/yc/pdf/ocpaper3.pdf (accessed 15 July 2009).

Page, E.C. and Jenkins, B. (2005) *Policy Bureaucracy: government with a cast of thousands*, Oxford: Oxford University Press.

Paris, R. (2004) *At Wars End: building peace after civil conflict*, Cambridge: Cambridge University Press.

Paris, R. and Sisk, T. (2009) 'Understanding the Contradictions of Postwar Statebuilding', in R. Paris and T. Sisk (eds) *The Dilemmas of Statebuilding: confronting the contradictions of postwar peace operations*, Abingdon: Routledge.

Park, A.S.J. (2006) '"Other Inhumane Acts": forced marriage, girl soldiers and the Special Court for Sierra Leone', *Social and Legal Studies*, 15(3): 315–337.

—. (2008) 'Consolidating Peace: rule of law institutions and local justice practices in Sierra Leone', *South African Journal on Human Rights*, 24(3): 536–65.

Peacebuilding Support Office (2007) 'Briefing Paper on Local Governance and Democracy in Post-Conflict Sierra Leone: emerging issues and implications for peace and development'. Online, available at: http://157.150.195.10/peace/peacebuilding/Country-Specific%20Configurations/Sierra%20Leone/01.11.07%20briefing%20paper%20SL%20other%20info.pdf (accessed 8 June 2010).

Peake, G. (2004) *Policing the Peace: police reform experiences in Kosovo, Southern Serbia and Macedonia*, London: Saferworld.

Peake, G., Scheye, E. and Hills, A. (2008) 'Conclusion', in G. Peake, E. Scheye and A. Hills (eds) *Managing Insecurity: field experiences of security sector reform*, London: Routledge.

Penfold, P. (2009) 'The Special Court for Sierra Leone: a critical analysis', in L. Gberie (ed.) *Rescuing a Fragile State: Sierra Leone 2002–2008*, Waterloo, ON: Wilfred Laurier University Press.

Penketh, A. (2008) 'It might just as well have been his old master's voice', The Independent. Online, available at: http://www.independent.co.uk/opinion/commentators/anne-penketh-it-might-just-as-well-have-been-his-old-masters-voice-811845.html (accessed 11 November 2008).

Peters, G. (2001) *The Politics of Bureaucracy*, 5th edn, London: Routledge.

Peters, K. (2006) 'Footpaths to Reintegration: armed conflict, youth and the rural crisis in Sierra Leone', PhD dissertation, Wageningen University.

— (2008) Personal interview, 14 October.

Peters, K. and Richards, P. (1998) 'Why we fight: voices of youth combatants in Sierra Leone', *Africa* 68(2): 183–208.

Pham, J.P. (2006) *The Sierra Leone Tragedy: history and global dimensions*, New York, NY: Nova Science Publishers.

Porteous, T. (2005) 'British Government Policy in sub-Saharan Africa under New Labour', *International Affairs*, 81(2): 281–97.

—. (2008) *Britain in Africa*, London: Zed Books.

Powlick, K.M. (2007) 'The Economics of Intrastate Conflict: observations from the case study of Sierra Leone', Economists for Peace and Security. Online, available at: http://www.epsusa.org/publications/newsletter/2007/june2007/powlick.pdf (accessed 26 June 2009).

Ranger, T. (1983) 'The Invention of Tradition in Colonial Africa', in E. Hobsbawm and T. Ranger (eds) *The Invention of Tradition*, Cambridge: Cambridge University Press.

Rawnsley, A. (2000) *Servants of the People: the inside story of New Labour*, London: Hamish Hamilton.

Rennie, N. (2006) 'Silenced Injustices in Moyamba District', Sierra Leone Justice Sector Development Programme. Online, available at: http://www.britishcouncil.org/silence_injustices_in_moyamba_district.pdf (accessed 7 June 2013).

Reno, W. (1995) *Corruption and State Politics in Sierra Leone*, Cambridge: Cambridge University Press.

—. (1998) *Warlord Politics and African States*, Boulder, CO: Lynne Rienner.

Richards, P. (1996) *Fighting for the Rainforest*, London: James Currey.

—. (2005) 'Green Book Millenarians? The Sierra Leone war within the perspective of an anthropology of religion', in N. Kastfelt (ed.) *Religion and African Civil Wars*, London: Hurst & Company.

—. (2006) 'Agrarian Underpinnings of the Sierra Leone Conflict', in P. Kaarsholm (ed.) *Political Culture and Development in Africa*, Oxford: James Currey.

Rotberg, R. (2003) *State failure and state weakness in a time of terror*, Washington DC: Brookings Institution Press.

Sandy, J., Director, Public Sector Reform Unit (2009) Personal interview, 27 March.

Sannerholm, R. (2007) 'Legal, Judicial and Administrative Reforms in Post-Conflict Societies: beyond the rule of law template', *Journal of Conflict and Security Law*, 12(1): 65–94.

Sannoh, M., District Security Committee Coordinator, Bo District (2009) Personal interview, 18 March.

Sawyer, E. (2008) 'Remove of Reform? A case for (restructuring) chiefdom governance in post-conflict Sierra Leone', *African Affairs*, 107(428): 387–403.

Scheye, E. (2008) 'Unknotting Local Ownership Redux: bringing non-state/local justice networks back in', in T. Donais (ed.) *Local Ownership and Security Sector Reform*, Berlin: Lit Verlag.

—. (2009a) 'State-Provided Service, Contracting Out and Non-State Networks: justice and security as public and private goods and services', The International Network on Conflict and Fragility, Paris: Organisation for Economic Cooperation and Development.

—. (2009b) 'Pragmatic Realism in Justice and Security Development: supporting improvement in the performance of non-state/local justice and security networks', Clingendael Conflict Research Unit. Online, available at: http://www.clingendael.nl/sites/default/files/20090707_cru_local_justice_scheye.pdf (accessed 7 June 2013).

Scheye, E. and Andersen, L. (2007) 'Conclusion: toward a multilayered approach to security', in L. Andersen, B. Møller and F. Stepputat (eds) *Fragile States and Insecure People? Violence, security and statehood in the twenty-first century*, New York, NY: Palgrave Macmillan.

Schroven, A. (2006) *Women after War: gender mainstreaming and the social construction of identity in contemporary Sierra Leone*, Berlin: Lit Verlag.

Schümer, T. (2008) *The New Humanitarianism: Britain and Sierra Leone, 1997–2003*, London: Palgrave Macmillan.

Scott, J.C. (1985) *Weapons of the Weak: everyday forms of peasant resistance*, New Haven, CT: Yale University Press.

—. (1998) *Seeing like a State*, New Haven, CT: Yale University Press.

Sedra, M. (2006) 'European approaches to security sector reform: examining trends through the lens of Afghanistan', *European Security*, 15(3): 323–38.

—. (2007) 'Security Sector Reform in Afghanistan: an instrument of the state-building project', in L. Andersen, B. Møller and F. Stepputat (eds) *Fragile States and Insecure People? Violence, security and statehood in the twenty-first century*, New York, NY: Palgrave Macmillan.

Sen, A. (2000) 'Why Human Security?' Paper presented at the International Symposium on Human Security. Online, available at: http://www.humansecurity-chs.org/activities/outreach/Sen2000.pdf (accessed 15 May 2010).

Short, C. (1999) 'Security Sector Reform and the Elimination of Poverty', Speech given at the Centre for Defence Studies, King's College London. Online, available at: http://www.clareshort.co.uk/speeches/DFID/9%20March%201999.pdf (accessed 7 June 2013).

—. (2000) 'Clare Short Speaks on Globalisation', Guardian Unlimited Talk Board Session. Online, available at: http://www.guardian.co.uk/world/2000/dec/13/globalisation (accessed 8 November 2008).

—. (2002) 'Hansard Written Answers'. Online, available at: http://www.publications.parliament.uk/pa/cm200102/cmhansrd/vo020724/text/20724w10.htm (accessed 25 June 2009).

Sierra Leone Court Monitoring Programme (2006) 'Customary Law Users Guide'. Online, available at: http://www.slcmp.org/drwebsite/manager/uploads/1/SLCMP Customary_Law_Manual_Final.pdf (accessed 28 September 2009).

Sklar, R. (2003) 'The Premise of Mixed Government in African Political Studies', in O. Vaughan (ed.) *Indigenous political structures and governance in Africa*, Ibadan: Sefer Books Ltd.

Smith, G.H. (1997) 'The Dichotomy of Politics and Corruption in a Neopatrimonial State: evidence from Sierra Leone, 1968–1993', *Issue: A Journal of Opinion*, 25(1): 58–62.

Smits, R. and Wright, D. (2012) 'Engagement with non-state actors in fragile states: narrowing definitions, broadening scope', Clingendael Conflict Research Unit Report. Online, available at: http://www.clingendael.nl/publications/2012/20121200_cru_engagement_with_nsa_in_fragile_states.pdf (accessed 7 June 2013).

Sriram, C.L. (2009) '(Re)building the rule of law in Sierra Leone: beyond the formal sector', Paper presented at the International Studies Association Convention, New York. Online, available at: http://www.allacademic.com/meta/p313198_index.html (accessed 4 October 2009).

Statistics Sierra Leone and ICF Macro (2009) 'Sierra Leone 2008 Demographic and Health Survey: key findings', Calverton, MD: Statistics Sierra Leone and ICF Macro. Online, available at: http://www.measuredhs.com/pubs/pdf/SR171/SR171.pdf (accessed 7 June 2013).

Stepputat, F, Andersen, L. and Møller, B. (2007) 'Introduction: security arrangements in fragile states', in L. Andersen, B. Møller and F. Stepputat (eds) *Fragile States and Insecure People? Violence, security and statehood in the twenty-first century*, New York, NY: Palgrave Macmillan.

Stern, M. and Öjendal, J. (2010) 'Mapping the Security-Development Nexus: conflict, complexity, cacophony, convergence?' *Security Dialogue*, 41(5): 5–30.

Stone, C., Miller, J., Thornton, M. and Trone, J. (2005) 'Supporting Security, Justice and Development: lessons for a new era', London: Department for International Development and Vera Institute of Justice.

Straw, J. (2002) 'Failed and Failing States', Speech given at the European Research Institute, University of Birmingham. Online, available at: http://www.eri.bham.ac.uk/events/jstraw060902.pdf (accessed 17 November 2008).

Stringer, R., Security Sector Reform Advisor, DFID (2009) Personal interview, 11 February.

Tangri, R. (1978) 'Central-Local Politics in Contemporary Sierra Leone', *African Affairs*, 77(307): 165–73.

Tarawali, I., District and Provincial Security Coordinator, Office of National Security (2009), Personal interview, 24 February.

Teale, L. (2007a) 'The Registration of Customary Marriage and Divorce Bill: a discussion', Sierra Leone Court Monitoring Program. Online, available at: http://www.carl-sl.org/home/index.php?option=com_content&view=article&id=197:the-registration-of-customary-marriage-and-divorce-bill-a-discussion&catid=10:commentaries&Itemid=21 (accessed 5 October 2009).

—. (2007b) 'The Domestic Violence Bill: A Discussion. Sierra Leone Court Monitoring Program'. Online, available at: http://www.carl-sl.org/home/index.php?option=com_content&view=article&id=52:by-lotta-teale&catid=4:articles&Itemid=23 (accessed 5 October 2009).

Thomas, N.W. (1916) *Anthropological Report on Sierra Leone: part 1 law and custom*, London: Harrison & Sons.

Thompson, N. (2002) 'In Pursuit of Justice: a report on the judiciary in Sierra Leone', Commonwealth Human Rights Initiative. Online, available at: http://www.humanrightsinitiative.org/publications/ffm/sierra_leone_report.pdf (accessed 7 June 2013).

Trubek, D.M. (2003) 'The "Rule of Law" in Development Assistance: past, present and future', University of Wisconsin-Madison. Online, available at: http://www.law.wisc.edu/facstaff/trubek/RuleofLaw.pdf (accessed 7 June 2013).

Truth and Reconciliation Commission for Sierra Leone (2004) 'Witness to Truth: final report of the Truth and Reconciliation Commission for Sierra Leone'. Online, available at: http://www.trcsierraleone.org/drwebsite/publish/index.shtml (accessed 17 January 2009).

Tshombe Kargoi the 2nd, M., Paramount Chief, Wunde Chiefdom, Bo District (2009), Personal interview, 19 March.

Turpin, J. (1998) 'Many Faces: women confronting war', in L.A. Lorentzen and J. Turpin (eds) *The Women and War Reader*, New York, NY: New York University Press.

Ubink, J. (2008) *Traditional Authorities in Africa: resurgence in an era of democratization*, Leiden: Leiden University Press.

Ubink, J. and McInerney, I. (eds) (2011) *Customary Justice: perspectives on legal empowerment*, Rome: IDLO. Online, available at: http://www.idlo.int/Publications/CustomaryJustice3.pdf (accessed 7 June 2013).

Ucko, D. (2008) 'Militias, tribes and insurgents: the challenge of political reintegration in Iraq', *Conflict, Security and Development*, 8(3): 341–73.

UNCHR (2001) 'Sierra Leone: Report on Female Genital Mutilation (FGM) or Female Genital Cutting (FGC)', 1 June, available at http://www.unhcr.org/refworld/docid/46d5787cc.html (accessed 17 August 2009).

United Nations Children's Fund (2005) 'At a Glance: Sierra Leone'. Online, available at: http://www.unicef.org/infobycountry/sierraleone_statistics.html (accessed 31 August 2010).

—. (2007) 'Sierra Leone: multiple indicator cluster survey 2005'. Online, available at: http://www.childinfo.org/mics3_surveys.html (accessed 7 June 2013).

United Nations Department of Peacekeeping Operations (2012) 'The United Nations SSR Perspective'. Online, available at: http://www.un.org/en/events/peacekeepers-day/pdf/securityreform.pdf (accessed 7 June 2013).

United Nations Development Program (1994) 'New Dimensions of Human Security', Human Development Report, New York: UNDP. Online, available at: http://hdr.undp.org/en/reports/global/hdr1994/chapters/ (accessed 7 June 2013).

—. (2008) 'Human Development Report 2007/2008, Sierra Leone'. Online, available at: http://hdrstats.undp.org/countries/country_fact_sheets/cty_fs_SLE.html (accessed 3 September 2009).

United Nations Disarmament Demobilisation and Reintegration Resource Centre (undated) 'Country Programme: Sierra Leone'. Online, available at: http://www.unddr.org/countryprogrammes.php?c=60 (accessed 7 November 2008).

United Nations Population Fund (2005) 'Gender-based Violence in Sierra Leone: a case study', New York, NY: United Nations Population Fund.

United Nations Secretary-General (2008) 'Securing Peace and Development: the role of the United Nations in supporting security sector reform', Report of the Secretary-General, A/62/659 – S2008/39. Online, available at: http://issat.dcaf.ch/content/download/421/2650/file/UN%20SG%20Report%20on%20SSR.pdf (accessed 7 June 2013).

United Nations Security Council (2008) 'Security Council Presidential Statement Emphasises Security Sector Reform Essential Element of Post-Conflict Stabilisation, Reconstruction', 5889th and 5890th Meetings. Online, available at: http://www.un.org/News/Press/docs/2008/sc9327.doc.htm (accessed 10 August 2010).

United States Department of State (2009) '2008 Human Rights Report: Sierra Leone', Bureau of Democracy, Human Rights and Labor. Online, available at: http://www.state.gov/g/drl/rls/hrrpt/2008/af/119023.htm (accessed 17 August 2009).

Unruh, J. (2008) 'Land Policy Reform, Customary Rule of Law and the Peace Process in Sierra Leone', *African Journal of Legal Studies*, 2(2): 94–117.

Unsworth, S. (2009) 'What's politics got to do with it? Why donors find it so hard to come to terms with politics and why this matters', *Journal of International Development*, 21(6): 883–94.

—. (2010) *An Upside Down View of Governance*, Brighton: Centre for the Future State, Institute of Development Studies.

Vangahun, A.B., Paramount Chief, Nongowa Chiefdom, Kenema District (2009) Personal interview, 20 March.

Varvaloucas, A., Koroma, S., Turay, M. and Saddiqi, B. (2012) 'Improving the Justice Sector: law and institution-building in Sierra Leone', in O.E.G. Johnson (ed.) *Challenges and Policy Issues in Early 21st Century Sierra Leone*, London: International Growth Centre and the Bank of Sierra Leone.

Vaughan, O. (2005) 'Introduction', in O. Vaughan (ed.) *Tradition and Politics: indigenous political structures in Africa*, Trenton, NJ: African World Press.

Vincent, J.B.M. (2012) 'A Village up View of Sierra Leone's Civil War and Reconstruction: multilayered and networked governance', Research Report No. 75, Institute for Development Studies. Online, available at: http://www.ids.ac.uk/files/dmfile/RR75.pdf (accessed 7 June 2013).

Vinci, A. (2008) 'Anarchy, Failed States, and Armed Groups: reconsidering conventional analysis', *International Studies Quarterly*, 52(2): 295–314.

Viner, P., Coordinator, Justice Security Development Programme (2009) Personal interview, 27 February.

Waddell, N. (2006) 'Ties that Bind: DFID and the emerging security and development agenda', *Conflict, Security and Development*, 6(4): 531–55.

Wambura Kimathi, L. (2005) 'Non-state Institutions as a Basis of State Reconstruction: the case of justice systems in Africa', Paper presented at CODESRIA's 11th General Assembly. Online, available at: http://www.codesria.org/IMG/pdf/kimathi.pdf (accessed 7 June 2013).

Weaver, O. (1995) 'Securitization and De-securitization', in R. Lipschutz (ed.) *On Security*, New York, NY: Columbia University Press.

Weber, M. (1968) *Economy and Society: an outline of interpretive sociology*, Vol. III, edited by G. Roth and C. Wittich, New York, NY: Bedminster Press.

—. (1972) 'Politics as a vocation', in H.H. Gerth and C.W. Mills (eds) *From Max Weber*, Oxford: Oxford University Press.

—. (1978) *Economy and Society: an outline of interpretive sociology*, Vol. I, edited by G. Roth and C. Wittich, Berkley, CA: University of California Press.

White, M., West Africa Regional Conflict Advisor, former Security Sector Advisor; and former-Programme Manager, Sierra Leone, DFID (2008a) Personal phone interview, 16 October.

—. (2008b) 'The Security and Development Nexus: a case study of Sierra Leone 2004–2006', Working Paper No. 4, Security System Transformation in Sierra Leone, 1997–2007, Birmingham: Global Facilitation Network for Security Sector Reform. Online, available at: http://www.ssrnetwork.net/documents/Publications/SierraLeoneWPs/working%20paper%204.pdf (accessed 7 June 2013).

—. (2009) 'Security and Development in Sierra Leone: DFID's approach', in L. Gberie (ed.) *Rescuing a Fragile State: Sierra Leone 2002–2008*, Waterloo, ON: Wilfred Laurier University Press.

Wickham-Jones, M. (2000) 'Labour's trajectory in foreign affairs: the moral crusade of a pivotal power?' in R. Little and M. Wickham-Jones (eds) *New Labour's Foreign Policy*, Manchester: Manchester University Press.

Willett, S. (2005) 'New Barbarians at the Gate: losing the liberal peace in Africa', *Review of African Political Economy*, 32(106): 55–76.

Williams, P. (2001) 'Fighting for Freetown: British military intervention in Sierra Leone', *Contemporary Security Policy*, 22(3): 140–68.

Williams, R. (2002) 'Development Agencies and Security-Sector Restructuring', *Conflict, Security and Development*, 2(1): 145–9.

Wilson, P., Libra Advisory Group (2008) Personal interview, 6 October.

Wood, G. (2008) 'The Politics of Development Policy Labelling', *Development and Change*, 16(3): 347–73.

World Bank (2005) 'Republic of Sierra Leone Joint IDA-IMF Staff Advisory Note on the Poverty Reduction Strategy Paper'. Online, available at: http://www-wds.worldbank.org/external/default/WDSContentServer/WDSP/IB/2005/04/15/000090341_20050415102633/Rendered/PDF/31775.pdf (accessed 7 June 2013).

World Bank (2011) 'Conflict, Security and Development', World Development Report 2011. Online, available at: http://siteresources.worldbank.org/INTWDRS/Resources/WDR2011_Full_Text.pdf (accessed 7 June 2013).

Wulf, H. (2004) 'Security sector reform in developing and transitional countries', Berghof Research Centre for Constructive Conflict Management. Online, available at: http://www.berghof-handbook.net/documents/publications/dialogue2_wulf.pdf (accessed 7 June 2013).

Young, C. (2004) 'The End of the Post-Colonial State in Africa? Reflections on changing African political dynamics', *African Affairs*, 103(410): 23–49.

Young, M., Mende Tribal Head, Freetown (2012) Personal interview, 24 October.

Zack-Williams, T. (2002) 'Introduction: Africa at the millennium', in T. Zack-Williams, D. Frost and A. Thomson (eds) *Africa in Crisis: new challenges and possibilities*, London: Pluto Press.

Index